T0341177

ROUTLEDGE LIBRARY EDITIONS: ENERGY RESOURCES

Volume 2

PRIORITIES IN NUCLEAR TECHNOLOGY

PRIORITIES IN NUCLEAR TECHNOLOGY

Program Prosperity and Decay in the
United States Atomic Energy Commission,
1956–1971

IRVIN C. BUPP

Routledge
Taylor & Francis Group

LONDON AND NEW YORK

First published in 1988 by Garland

This edition first published in 2019
by Routledge
2 Park Square, Milton Park, Abingdon, Oxon OX14 4RN

and by Routledge
52 Vanderbilt Avenue, New York, NY 10017

Routledge is an imprint of the Taylor & Francis Group, an informa business

British Library Cataloguing in Publication Data
A catalogue record for this book is available from the British Library

ISBN: 978-0-367-23168-2 (Set)
ISBN: 978-0-429-27857-0 (Set) (ebk)
ISBN: 978-0-367-23087-6 (Volume 2) (hbk)
ISBN: 978-0-429-27827-3 (Volume 2) (ebk)

Publisher's Note
The publisher has gone to great lengths to ensure the quality of this reprint but points out that some imperfections in the original copies may be apparent.

Disclaimer
The publisher has made every effort to trace copyright holders and would welcome correspondence from those they have been unable to trace.

PRIORITIES IN
NUCLEAR TECHNOLOGY

PROGRAM PROSPERITY
AND DECAY IN THE
UNITED STATES ATOMIC
ENERGY COMMISSION,
1956–1971

IRVIN C. BUPP

GARLAND PUBLISHING, INC.
NEW YORK & LONDON 1988

Library of Congress Cataloging-in-Publication Data

Bupp, Irvin C.
Priorities in nuclear technology.
(Harvard dissertations in American history and
 political science)
Thesis (Ph. D.) — Harvard University, 1971.
Bibliography: p.
1. Nuclear industry — Government policy — United States.
2. U.S. Atomic Energy Commission. I. Title. II. Series.
HD9698.U52B79 1988 353.0087'22 88–30973
ISBN 0–8240–5117–3

PREFACE

Virtually no one still believes that policy-making and administration are separate functions. On a number of related issues, however, consensus remains elusive. Within government there is puzzlement about why some public policies succeed and others do not, without apparent regard to their objective merit. From a different perspective, many have supposed at least part of the explanation to lie in the characteristics of the administrative structure itself. Public policies, according to this view, are the products of an inert bureaucratic apparatus muddling through today's problems with yesterday's programs.

This study is written for two audiences, roughly corresponding to these two concerns. To the first, I want to argue that in the main public policies prosper or falter because of their political consequences; to the second, that the same policies are often the outcome of a lively entrepreneurial process which resembles Nineteenth Century capitalism more than Twentieth Century socialism.

The programs and personnel of the Atomic Energy Commission are the empirical foundation for these arguments. The data generated by that agency's annual budget-making cycles, collected over time and organized by program, will be used as evidence to test some propositions about policy formation within the executive branch of government. My concern here will be with questions of _where_ and _how_ priorities are established in a complex institutional environment. To answer the more fundamental causal question of _why_ some programs prosper while others whither or die, I will turn to more historical analysis and compare the fortunes of several of AEC's efforts to develop applied nuclear technology.

Chapter I, then, sets the stage. A narrative summary of the fiscal year 1967 budget cycle (fall, 1965) within the AEC, it provides a background for the subsequent quantitative and historical analysis. The main theoretical arguments about priority establishment are deployed in Chapter II. At issue is the extent to which recent scholarly attention to the regularities of the budgetary process has obscured evidence about how priorities are determined in government. I will show that budgetary data can tell us more about public administration than the fact that officials use a repertoire of techniques to simplify complicated situations.

Chapters III and IV are case studies of two AEC programs-- civilian power reactor development and peaceful nuclear explosives. Though my principle theme is the causes of their respective turns of fortune, it will become apparent that the histories of these two endeavors bracket an abiding normative issue of American government. In the development of new technology, how active should government be and what is its proper role vis-a-vis the private sector?

Chapter V returns to the problem of priority setting. There was little doubt from the outset that the AEC budgetary data provided a behaviorally interesting dependent variable (the notion of "program prosperity," operationalized in Chapter II). What was a good deal less certain was whether the same information could also be manipulated to yield independent variables. The keystone of Chapter V is a frankly innovative attempt to do just this. Building upon the results of this measurement exercise, a simple test is then proposed and executed to test a specific causal hypothesis about how priorities are established in government. The chapter concludes with a brief assessment of the validity of the experiment.

Throughout Chapters I - V the AEC and its programs are used to illustrate what, hopefully, are general problems of public administration. Naturally there is a danger in this, especially with an agency having so many obviously unusual characteristics. (As Doug Price observed at an early stage of this study, "For studying ships, the AEC is a submarine.")

Chapter VI is about the AEC. It is an attempt to explain why time and again AEC programs have been technical triumphs and political catastrophies. To answer this question, I attempt to combine the insights from both the systematic and the historical analyses of Chapters I - V with some well-known literature on public administration and organizational behavior.

It should also be said that this entire study is an experiment of an altogether different sort; it tests the proposition that the conflict of interests between the scholar and the administrator is not absolute. As is obvious from the opening pages, my research was extraordinarily dependent upon the Commission's internal records, many of which, even when they are not "classified," are highly confidential for valid administrative and political reasons. Some two years ago I proposed to the Secretary to the Commission, Mr. Woodford B. McCool, that the study I had in mind be undertaken as part of the ongoing research program of the Historian's Office. Mr. McCool readily agreed to support that highly unusual proposal and was subsequently instrumental in securing the approval of the Commission itself for the project. Subject only to the stipulation that I submit a copy of my final results to the Division of Classification for review on national security matters, I was given a virtual _carte blanche_ to use the official files of the Office of the Secretary for my research. Once again the key factor was Mr. McCool's confidence in the value of independent scholarship and his personal trust in me. For these reasons, among the many debts incurred over the past months, that owed to this remarkable public servant is perhaps primary.

As might be imagined, association with the AEC Historian's Office proved to be of vast practical value. Not the least of such benefits was the continuous advice and assistance of Richard G. Hewlett, the Chief Historian. I am especially grateful for his help on Chapters II and III.

For her work in arranging complicated interview schedules with busy executives and for seeing to a variety of other administrative details, I want to thank Miss Betty Wise of the Historian's Office.

Many of the records I needed both to compile the budgetary data set and to develop the case studies would doubtless remain sequestered in AEC vaults had it not been for the assistance of Mrs. Velma Early of the Secretariat's Reference and Reproduction Branch. For this assistance and for her unfailing cheer in the face of endless stupid questions, I am enormously grateful.

My friends at Harvard, John F. Beatty, Jr., Gary R. Orren, and William Schneider, provided a running commentary on an array of substantive, methodological, and editorial points. The cumulative effect of this sort of help can, of course, be the difference between the success and the collapse of an intellectual enterprise.

I am indebted to Fred Bookstein for his contribution of massive methodological aid on an embarrassing number of occasions. (Though I fear it had less visible effect, I am also grateful to him for insisting that I read George Orwell's "Politics and the English Language" as a condition for his help on numerical matters.)

The empirical standards to which I attempt to adhere throughout the study are due to the teaching of H. Douglas Price. His stress upon the need to confront specified causal theories with evidence was the inspiration for the quantitative analyses in Chapters II and V. I also benefited in the early stages of my research from his flawless critical sense in pointing out theoretical booby traps and smoke screens.

Dean Don K. Price has been enormously generous of his time and judgment. I am grateful for his attention in reviewing early drafts of much of this material; I am grateful, in addition, for his strong personal support, interest--and patience in tolerating an often preoccupied teaching assistant.

It is of course customary to absolve all those whose aid one acknowledges from responsibility for the shortcomings of the final product. I hereby do so. However, one person has been so intimately involved in every aspect of the research, so helpful on matters from the most fundamental to the most trivial, that his right to escape under this clause is dubious at best. Peter B. Natchez has been critical to this exercise from conception through execution, and review. He is clearly entitled to share the credit for most of its strength, and I suppose following tradition immune to criticism for its weakness.

My mother, Mrs. Helen C. Bupp, falls in a different category. The truth is that what follows simply could not have been written without her services as executive secretary, typist, proof-reader, and even courier.

Finally, a nod to an old friend and teacher, Claire G. Walker. Her contributions, though distant in time and remote in sub-ject, were nonetheless as real and were surely as important as the more proximate ones of my colleagues, associates and friends at Harvard and in the AEC.

Again traditions being what they are, one cannot conclude a statement of acknowledgment without reference to one's wife. I have one, and she performed, no less well I am confident than the spouses of countless other thesis-writers, all the supportive tasks expected of her. In Alice's case, I am especially grateful for her patience, humor, and consumptive function--both as support and as incentive.

ICB

TABLE OF CONTENTS

Page

PREFACE   ii

LIST OF TABLES   ix

CHAPTER

    I.   FISCAL YEAR 1967   1

    II. THE POLITICS OF PROGRAM PROSPERITY   67

    III. THE AEC'S CIVILIAN POWER REACTOR PROGRAM   123

    IV. PLOWSHARE   162

    V.   THE CONSEQUENCES OF ADMINISTRATION   213

    VI. ORGANIZATIONAL ADAPTABILITY AND
         PROGRAM PROSPERITY   272

APPENDIX

    A. OPERATING EXPENSES IN $ MILLIONS FOR
        23 AEC PROGRAMS BY STAGE, FY 1958 -
        FY 1972   311

    B. METHODOLOGICAL APPENDIX TO CHAPTER V   324

BIBLIOGRAPHY   333

LIST OF TABLES

Table		Page
I - 1	Commission Review FY 1967 Budget Summary by Program, Operating Expenses, Capital Equipment and Construction	17
I - 2	FY 1967 - Staff Reductions to Meet B oB Directive	39
I - 3	Commission Revisions	43
I - 4	B oB Mark-up of AEC Budget	46
I - 5	Appeals to B oB Mark-up Approved by Commission	50
I - 6	B oB Restoration of AEC FY 1967 Budget Appeals	53
I - 7	Staff Recommendations	59
I - 8	Per Cent Change in Operating Expenses by Program	65
II -10	Correlations Among Budgetary Stages of 23 AEC Programs Pooled Across FY 1958-FY 1972	79
II -11	Total of Each Budget Stage for 23 AEC Programs	102
II -12	Four AEC Programs Histories Expressed as "Prosperity Scores"	104
II -13	Arithmetic Mean of Prosperity Change Scores, FY 1958-FY 1972, 23 AEC Programs	107
II -14	Rank Order of Program Strength	110
II -15	Four-fold Categorization of AEC Program Histories FY 1958-Fy 1972	112
II -16	Prosperity Change Score Correlations	117
V -17	Raw Materials Budget	217
V -18	Deviations From Fair Share - GM	239
V -19	Deviations From Fair Share - Commission	242
V - 20	Preliminary Regression Analysis, Civilian Power	256
V -21	Regression Analysis, Civilian Power	258
V -22	Regression Analysis, Plowshare	262
V -23	Regression Analysis, Rover	264
V -24	Summary of Regression Results, All Programs	266

CHAPTER I

FISCAL YEAR 1967

1. Introduction

On Tuesday, January 1, 1966, the Joint Committee on
Atomic Energy (JCAE) began hearings on H. R. 12292; S.2823, the
Atomic Energy Commission's Proposed Authorization Bill for Fiscal
Year 1967.[1] Welcoming the Committee members and witnesses,
Chairman Holifield said he expected the review of the proposed AEC
budget to extend over the next several weeks, and to serve the purpose,
"not only of examining in detail the AEC's proposed budget for the next
fiscal year, but also (of) inquiring into the progress of the AEC's programs generally and into government-industry cooperative projects."[2]

The ensuing hearings did require considerable time and produced three volumes of testimony and supporting documents. The Joint

---

[1] FY 1967 Authorization Hearings, p. 1. (See "Short Title
Index" for complete citation.)
   In 1963, Section 261 of the Atomic Energy Act of 1954 was
amended (Public Law 88-72) requiring the Atomic Energy Commission
to submit to Congress a draft bill encompassing authorization for all
appropriations needed by the Commission to carry out its programs in
the coming fiscal year. The ensuing annual "authorization hearings"
before the Joint Committee on Atomic Energy provide an almost definitive record of the Commission's unclassified activities since 1963.

[2] Ibid. The AEC operates under two appropriations from Congress, one headed "Operating Expenses," the other, "Plant and Capital

Committee heard from virtually the entire AEC senior staff, from repre-

sentatives of a variety of other federal agencies participating in atomic

energy programs, and from several government contractor representa-

tives. On the whole, the record of these hearings, along with their

counterparts in other years, contain massive support for the well-known

Green and Rosenthal analysis of the relationship between the Atomic

Energy Commission and an extraordinarily cohesive, privileged and

active Congressional committee. [3]   According to the authors of this

influential study, the existence of such a sovereign combined with the

absence of any significant external constituency and a cumbersome

form of internal administration produced progressive isolation of the

Atomic Energy Commission from the President. [4]

In broad outline these observations remain substantially

correct, and any account of AEC behavior must begin by recognizing

the continuing influence of the Joint Committee upon the agency. Yet,

---

Equipment. " Under the latter, the draft authorization bill sets out
the construction projects to be initiated during the fiscal year, as well
as obligations required for the acquisition of capital equipment not related to construction projects (e. g. , computers), and for planning and
design work on future construction projects. Authorization for these
last two items was not required under Section 261 prior to the 1963
amendment. Nor was authorization for "operating expenses, " the
heading which covers the costs of all the Commission's programmatic
activities.

[3] Harold P. Green and Alan Rosenthal, Government of the
Atom (New York: Atherton Press, 1963).

[4] Ibid. , p. 113

consider Glenn T. Seaborg's opening statement on that January afternoon.
He first noted that the AEC's proposed budget of $2,274.3 million for
fiscal year 1967 represented a $103 million decrease below the amount
appropriated for the Atomic Energy Commission programs in fiscal year
1966. Nevertheless, even with this reduction in the overall budget, the
Commission was proposing "several significant new projects and program
expansions in 1967."[5] Continued expansion was being proposed in the
development of fast breeder reactors, and increased emphasis would be
given to the heavy-water organic-cooled reactor programs. Increased
program efforts were also planned for naval propulsion reactors, radioisotope-powered auxiliary power sources for both space and terrestrial
application, nuclear safety research and development and the application
of nuclear power to the desalination of sea water. The proposed budget
also provided for expansion of AEC activities in basic physical and biomedical research and in several areas of applied research and development: the use of nuclear explosives for non-weapons purposes, and the
development of new isotopic power and heat-source fuels. The Commission proposed to expand its support for traineeships in nuclear engineering and its dissemination of technical information. Finally, such
hitherto relatively minor programs as mathematics research, radiation
chemistry, and research on transplutonium elements were also to grow.[6]

---

[5] FY 1967 Authorization Hearings, p. 5

[6] Ibid.

Dr. Seaborg pointed out that the Commission had been "able to finance
these increases within a lower total budget level because of a continuing
downward trend in military requirements and a very careful review of
all AEC programs which had led to the curtailment or elimination of
certain lower priority activities. "[7]

At the time of these hearings, AEC programs can be grouped
into four major functional categories: the procurement of uranium ore;
the production of enriched uranium, plutonium, and tritium (known col-
lectively as "special nuclear materials") for weapons and non-weapons
purposes; the production, testing, and surveillance of nuclear weapons,
including research and development on new systems; and pure and applied
research in the fields of power-producing reactors, physical, biological
and medical sciences, the use of radioisotopes and the peaceful uses of
nuclear explosives. In addition, the AEC operating budget provided for
two major "support" programs: "training, education and information, "
encompassing a broad array of grants and loans for fellowships and
traineeships in various nuclear fields, a technical information program, and the AEC's public relations activities; and "program direction and administration, " a catch-all administrative category. It
is apparent from even the most cursory review of the twenty-five year
history of the AEC that these various activities have not commanded

---

[7] Ibid. (emphasis supplied).

fixed proportions of the total agency budget. They have instead fluctuated widely, obviously reflecting, among other things, the Commission's varying levels of activity in connection with the cold war, the partial realization of many non-weapons applications of nuclear energy, and the emergence of new national priorities such as space exploration and certain types of basic research. The interesting point in Seaborg's 1966 statement is its explicit recognition of the fact that such variation involves a process of priority-setting within government. The curtailment of some activities in order that others might survive or even grow implies the establishment of at least a loose set of priorities which in this case, since we are dealing with an agent of the federal government, in part determine the authoritative allocation of national values. The ungainly headings, "fast breeder reactor program" or "isotopic power and heat-source fuels program" camouflage a process of fundamental social importance. The pertinent issue is: Why is the government doing some things rather than others? As usual, conventional wisdom supplies an inventory of answers. On the one hand, Washington folklore variously ascribes causal pre-eminence to the Bureau of the Budget, powerful Congressional committee chairmen, aggressive program directors, Presidential staffers, or sundry combinations of the foregoing. Alternatively, recent scholarly studies of the public budgetary process suggest that the yearly outcomes are controlled by last year's budget;

that the behavior of the participants is, in effect, strongly auto-regressive.[8]

Actually, we know very little about the relative significance of the numerous participants in the federal budget-making process. We do not really know, that is to say, who or what does make a difference in the setting of national priorities. Investigation of this question is, broadly stated, the chief purpose of what follows. Some pertinent theoretical issues will be taken up in Chapter II. As a preliminary, though, I want to review in some detail an unusual set of data.

In the summer of 1965 President Johnson directed all departments and most agencies of the federal government to recast their budget formats into "output" or program-based schedules. For the AEC, however, this required only relatively minor changes; since from its creation in 1947 the agency had for the most part allocated its resources on an output basis. Thus, the operating costs which had traditionally been

---

[8] See, for example, J. P. Crecine, "The Defense Department Budgetary Process." (Unpublished paper presented at the 64th Annual Meeting of the American Political Science Association, Washington, D. C., September, 1968.) The point about the behavior of the participants being seen as "auto-regressive" is also made by John E. Jackson of Harvard University in an unpublished paper, "A Research Strategy on National Priority Determination."

On the matter of capital folk wisdom, see William D. Carey, "Roles of the Bureau of the Budget" and William M. Capron, "The Impact of Analysis on Bargaining in Government," both reprinted in James W. Davis, Jr., ed., Politics, Programs, and Budgets: A Reader in Government Budgeting, (Englewood Cliffs, N. J.: Prentice-Hall, Inc., 1969).

shown under the "raw materials" and "special nuclear materials" pro-

grams were modified slightly and several new categories presented:

e. g. , "uranium for future reactors, " and "sale and lease of source

material. " A few "supporting" activities, such as "general reactor

technology, advanced systems, and nuclear safety, " were re-allocated

to other categories in the field of reactor development. The compata-

bility of the Commission's traditional budgetary practices with the re-

quirements of the new Planning, Programming and Budgeting (PPB)

system contrasted sharply with the situation in other federal agencies.

Prior to 1965, the practice of anything resembling output budgetry was

extremely rare.[9] Virtually all other departments, agencies and bureaus

adhered to the traditional method of drawing up their budgets according

to such administrative categories as "personnel, " "maintenance, " etc.

As is now widely recognized, such categories are acceptable only from

the standpoint of administrative efficiency narrowly defined. The com-

mander of a military base, for instance, has a legitimate interest in

knowing how many motor vehicles or typewriters he is responsible for

---

One related editorial point: In 1970 the Bureau of the Budget became the Office of Management and Budget. Throughout this study
I will consistently ignore this fact and refer to the agency by its old name.

[9] Virginia Held, "PPBS Comes to Washington, " reprinted in
Davis, op. cit.

at any given time, irrespective of the purpose for which this equipment is meant to be used. For almost anyone else, however, it is the purpose which is important. What proportion of the base's activities are being used for "training," as opposed to, say, logistic support? The point of "program" or "output" budgeting is to identify proposed and actual resource allocations according to the ultimate objects of the expenditure, thus allowing one meaningfully to ask what is being done with the money.[10]

This is precisely the question which AEC budget records permit us to ask. For example, when the five AEC Commissioners met on September 2, 1965, to begin consideration of their General Manager's recommendations for FY 1967, their attention was immediately called to an "analysis of program priorities" which broke down the total proposed operating budget into the following functional categories: raw materials, special nuclear materials, weapons, reactor development, physical research, biology and medicine, training, education and information, isotopes development, Plowshare, community, community program direction and administration, construction, planning and design, security investigations, cost of work for others, revenues applied, and increase or decrease in selected resources. Actually this

---

[10] The literature on PPB is by now vast. Easily the most useful single reference is: Inquiry of the Subcommittee on National Security and International Operations of the Committee on Government Operations, Planning, Programming, and Budgeting, 91st Congress, 2d Sess., (Washington, D.C.: Government Printing Office, 1970). The material introduced in support of the testimony at these hearings contains full and current bibliographic references to the pertinent official and scholarly literature. See also: Fremont J. Lyden and Ernest G. Miller, (eds.) Planning, Programming, Budgeting: A Systems Approach to Management (Chicago, Ill.: Markham Pub. Co., 1968).

particular breakdown does not accurately reflect the way AEC activities
are dealt with within the government either before or after the 1965
Presidential (PPB) directive. Its most serious shortcoming is the
generality of the category "reactor development, " a heading which
encompasses an extraordinarily diverse range of endeavors that are
never considered as an aggregate unit. Other headings such as "community" or "security investigation" represent vestigial or trivial enterprises to which little real attention is paid, while still a third group--
"increases or decreases in selected resources"--are obviously not
programs at all. There is a more general point, however, which must
be met at the outset. Several critics have noted that there is an inherently subjective component to the whole concept of a program. Just
what is meant by an "end-product" or a "program" is not unambiguous.
In Aaron Wildavsky's words: "Programs are not made in heaven.
There is nothing out there that is just waiting to be found. Programs
are not natural to the world; they must be imposed on it by men. . . .
There are just as many ways to conceive of programs as there are of
organizing activity. "[11] Whether something is "really" a program in
the end depends in part upon the perspective from which one approaches

---

[11] Aaron Wildavsky, "The Political Economy of Efficiency:
Cost-Benefit Analysis, Systems Analysis and Program Budgeting, " reprinted in Davis, op. cit.

the matter. The perspective I have chosen represents a compromise between strict adherence to what the AEC itself, i. e. , its Commissioners and senior operating staff, would consider a "real" program and the constraints of limited time and research assistance. After some experimentation, I settled upon twenty-three exclusive but not exhaustive "programs" whose aggregate total comprises roughly 90 per cent of all AEC operating activities at any time between the mid-1950's and the early 1970's. It would be difficult to defend several of these as meaningful output or end-product categories. But all at worst are relatively specific and what is more important, because of the AEC management practices already noted, it is possible to trace the history of each over a much longer period than would normally be the case for the activities of a public agency. For the purpose of inquiring into the process of governmental priority-setting, this provides a second dimension to an already valuable data set. The question of who or what makes a difference cannot only be asked in terms of socially and politically meaningful categories, it can also be framed in terms of effects over time.

But there is yet a third dimension to AEC budgetary data; a dimension which suggests an even more intriguing possibility. For each of the AEC's annual budgetary cycles one can isolate several discrete and usually comparable "stages" where the agency's programs are acted upon by different participants. The question which naturally comes to mind is whether a set of comparable stages replicated at the program level across a number of years contains any information pertinent to how priorities are established within government. The answer is by no means self-evident. Certainly it is possible on a priori grounds to argue persuasively to the contrary. For one thing there is a sophisticated and growing analytic tradition within political science which views bureaucratic budgeteers as cognitive satisficers concerned with problem-solving rather than priority-setting. To the degree this view is correct, much of what happens during the budget cycle can be reduced to a set of rules used to simplify a potentially complex and therefore distressing situation. A second approach might argue that even if the problem-solving perspective is misguided, whatever information the stage data provides about the relative impact of various political forces will be ambiguous at best, and probably spurious. The behavior of the participants in the budgetary process according to this more telling criticism must be accounted for in terms of the antecedent political and economic variables about whose relative impact we are really concerned when we ask: "What counts?" There is very little to be said other than that the point is well taken. The problem is that data on these "real" political variables are notably rare. In its absence there seems to be small harm in exploring what is available, the evidence generated by the governmental budgetary process itself, as a possible though hardly guaranteed or foolproof source of information about the matters which intrigue us.

As a means of becoming familiar with both the federal budgetary process as it applies to the AEC and with some of the substantive programmatic issues involved, let us now return to fiscal year 1967 and pick up the review process with the Commissioners' September, 1965 discussions of the program levels recommended by their senior staff.

2. The FY 1967 Budget Cycle Begins

To the participants the salient fact about each of the AEC's annual budgetary cycles is its individuality. Among the professionals who make the Commission's budgets, the prevailing attitude toward putative theories of the budgetary process is a genial skepticism that any set of generalizations can capture the unique flavor of each year's "exercise." Certain years, moreover, remain in their memories as especially unusual. In retrospect, 1965 is seen as such a year. On June 18 the President directed the AEC to establish a "budget task force" consisting of the Chairman, the General Manager, and the Controller to undertake a "special priority analysis" of the funding levels the agency intended to request for fiscal year 1967. In this analysis, all contemplated program increases above levels approved for FY 1966 were to be assigned to one of two priority groups. The task

force was then to identify specific reductions in other ongoing activities

which might be made to finance the increases assigned to the higher of

the two priority categories. The AEC, that is to say, was to assign to

this latter category only those increases above FY 1966 funding levels

which were considered to be of such importance that they should be pro-

vided even at the expense of cutbacks in other programs. All other pro-

posed increases were to be assigned to the lower priority category.[12]

This was an unusual directive, for typically the opening

rounds of AEC's budget cycles are a good deal less formal. In late

spring the agency submits to the Bureau of the Budget (BoB) a "flash"

or "preview" budget and receives in the following weeks through its

budgetary staff a series of informal estimates or guidelines about the

amount of expansion that is likely to be considered reasonable in light

of the administration's own program priorities. In 1965 the President's

early escalation of these preliminary exchanges was correctly seen as

evidence of serious intent on the part of the administration to hold the

Commission's program growth to a bare minimum in the coming fiscal

year. The combination of Vietnam and the Great Society was, of course,

---

[12] AEC 1181/6--"Analysis of Program Priorities, FY 1967 Budget Review," July 7, 1965. (See Bibliography for explanation of internal AEC documentation.)

the reason for the President's concern. The summer of 1965 was the period when the Johnson Administration was attempting to fund a major and growing foreign military commitment without sacrificing its new domestic anti-poverty and welfare programs. It was clear to all within the AEC at the time that in these circumstances it was going to be extremely difficult to secure administration approval for continued growth of AEC programs which in large part had little to do with either the war on poverty or the war on the Viet Cong.[13]

The total AEC budgets (new obligational authority) for FY 1965 and FY 1966 had been $2.625 billion and $2.377 billion, respectively. The spring 1965 "preview" to the BoB of the FY 1967 budget had totaled $3.141 billion. On July 8 the Commission and its staff completed the Presidentially directed "special priority review" and agreed upon a new submission to the Bureau which came to $2.516 billion, $625 million less than the earlier preview, but $139 million above the approved level for FY 1966.[14] Dr. Seaborg and the other members of the "special budget task force" met with President Johnson on July 14, 1965. During the course of this discussion both the President

---

[13] Comments to this effect by both the AEC Commissioners and senior program staff were quite common during all of the meetings and discussions on the FY 1967 budget throughout the summer and fall of 1965.

[14] AEC 1181/9, "FY 1967 Budget," August 26, 1965, p. 5; see also Minutes of Commission Meeting 2121, July 8, 1965.

and his budget director repeatedly emphasized their intent to require all
agencies and bureaus to identify savings and reductions in ongoing activities as a prerequisite to administration consideration of proposed new
programs and program expansions in FY 1967.[15]

Following this mid-summer trauma, the FY 1967 budget
process temporarily reverted to a more normal pattern. Within the
AEC the real beginning of a typical budget cycle is the consideration
by the General Manager and his "Budget Review Committee"--the
Controller and the Commission's several assistant general managers--
of the requests of the Commission's program divisions.

The General Manager and Controller undertake their review
with an eye toward working the Commission budget down to what they
judge to be a feasible figure which is regularly exceeded by the raw
aggregation of division requests. Though the General Manager may have
in hand more or less specific guidance from the Bureau of the Budget
about the magnitude of this figure, its actual determination is usually a
matter of judgment. The basis of this judgment is the network of informal
"working" relationships among AEC budget staff and their counterparts in
BoB. In the case of the AEC this is a particularly strong network due

---

[15] Minutes of Commission Meeting 2138, September 2, 1965.

largely to the work of John P. Abbadessa, who has been the Commission's controller since 1960. Abbadessa is widely regarded as one of Washington's ablest budget officers. His information about BoB intent and administration fiscal policy in any given year is usually extraordinarily sound and is respected as such by his superiors within the Commission.

The General Manager's recommendations, along with the original requests, are the agenda for a series of meetings between the Commissioners and the AEC program staff. Each program director is given the opportunity to appear before the Commission to explain his own request and to appeal the General Manager's reduction, if any. The Commission may occasionally retire into executive session to consider differences among its staff; but such disagreements are usually settled out of hand with a minimum of formality. The result of these deliberations is a new budget which is almost always a compromise between the General Manager's recommendations and the original requests. This budget constitutes the official agency request to the administration and is normally transmitted to the BoB by mid-September.

The Commission convened on the afternoon of September 2, 1965 for the first session of the review of the proposed FY 1967 budget. Observing that the aggregated division requests had totaled $3.053 billion, the Controller informed the Commissioners that the General Manager was recommending an FY 1967 request for $2.629 billion. (The "spring preview" and the "special priority review" totals had been $3.141 billion

and $2.516 billion, respectively.) He then invited the Commissioners'

attention to the breakdown of this total by program shown in Table 1.[16]

TABLE 1

Commission Review FY 1967 Budget

Summary by Program, Operating Expenses,
Capital Equipment and Construction
($ thousands)

Program	Program Division Request	General Manager's Recommendation
Raw Materials	$163,105	$163,105
Special Nuclear Materials	396,783	383,358
Weapons	816,655	779,245
Reactor Development	786,631	674,731
Physical Research	557,757	386,030
Biology and Medicine	127,950	110,200
Training, Education & Information	22,857	21,016
Isotopes Development	39,100	20,800
Plowshare	31,760	23,705
Community	13,342	11,837
Program Direction & Administration	88,177	87,773

Source: AEC 1181/9, August 26, 1965, pp. 18-20.

---

[16] Minutes of Commission Meeting 2138, September 2, 1965.

In his judgment the "major policy issues" in this year's review process would be the future of the "Plowshare" program, the level of research and development to be associated with the "civilian power reactor" program, and the AEC request for funds to build a "Meson facility at Los Alamos.[17] Plowshare is the AEC effort to develop peaceful uses for nuclear explosive devices. Initially conceived by one of the weapons laboratories in 1957, the program has throughout its history been enormously controversial both within and outside government. Some of the political issues involved in these controversies will be explored in detail later.[18] The civilian power program, for which the General Manager was recommending an operating budget of $94.9 million for FY 1967, is a major component of the general program category shown in Table 1 as "Reactor Development." A nuclear reactor is a machine in which the controlled fissioning of radioactive material, normally uranium enriched in the isotope, U-235, yields both new radioactive material and energy. Depending upon the purpose for which the reactor design has been optimized, either of these may be regarded as a "waste product." Originally, of course, the energy was the waste product as reactors were used to produce the isotope plutonium-239 for nuclear weapons. The

---

[17] Ibid.

[18] See Chapter IV, below.

civilian power program represents the AEC's main effort to realize the
commercial potential of the controlled fission energy as a heat source
for the generation of electrical power. We will develop these matters in
some detail shortly.[19]

The "Meson facility" to which the Controller referred was
a proposed $40 million particle accelerator for use in what physicists
at the time were beginning to refer to as "medium energy research."

By custom the Commission begins its "September review"
with the raw materials, special nuclear materials, and weapons programs. In 1965 the procurement of raw materials received only cursory
attention since all of the recommended funds represented the costing out
of contractual commitments made several years previously and no policy
changes in this area were then contemplated.[20] A fairly lengthy discussion was, however, occasioned by the $6 million reduction in the "special
nuclear materials" proposed by the General Manager. Dr. Seaborg expressed substantial interest in the potential use of the Commission's
plutonium production facilities for non-weapons purposes. He believed
this to be a growing area where additional funds would shortly be required.

---

[19] See Chapter III, below.

[20] Minutes of Commission Meeting 2139, September 3, 1965.

There was no disagreement among the Commissioners with the position taken by the Chairman, and the discussion produced a tentative decision to increase the proposed special nuclear materials budget by $1 million. [21]

Even though the weapons budget had been reduced by $15 million during the General Manager's review, this program too received only cursory attention from the Commission. The program director informed the Commissioners that the proposed cuts would not have any serious impact on his division's activities. [22]

The next matter to be taken up did produce substantial debate. The Controller informed the Commission of the BoB's firm intent to hold the joint AEC - NASA program to develop a nuclear space rocket (Rover) to its FY 1966 funding level. The Commission had placed a $2.8 million increase in operating expense for Rover in the high priority category during the mid-summer review exercise. [23] The General Manager's recommended budget provided for a similar increase, though it did represent a slight ($700,000) reduction from the program division request. [24] In the fall of 1965 the AEC was very anxious indeed to protect Rover. Since the debate over the priority to be attached to this program

---

[21] Ibid.

[22] Ibid.

[23] Minutes of Commission Meeting 2121, July 8, 1965.

[24] AEC 1181/9, op. cit., p. 6.

was to become one of the most sharply defined issues as the AEC's

FY 1967 budget cycle progressed, it will be helpful to pause momentar-

ily to set out some of the relevant historical and technical circumstances.

As we shall eventually see, the background of Rover is typical of a great

many AEC activities; not only in its genesis and subsequent history, but

also in its eventual outcome.

First, in discussing Rover one must begin as with virtually

every AEC developmental program with recognition of the peculiar aura

which surrounded the atom in post-war Washington.[25] There was general

consensus among both politicians and scientists that nuclear energy was a

practical, as distinct from a theoretical, discovery of quite literally

epochal significance. Though the specifics were a bit foggy, the potential

practical applications of this huge new energy source seemed obvious--

electrical power, propulsion, excavation, etc. Only a few engineering

details needed to be worked out.

Development of explosive applications for military use, however,

temporarily commanded almost all of the AEC's administrative, technical,

---

[25] For a fascinating perspective on this point, see David E.
Lilienthal, The Atomic Energy Years, 1945-1950, (New York: Harper
& Rowe, 1964). The definitive references, though, are Richard G.
Hewlett and Oscar E. Anderson, Jr., The New World, 1939-1946, A
History of the USAEC, Vol. I, and Richard G. Hewlett and Francis
Duncan, Atomic Shield; 1947-1953, A History of the USAEC, Vol. 2,
(University Park, Pa.: Penna. State University, 1962 and 1969).

and financial resources, and it was several years before any sustained

priority was attached to non-military nuclear programs. In time, though,

and as resources were thought to permit, a wide array of non-weapons

research and development efforts were undertaken by the Commission.[26]

For several years prior to the Kennedy Administration, AEC had funded

Rover as a promising but rather low priority "level-of-effort" project

at the Los Alamos Scientific Laboratory.[27] President Kennedy's 1961

decisions up-grading the national space effort had an almost immediate,

and, of course, salutary impact upon Rover; within the AEC its operat-

ing budget more than doubled from $30 million to $74 million in the first

years of the new Democratic Administration. AEC and NASA proclaimed

nuclear rockets to represent the most important potential advance in

rocketry then forseeable for the "post-Apollo" period, capable of offering

---

[26] Hewlett and Duncan, op. cit., see especially Chaps. 7 and 8.
Two important themes emerge from the Hewlett and Duncan narrative.
The first, and most significant, was the surprising disarray and poverty
of the weapons production and development capability inherited by the AEC
from the Army's Manhattan District. Regardless of one's normative
assessment of the desirability of the Commission's accomplishments in
this area, AEC's transformation of the weapons complex was a truly heroic
administrative and technical achievement. A second theme of the early
years of the AEC is the astonishing degree to which the attention of its
already pressed top management was absorbed by frivolous matters of
personnel and material "security."

[27] In the Washington research and development lexicon the
term "level-of-effort" signifies the existence of a consensus that in the
absence of startling technical development a program should "grow" only
at a rate large enough to balance monetary inflation.

substantial improvement over chemical rockets on a number of performance dimensions critical to extra-lunar or deep space missions. In 1963
the two agencies announced a major reorientation of the program, with
the emphasis now to be on component, subsystem, and engine system
analysis and extensive ground testing. [28] This was a much more am-
bitious program specifically geared to providing the design and operating
experience necessary for development of an actual flight system. At the
working level among laboratory scientists and engineers the clear expectation was that the "requirement" for such a flight system was imminent.
It should be emphasized that this was no small undertaking. Several hundred millions of dollars were now being allocated to a broadly based research, technology and engineering effort specifically directed toward
the development of flight systems. That amount of money pays a lot of
salaries, builds a lot of hardware, and supports a lot of expectations.
The place where these expectations were centered was Los Alamos.

Both Los Alamos and the AEC weapons laboratory at
Livermore, California have been extremely anxious to diversify their
operations since the mid-fifties; in fact, this desire was the source of
most of the new ideas for nuclear research and development which com-
peted for support in the 1960's. On the basis of the 1963 reorientation

---

[28] FY 1965 Authorization Hearings, pp. 482-523.

Rover had come to represent a major effort at diversification by Los Alamos. Its success was believed, by the laboratory, the AEC, and Clinton Anderson, Senior Senator from New Mexico and a highly influential member of the JCAE, to be vitally important to the laboratory's future. The laboratory's future was in turn considered vitally important to the Commission. For these reasons the success of Rover was seen by most of the government nuclear community as uncommonly crucial.

And Rover, like so many similar research and development programs, was successful--on its own terms. Justifying his program before the JCAE in March of 1966 the Director could point to an impressive string of technical achievements. [29] On engineering grounds Rover was clearly repaying the investments made by AEC and NASA. There appeared to be no technical reason why the expectations on which the program had been expanded several years earlier would not soon be wholly met. The trouble was that in early 1966 nobody seemed to want the final product. For the AEC and its laboratory this was an intensely frustrating and all too familiar state of affairs. Time and again, as the Commission saw it, the government had made enormous material and administrative investments to "realize the potential of the atom." With

---

[29] FY 1967 Authorization Hearings, pp. 209-244. For a definitive, though technical account, see, Holmes F. Crouch, Nuclear Space Propulsion, (Granada Hills, California: Astronuclear Press, 1965).

rare exceptions these investments had produced striking technical

progress on the engineering and physical frontiers in question only

to be thwarted by "political" factors beyond the Commission's control.

One of the Commissioners noted during their review of

the General Manager's FY 1967 budget recommendations that in the

fall of 1965 this now seemed to be precisely the danger to Rover. The

other Commissioners agreed that the entire "post-Apollo" space pro-

gram was going to be notably vulnerable to the severe budgetary con-

straints caused by an apparently sincere administration desire not

to sacrifice its Great Society programs to the exigencies of a major

war.[30] They were, of course, correct.

Many of the same considerations were on the Commission-

ers' minds when they turned to the next item on their budget agenda,

the SNAP program. SNAP is a felicitous acronym for "System for

Nuclear Auxiliary Power" and actually comprises a series of hetero-

geneous projects (SNAP-10A, SNAP-50, etc.), each directed toward

the development of a specific nuclear energy source for space and terres-

trial applications.[30a] It is normally one or more of these particular pro-

jects, as distinct from the entire "program," which is the object of de-

bate during the budget review process.   During the meeting in question

---

[30] Minutes of Commission Meeting 2139, September 3, 1965.

[30a] Details on many of these projects can be found in Robert
F. Loftness, Nuclear Power Plants, (Princeton, N. J.: Van Nostrand
Co., 1964).

attention was focused upon "SNAP-50," a relatively large radioisotope-powered electrical generator for "post-Apollo" space missions. Like Rover, the salient characteristic of SNAP-50 and its companion projects was their dependence upon another agency's "mission requirement" for justification. In agreeing to augment the General Manager's recommendation for the project by $2 million, the Commissioners again shared expressions of deep concern for the effect of the "requirements" system upon their programmatic activities. Under the groundrules of this system, a "supplier agency" like AEC had to rely wholly upon the needs of its "customers," NASA in this case, to justify continuation or expansion of programs which from the Commission's own perspective were highly successful on technical grounds. Among the Commission and its staff the prevailing view was (and remains) that the AEC ought to have authority to continue hardware developmental programs like SNAP-50 through the "demonstration phase," even in the absence of firm mission requirements, on the basis of its own technical judgment. The basic argument was that a system which permitted technically successful programs to evaporate at the point of highest promise was extremely wasteful of the country's scientific and administrative resources and placed an unfair burden upon scientists, engineers and administrators who were rarely certain from year to year that their endeavors would continue to be supported, regardless of the excellence of their work.

The decision on SNAP-50 concluded Meeting 2138; the Commissioners adjourned until the following morning, when, according to custom, an entire budget session would be devoted to review of Admiral Rickover's naval propulsion reactors program.

The Admiral and his staff began the meeting with their usual impressive "briefing" on the current status, accomplishments, and objectives of the naval reactors program. One of the Commissioners asked why the level of research and development for the naval reactor program had increased over the period FY 1965 - FY 1967. (Only figures for three years are normally shown in the budget papers prepared for the Commissioners.) This fact seemed somewhat "anomalous" to him in view of the forthcoming phase-out of the Polaris program. Admiral Rickover justified the increases in terms of various technical needs, such as reactor cores with increased performance capabilities, and the matter was not pursued. The Admiral had requested about $100 million in research and development funds for FY 1967. The General Manager had made no changes in this request. Neither did the Commission. The discussion consumed a bit more than two hours.[31]

---

[31] During the Rickover discussion there was a brief exchange of more than passing interest as an illustration of many of the things we will be talking about.

One of the Commissioners asked Admiral Rickover if there were any studies in progress in the Pentagon which might have an adverse effect upon a decision to build (another) nuclear-powered

The afternoon session began with consideration of the Plow-share program to develop non-weapons uses for nuclear explosives, one of the programs which the Controller had predicted would be a major issue with the Administration as the budget cycle progressed. Since we will later want to review this fascinating enterprise in considerable de-tail, it will suffice to note here that Plowshare in a sense was the "Rover" of the other weapons laboratory, Livermore. It respresented a major ef-fort by Livermore to develop non-weapons applications for its consider-able technical expertise.

This particular discussion of the Plowshare program began with the General Manager and the Controller stressing for the Commis-sion the BoB's hostility to Plowshare. (The Commission was already very well aware of this fact.) One of the Commissioners questioned the "realism" of the proposed excavation program for FY 1967. The Admin-istration was known to be extremely reluctant to authorize any nuclear explosions which might be interpreted as a violation of the Limited Test Ban Treaty. The proposed budget was, however, strongly defended by

---

aircraft carrier. The Admiral thought there probably were such studies. A member of his staff commented that a recent internal Pentagon study of tactical air warfare was said to have convinced Secretary McNamara that two additional attack carriers would be necessary in 1969-1971. Rickover observed that the Pentagon was "being subjected to industrial pressure to revive the Aircraft Nuclear Propulsion Program." (Minutes of Commission Meeting 2139, September 3, 1965.)

John Kelly, Program Director. He was supported by other Commission staff who argued that the proposed program to develop suitable clean nuclear explosives was necessary in order to make Plowshare a credible alternative in constructing a new interoceanic canal. The Commission, however, chose not to restore the reductions made by the General Manager.[32]

The next matter to be discussed, cooperative power reactor development, is a program which wholly resists concise summarization. I will return to it in the context of an extended assessment of the Commission's civilian power reactor development efforts.[33] The present discussion was limited to brief comment upon a particular project which involved a cooperative arrangement with the State of California for construction of a very large reactor to desalinate sea water as well as generate electricity.[34] The Commission added $2.0 million to the General Manager's budget for this project.[35]

The General Manager's reductions in the Euratom program were noted without comment by the Commission as it turned to merchant

---

[32] Minutes of Commission Meeting 2140, September 3, 1965.

[33] See Chapter III, below.

[34] This cooperative enterprise involved the AEC, the Department of Interior, and the Metropolitan Water District of Southern California. The proposed reactor would have produced 1500 megawatts of saleable electricity and 150 million gallons of fresh water per day. For more information see FY 1967 Authorization Hearings, pp. 611-612, pp. 621-622, and pp. 781-788. Also for further information on this project see FY 1968 Authorization Hearings, pp. 860-876.

[35] Minutes of Commission Meeting 2140, September 3, 1965.

ship reactors. In the fall of 1965 this was a troubled program. Only

two days previously the Commission had met with the new Undersecretary

of Commerce, Allen S. Boyd, for the second time in three months to dis-

cuss the future of federal efforts to develop a commercially viable nuclear

maritime capability for the United States.[36] Fundamental differences

had crystallized during the first meeting. AEC technical staff strongly

believed that the whole maritime reactor program should be reoriented

around a government built and operated land-based test facility. Several

reactor manufacturers were currently claiming the ability to produce

"off-the-shelf" reactors allegedly suitable for immediate incorporation

in merchant vessels. The AEC technical staff had argued that on the

basis of present knowledge and experience the AEC was in no position

to underwrite the economy or efficiency of such a power plant. Only a

government test facility could meet this need.

The Department of Commerce and the Maritime Adminis-

tration were much more interested in a shipbuilding than a testing pro-

gram, and were highly reluctant to concur with AEC plans for an ex-

pensive new facility. The Commerce Department was also sensitive to

the degree to which AEC's safety requirements were inhibiting the reali-

---

[36] The first meeting was held on July 8, 1965, the second
on September 1, 1965. Summary Notes of both discussions are on file
in the Office of the Secretary, USAEC.

zation of nuclear maritime power. The specific point at issue was the
AEC requirement that a tugboat had to "stand by" a nuclear vessel for
the full period such a vessel was in harbor. Another point of tension
between the two agencies involved what AEC considered to be the Maritime Administration's chronic inability to produce definitive economic
studies of various trade routes comparing the marginal advantages and
cost effectiveness of nuclear and conventional power for various types
of cargoes. Though not all of these issues had been settled during the
two lengthy discussions, the Commissioners came away from them with
the feeling that some real progres s had been made toward coordinating
the agencies' approaches. The BoB was on record to the effect that
"full agreement" between the Maritime Administration and the AEC on
a specific program was a necessary condition to further funding of the
entire effort.

On a personal level the Commissioners felt that in their
frank exchanges with the obviously intelligent Boyd some real progress
had been made. They were therefore visibly hesitant about the budgetary
actions now proposed by the General Manager, questioning whether the
recommended reductions in the program's operating budget were consistent with agreements reached with Boyd. The director of reactor development apparently believed they were for he did not object to the General
Manager's cuts. The Commission, however, demurred and decided to

increase the operating budget for merchant ship reactors from $3 million
to $5 million.[37]

"Army power reactors" and "general reactor technology"
received only cursory attention. A brief discussion of "advanced systems" ended in agreement to add $1 million to support a project at Los
Alamos.[38]

The director of reactor development did make an effort to
persuade the Commission to increase the budget for nuclear safety.
While agreeing that expansion of this program was highly desirable,
the Commission did not modify the General Manager's recommendation,
and thus completed their review of the operating budgets for all of the
civilian and military reactor development programs. They went on,
however, to what was to be the first of many discussions of the major
policy issue of the AEC's FY 1967 budget: the request of the division
of reactor development for $75 million to construct a fuel testing facility
for breeder reactors. Although the project had been included in both the
May budget preview and the special mid-summer review, Chairman
Seaborg was not persuaded that such a facility was necessary, while
reactor development technical staff, particularly the division director,

---

[37] Minutes of Commission Meeting 2140, September 3, 1965.
[38] Ibid.

believed it quite imperative. After a lengthy technical exchange between Seaborg and the division director, inclusion of the project in
the AEC September budget was approved, and the meeting adjourned.

At the meeting the following day,[39] the Commission concluded its review of the General Manager's recommended budget, considering: physical research; biology and medicine; training, education
and information; isotopes development; "community;" and program direction and administration. The most significant discussion concerned
the construction of particle accelerators (physical research program).
One of the Commissioners was dubious about the amount proposed for
such facilities in light of the stringency of the rest of the budget.[40] This
particular Commissioner would doubtless have rated reactor development
in general as much more important to AEC than physical research. During the discussion, the Controller explained his understanding of the BoB
attitude toward the major new items in the AEC FY 1967 budget. In com-
puting its "target figures" the Bureau, according to Abbadessa, had essentially taken the FY 1966 budget and added $75 million for the fast fuels
test facility (FFTF), $49 million for the "Alternating Gradient Synchrotron"
(AGS)--one of the particle accelerators, and $3 million for architect-
engineering work on the heavy water organic cooled reactor (part of the

---

[39] Minutes of Commission Meeting 2141, September 7, 1965.
[40] Ibid.

cooperative power program). The Bureau figure did not include funds for the Meson physics facility at Los Alamos, another accelerator. Though the BoB target figures in no way bound the AEC in terms of its final budget, it was possible that if the Commission deleted the FFTF or the AGS, the Bureau of the Budget would simply reduce the total agency budget by a similar amount.[41]

Consideration of the biomedical program proceeded in the context of an accompanying policy paper which proposed a significant (more than 20 per cent) long-term expansion of the biomedical research program at Oak Ridge National Laboratory (ORNL).[42] The discussion produced no agreement on this policy issue, which, it is probably safe to say, was not considered an especially high priority matter by the Commissioners. The General Manager's recommended budget for biology and medicine was approved.[43]

The training, education and information program was one regarding which Chairman Seaborg had, since 1961, made a point of taking a strong personal interest. Another expression of such interest during this meeting led to Commission agreement to add $2 million for

---

[41] Ibid.

[42] AEC 1185/1--"ORNL Biology Division Five Year Plan," August 20, 1965.

[43] Minutes of Commission Meeting 2141, September 7, 1965.

support of a "traveling exhibit" on nuclear energy and increased support for the New York Hall of Science.[44]

During discussion of the "isotopes development" program, the General Manager said he would now like to recommend a construction budget of $3.3 million rather than $1.0 million to provide for a new isotopic fuels testing facility. No one had any objections. Following very brief inspection of the proposed "community" and "program direction and administration" (PDA) budgets, the meeting was adjourned.

The following morning the Commission again convened; this time to review their actions during the preceding meetings. The Controller observed that the Commission's tentative adjustments to the General Manager's recommendations had resulted in a budget approximately $100 million above the Bureau target. The Commission had made no single major change in the General Manager budget; the differential was made up of a number of relatively small items. However, the proposed submission to the Bureau also included four items of major policy significance: 1) $75.0 million for the FFTF; 2) $43.5 million for conversion of the AGS; 3) $3.0 million for A-E and design of the Meson facility; and 4) $7.5 million in design funds for the 200 BEV accelerator. Mr. Abbadessa believed the Commissioners now needed to choose be-

---

[44] Ibid.

tween two alternatives; they could either review their tentative additions

to the General Manager's budget, or they could eliminate one or more

of the major items. The budget staff, for its part, intended to treat the

proposed 200 BEV accelerator as a separate policy issue to be dealt with

on its own merits throughout the coming negotiations with the Bureau of

the Budget. Mr. Abbadessa did not expect any problems in this regard.[45]

One of the Commissioners asked about the possibility of

treating the entire high energy physics program--both operating and

construction budgets--as a separate policy issue. Abbadessa was

skeptical that the administration would agree to such a tactic. A "head-

scratching" discussion followed. One senior staff member noted that

a point not obvious from a cursory inspection of the reactor development

budget was the extent to which increases in the entire civilian power pro-

gram was attributable to growth in the projects being administered by the

---

[45] Minutes of Commission Meeting 2142, September 8, 1965. Federal support for high energy physics research was in fact a major executive policy issue in its own right during 1965 and 1966. For further background see High Energy Physics Research, Hearings before the Subcommittee on Research, Development, and Radiation of the Joint Committee on Atomic Energy, 89th Cong., 1st Sess., March 2-5, 1965. The material in pp. 73-77 and pp. 118-128 is especially pertinent as background to the 200 BEV accelerator.

Now under construction at the National Accelerator Laboratory in Batavia, Ill., the facility had been initially recommended in April, 1963 by a panel of scientists (the Ramsey Panel) appointed jointly by the AEC and the President's Science Advisory Committee to review all aspects of the national high energy physics program.

division of naval reactors. The "seed and blanket" prototype accounted
for a very large proportion of the increase in total reactor development
funding.[46] The Commissioners agreed that increases in Admiral Rickover's civilian power development programs placed severe constraints
on the rest of the Commission's budget in general and the reactor development budget in particular.

There was general discussion of eliminating one of the four
major items noted by the Controller, but the consensus was that this
would simply result in the total AEC budget being reduced by an equivalent amount. Further, it was agreed that it was far too early in the
review process for the Commission to remove a major item from its
budget. There was also discussion of the Commission's submitting a
budget $100 million above the Bureau of the Budget target. The Com-
mission decided to "sleep on the matter" while the Controller attempted
to develop some further alternatives. Overnight Abbadessa and his staff
managed to produce a breakdown of the excess $100 million which divided

[46] Admiral Rickover had requested $22 million in operating
funds to support development of a prototype of this concept. The General
Manager had not reduced the request. See AEC 1181/11, "Statistical
Tables for FY 1967 Budget Estimates," August 26, 1965, p. 11. For
further information on the "seed and blanket" concept, see FY 1967
Authorization Hearings, pp. 595-609.

the increments among three priority categories in a manner consistent with both Commission decisions made during the previous budget
sessions and the prior transmittals to the Bureau of the Budget. The
General Manager reported that all of the Commission's senior staff
had agreed to the priority listings, with the understanding that every
effort would be made to secure final administration approval of the
"Priority A" items.

The Commission then formally approved a final budget
as follows:

	(In $ thousands)
Operating Expenses	$2,234,775
Capital Equipment	178,206
Construction	254,515
Total New Obligational Authority	$2,667,496

3. Bargaining with the Bureau

During October, the Bureau of the Budget normally returns
its "mark-up" or reductions in the agency budget as the opening move in
a series of exchanges that extends into December when the Presidential

budget for the coming fiscal year is finally set within the Executive Branch. Though the characteristics of this "appeals process" do vary from year to year, the developments of October, 1965 were atypical of the normal pattern of exchanges between the Bureau of the Budget and the Atomic Energy Commission; in late October the Commissioners were flatly instructed to reduce the September submission by $122 million, to be apportioned by the Commission as it chose.[47] In effect, the Bureau of the Budget directive left the Commission with the problem whose resolution had been avoided during the concluding sessions of the September review. The Commissioners either had to eliminate one or more of the major facility requests or agree upon reductions in the operating budget. The General Manager had developed a set of recommendations on the assumption that the Commission would choose the latter alternative.[48] The General Manager's proposed actions are reflected in Table 2.

---

[47] Minutes of Commission Meeting 2153, November 8, 1965.

[48] AEC 1181/17, "FY 1967 Budget Estimates," November 7, 1965, p. 1.

TABLE 2

FY 1967
Staff Reductions to Meet BoB Directive

Operating Expenses

1.	Special Nuclear Materials	$ 5,000		
2.	Weapons	20,000		
3.	Reactor Development	33,700 --------Apportioned as follows:		
4.	Research	8,000	1. Civilian	$ 6,000
5.	Biology and Medicine	1,000	2. Cooperative	2,000
6.	Training, Education		3. Merchant	1,000
	and Information	1,500	4. Naval	4,000
7.	Isotopes	2,300	5. SNAP	7,900
8.	Plowshare	2,600	6. General	3,000
		$74,100	7. Advanced	7,800
			8. Safety	2,000
				$33,700
	Income or Decrease			
	in Selected Resources	$29,955		

Capital Equipment

1.	Weapons	$ 2,000
2.	Reactors	1,000
3.	Research	4,500
4.	Biology and Medicine	1,600
5.	Isotopes	500
		$ 9,600

Construction

1.	Weapons	$ 3,745
2.	Reactors	2,000
3.	Research	300
4.	Isotopes	2,300
		$ 8,345

Operating Expenses	$74,100	
Income or Decrease in Selected Resources	29.955	
Capital Equipment	9,600	
Construction	8,345	$122,000

During discussion of the matter, the Chairman set out what seemed to him to be four possibilities. The Commission could: a) take the actions recommended by the General Manager; b) eliminate both large facilities, the AGS (high energy physics program) at $45.3 million, and the FFTF (civilian power program) at $75.0 million; c) eliminate only the FFTF and make up the remainder from reductions in the operating budget; and d) eliminate only the AGS, again meeting the balance from the operating budget. In his view, the disadvantage of the first was that several programs would lose momentum which the Commission had pains-takingly built up over the years.[49]

A rather rambling discussion ensued. The budget staff maintained that their suggested reductions were based on "tactical" judgments rather than on considerations regarding relative priorities of the damaged programs. The staff had cut those it believed "most vulnerable to BoB attack." Hence, the suggested $1 million reduction in the cooperative power program from funds earmarked for the arrangement with the State of California. These comments were elicited by the sharp questioning of a Commissioner with a strong interest in the California project.

Chairman Seaborg, in a series of subtle comments and

---

[49] Minutes of Commission Meeting 2153, November 8, 1965.

questions, allowed his preference for the third alternative to become
known. He specifically questioned the wisdom of reducing the merchant
ship program in view of the negotiations then in progress between AEC
and the Maritime Administration. It had, of course, been at Seaborg's
prodding that the initial General Manager recommendation for this program had been supplemented in September. The staff was now proposing to reverse that action. Seaborg also believed the proposed reductions
on Plowshare to be "highly undesirable, " since they would eliminate all
cratering experiments for the forthcoming fiscal year.[50]

The General Manager and budget staff argued that regardless
of Commission preferences certain programs and projects were sure
to be reduced or eliminated by the Bureau of the Budget at some point
in the review process. Likely candidates were weapons production, the
merchant ship program, the California cooperative arrangement (Cooperative Power Program), the MPRE project (SNAP program), SNAP-50,
and the "710" project (Advanced Systems). His suggested cuts had taken
these possibilities into account.

One of the Commissioners expressed preference for the
elimination of a major facility. There was discussion of the possibility
of asking only for "architect-engineer" funds at $5 million for the FFTF.

[50] Ibid.

This is a recognized budget convention which allows preliminary planning
and design for a construction project to proceed before full financial authorization has been granted. Naturally, approval of A-E funds establishes
a strong presumption that full authorization will be given at a later date.
Another Commissioner indicated support for the A-E ploy. The emerging
consensus called forth a spirited defense of the FFTF project by the division director. He argued that to request only A-E funds would constitute
a tacit deferral of the project which would have the effect of placing it in
contention with other high priority needs in his program.

The discussion carried over into an afternoon session.[51] The
Controller began by reporting success in persuading the Bureau to permit the
Commission to pick up $14 million of the $122 million by applying "under-
runs" from the FY 1966 weapons budget. The Commissioners returned
to an attempt to assess the relative importance of the FFTF and the AGS
projects. At issue with regard to the latter was the question of whether
support for high energy physics research in the FY 1967 budget was generally consistent with the stringency of the rest of the budget. The
counter argument concentrated upon technical reservations about the
FFTF. After extended debate and, of course, over the vigorous objections of the affected program director, these arguments carried the

---

[51] Minutes of Commission Meeting 2154, November 9, 1965.

day. The Commission agreed to include only $7.5 million in A-E money

for the FFTF, though the Controller observed that the Bureau of the

Budget would correctly assess this as a tactical maneuver rather than

a real budgetary reduction. On this basis the Commissioners were then

able to quickly decide on the following revisions to the General Manager's

recommendations.[52]

TABLE 3

Commission Revisions to General Manager Recommendations

Operating Expenses

1.	Special Nuclear Materials	$ 800	
2.	Weapons	14,000	
3.	Reactor Development	1,900	
4.	Research	2,000	$ 18,700

Increase or Decrease in Selected Resources   6,155

Capital Equipment

1.	Weapons	2,000	
2.	Reactors	1,000	
3.	Research	4,500	
4.	Biology and Medicine	1,600	
5.	Isotopes	500	9,600

Construction

1.	Weapons	3,745	
2.	Reactors	69,500	
3.	Research	300	73,545

| | | | $108,000 |

The outcome of these deliberations is probably worth a few addi-

tional observations. In the end the Commission had been obliged to

---

[52] Minutes of Commission Meeting 2154, November 9, 1965.

make a choice which it clearly would have preferred to avoid. Even though the "A-E" gambit was a recognized tactical maneuver, the Commission, by choosing this alternative, signalled the Bureau of the Budget that it was attaching a lower priority to the project than to some of its other activities, in this instance support for high energy physics research. The program staff was unsuccessful in achieving flat Commission commitment to what it considered an extremely important undertaking. The competitive strength of the project in future reviews would, as the division director saw, be affected by these events. The program director affected by the FFTF decision did however avoid total defeat.

In these terms, we are obviously observing the progress of an inherently political enterprise involving direct confrontation among different value orderings. This does not mean either that the budget process is all mindless incrementalism or that it is all tactics. It simply means that compromise is a likely outcome of a political confrontation. At this stage the crucial point is to recognize, indeed to highlight, the political nature of what is going on here. [53]

On December 1, 1965 the Commission received the official BoB "mark-up" of its FY 1967 budget request as amended by the Novem-

---

[53] See Chapter III, below, for more on the FFTF.

ber $122 million reduction (actually $108 million because of the allowed

carry-over). The "mark-up" involved additional reductions of $322 mil-

lion and provided for a total of $2.346 billion in new obligational author-

ity (NOA). The AEC was told that the administration regarded these new

cuts as an expression of the President's personal desire to apply very

strict budgetary controls to all federal programs, including those for the

"Great Society, " in light of the serious situation in Southeast Asia.[54] On

top of this the Bureau had identified even further reductions totaling $299.6

million as "a list of alternatives from which the President could make

selections in the event he personally wanted an overall budget for the

AEC of less than $2.346 billion. "[55] The Bureau had specifically noted,

however, that the Commission could substitute other items for those it

had listed in its supplementary cuts. Finally, the Bureau notified the

Commission that in preparing his budget for this fiscal year the Presi-

dent was primarily interested in reducing expenditures, even though re-

ductions were made on an NOA basis. Therefore, the Bureau of the

Budget would not allow plant projects and equipment requests to be sub-

stituted on a dollar-for-dollar basis for operating items.

---

[54] Memorandum of December 1, 1965, to the Commissioners from the Controller on file in the Office of the Secretary.

[55] Ibid.

TABLE 4

BoB Mark-up of AEC $2,667,496 Budget[56]
(In $ thousands)

I. Summary - NOA

	Budget Mark-up		Possible Additional Reductions	
	Reductions	Amount Left	Reductions	Amount Left
Operating Expenses	$234,213	$2,000,562	$151,800	$1,848,762
Capital Equipment	25,300	152,906	15,000	137,906
Construction Projects	62,090	192,425	132,800	59,625
Total	$321,603	$2,345,893	$299,600	$2,046,293

II. Detail for Operating Expenses

	BoB Mark-up	Possible Additional Reductions
Raw Materials	--	--
Special Nuclear Materials	-24,300	-14,000
Weapons	-33,000	-25,000
Reactor Development	-58,200	-69,600
Physical Research	- 9,000	-10,000
Biology and Medicine	- 1,000	--
Training, Education and Information	- 4,017	- 1,100
Isotopes Development	- 2,300	- 1,870
Plowshare	- 6,800	- 7,200
Community	--	--
Program Direction and Administration	- 1,596	- 3,000
Security Investigations	--	--
Cost of work for others	--	--
Other costs and credits	--	--
Subtotal	-140,213	-131,770
Revenues Applied	--	--
Increase or Decrease in Selected Resources	- 80,000	- 20,030
Total Obligations	-220,213	-151,800
Unobligated balance brought forward	- 14,000	--
Unobligated balance carried forward	--	--
New Obligational Authority	-234,213	-151,800

[56] Source: Statistical tables attached to memorandum from Controller dated December 1, 1965.

In summarizing the data in Table 4 for the Commissioners, the Controller emphasized several items. The proposed reductions would have a very substantial effect on the special nuclear materials production program. The "mark-up" alone would require the shutdown of three plutonium producing reactors; the possible further cuts would necessitate closing down two additional reactors. Either action would sharply reduce the government's production capacity for nuclear weapons material.

The reductions from the cooperative power program would effectively eliminate the contemplated California Metropolitan Water District cooperative arrangement. The Bureau of the Budget had, however, indicated that this particular deletion was made "without prejudice" and that the administration would entertain an amendment to the FY 1967 budget for this project after the Presidential budget had gone to Congress. Approval of such an amendment would depend upon the merits of the case and would require a coordinated program with the Department of Interior and a concrete financial commitment from the State of California, neither of which existed at the moment.

A further effect upon the cooperative power program would be to deny all additional support for Admiral Rickover's "seed and blanket" project, though, here again, the BoB said it would entertain an amendment. This reduction incidentally was not entirely unexpected.

The "seed and blanket" project had developed some unexpected technical problems and the status of the cooperative arrangement with a California utility was uncertain.[57]

The proposed reductions in the Euratom program represented a substantial proportion of that program's operating funds. In the case of merchant ship reactors, the reductions would effectively cancel the AEC program. The Bureau had specified that the $500,000 balance was to be used only for "conceptual" and "cost-effectiveness" studies. The $2.5 million reduction from "terrestrial auxiliary power systems" would defer the Commission's oceanographic reactor development effort in its entirety.

The reduction from the Rover program was only $1.0 million. The possible additional $40.0 million cut was an admittedly arbitrary figure representing the Bureau's intent to find some "midway level" for the program. The Bureau had stated that if the Commission believed no meaningful program could be conducted at a level less than the requested $80 million, consideration should be given to complete termination of the program. The BoB recognized that the drastic step reflected by the $40 million reduction would require a Presidential decision.

Plowshare also would be especially hard hit by the Bureau's action. The "mark-up" itself would cancel or defer several high priority

---

[57] FY 1967 Authorization Hearings, pp. 591 ff.

experiments, notably "Project Gasbuggy." The possible additional cuts would, in effect, eliminate the entire excavation technology program.

Construction projects had been considered by the Bureau on an individual case-by-case basis as the President was said to be particularly concerned with new starts on new facilities. The AEC request had included $7.5 million for preliminary design of the 200 BEV accelerator. This item was eliminated as part of the "mark-up." The Bureau of the Budget noted that to date there had been no specific site information and no clear indication that a decision on a site would be made on a time schedule requiring the $7.5 million in FY 1967. The BoB had reinstated the FFTF at the full $75 million. The AGS project was included in the "mark-up" at $45.3 million, but this entire amount was eliminated in the additional reductions, and the A-E on the Los Alamos Meson facility ($3.0 million) was eliminated in the "mark-up." Finally, the Commission had requested a biomedical laboratory and administration building at the Oak Ridge National Laboratory at $7.6 million. This facility was eliminated in the "mark-up," as was $7.0 million out of a requested $9.7 million for general accelerator improvements.

Following this review of the Bureau actions, the Commission adjourned, without comment, giving every indication of being a very unhappy group of men.[58] At a subsequent meeting[59] the following

decisions were quickly made without substantial debate:

TABLE 5

Appeals to BoB "Mark-up"
Approved by Commission at Meeting 2160[59]

	($ millions)
Special Nuclear Materials	$18.0
Weapons	9.0
Reactor Development	15.6
Physical Research	6.9
Biology and Medicine	7.6
Training, Education and Information	0.6
Plowshare	5.3
Subtotal	$66.0
Goods and Services on Order	18.0
Total Operating Expenses Appealed	$84.0

Within reactor development, the $15.6 million appeal was

divided among the civilian power program--$12.8 million; Euratom--

$1.5 million; and oceanographic research and development--$1.3 million.

The Commission also sought restoration of $3.0 million for

---

[58] As was the case for many of these meetings, I was the official rapporteur. At the time, it was perfectly clear the Commissioners were stung by the actions reported by the Controller.

[59] Minutes of Commission Meeting 2160, December 2, 1965.

capital equipment, split equally between special nuclear materials and physical research. Finally, several construction projects were appealed, notably $3.0 million in A-E funds for the Los Alamos Meson facility, $4.0 million in A-E funds for the 200 BEV accelerator, and $7.6 million for a biomedical research laboratory for the Oak Ridge National Laboratory. These, plus several minor projects, produced a total construction appeal of $17.6 million. The total appeal--operating plus capital equipment, plus construction, plus "goods and services on order"-- was $104.6 million.

These decisions were reached very quickly in semi-executive sessions with the Commissioners in effect accepting the recommendations of its General Manager and Controller. The program directors were not actually excluded from these deliberations, but all participants knew that the "groundrules" of these proceedings differed from those of earlier meetings in which the divisions had been appealing actions of the General Manager. During these meetings the Commission and its staff in a very real sense were acting as a unit in attempting to reach a consensus about which of the Bureau's reductions would have the most serious impact on the agency as a whole. Thus the director of the Plowshare program, for example, would never have thought to question the view that attacks to his program were measurably less important to overall Commission activities than attacks on special nuclear materials production operations. It is important to note in this regard the extraordinary harmony which characterized working relations within the AEC, both among the staff and between the Commission and its staff. By 1965 virtually all AEC senior staff had known and worked with each other for more than twenty years. They shared a common outlook and perhaps more important a common technical background. As a result the search for consensus regarding a response to the Bureau of the Budget cuts had few of the characteristics of an adversary proceeding and a complete absence of personal acrimony.[59a]

All of these factors were most evident in the discussion of the Bureau of the Budget's reduction in the special nuclear materials program. This was plainly regarded as the most serious single action taken by the Bureau, representing a further attempt by the administration to achieve a substantial cut-back in these operations.[60]

4. Presidential Decisions

The Bureau of the Budget granted $27.9 million of the $104.6 million appeal. The details are shown in Table 6.

_____

[59a] Again these are personal observations based on my presence at the discussions as rapporteur.

[60] See Chapter VI below.

TABLE 6

BoB Restoration of AEC
FY 1967 Budget Appeals
($millions)

	Amount Appealed	Amount Restored
Operating Expenses		
Special Nuclear Materials	$18.0	$12.0
Weapons	9.0	2.0
Reactor Development	15.6	5.8
Physical Research	6.9	0.0
Biology and Medicine	7.6	0.0
Training, Education and Information	0.6	0.0
Plowshare	5.3	0.0
Subtotal	$66.0	$19.8
Capital Equipment	3.0	1.5
Construction Projects	17.6	0.0
Goods and Services on Order	18.0	6.6
Total	$104.6	$27.9

The Commissioners met on December 8, 1965, to consider the Bureau of the Budget's restorations.[61] They had by now essentially exhausted their bargaining leverage with the Bureau; further attempts to rescue FY 1967 program funds would have to be made directly to the

---

[61] Minutes of Commission Meeting 2163, December 8, 1965.

President. By convention, such appeals had to be fairly limited and supported by the strongest possible case. Thus the tone of the discussion at Meeting 2163 was similar to that of the meetings preceding the appeal to the Bureau of the Budget.

There was instant agreement that Bureau failure to restore the full $18.0 million to special nuclear materials operations should be taken to the President. Discussion concentrated on developing the strongest possible case to support such an appeal, the details of which unfortunately remain classified.[62] The Commissioners agreed without comment to the General Manager's recommendation that $4.0 million of the remaining $6.0 million cut in weapons should also be appealed.

There was a reasonably lengthy discussion about appeal of reactor development items. The consensus was that at this point these projects were hopelessly lost. The director of the Bureau of the Budget (who would be present at the Chairman's meeting with the President) was certain to be particularly adamant here. The Chairman said he would make an effort to retrieve the requested test facility at $1.9 million on the basis of the employment dislocations which would occur at Argonne National Laboratory if the project were deferred.[63]

---

[62] One unclassified point: The Commissioners did note the desirability of pointing out to the President the effects of the reductions upon AEC's capacity to produce the isotope, Pu-239, then considered the prime candidate as a power source for the artificial heart. President Johnson was widely known to have a strong personal interest in the artificial heart program.

[63] Minutes of Commission Meeting 2163, December 8, 1965.

The Controller and one of the Commissioners discussed the redefinition of the Commission's oceanographic program as a "small terrestrial reactor for underwater use. " This would allow it to be funded under a program which Admiral Rickover and the Navy were already operating. Abbadessa indicated that he would call the Bureau director to see if he would go along with such an arrangement.

Chairman Seaborg was personally inclined to appeal all of the physical research items which the BoB had failed to restore. The Controller, however, urged caution. The two A-E construction items, along with an associated $2.0 million in operating money, should obviously be taken to the President. (None of the other senior staff or Commissioners demurred.) The BoB could be expected to be intransigent on the other reductions in view of the amount of growth the administration was already permitting in the physical research program. One of the Commissioners heartily agreed and the Chairman agreed, reluctantly, not to press the point.

There was extensive discussion of the Plowshare program, dominated by the Controller's extremely pessimistic assessment of the Bureau position. This judgment was not questioned by any of the Commissioners or program staff.

After some additional head-shaking, the Commission agreed the Chairman should take the following items to President Johnson:

	($ millions)
1) Operating expenses	
a) special nuclear materials program	$6.0
b) weapons program	4.0
2) Construction authority	
a) "Positron Accelerator"	1.9
3) Physical research program	
a) Meson research	2.0
b) 200 BEV Accelerator, A-E	4.0
c) Meson facility	3.0 $20.9

(Source: Memorandum of December 13, 1965 from the Secretary, "FY 1967 Budget Appeals")

Having made these decisions, however, the Commission proceeded into extended discussion of the serious threat to the Rover program posed by the BoB position. The issue was whether AEC ought to take the stand that "no meaningful program" could be carried out at a funding level below the requested $86.0 million. The program director, one of the Commissioners, and most of the senior staff ardently favored this tactic, arguing that any indication of AEC willingness to accept a reduction of the size identified by the Bureau of the Budget ($40.0 million) would delay the program at least ten years. The Commissioner who supported the staff made a forceful plea that in his discussions with the President the Chairman should not hint at any willingness to bargain about Rover.

Dr. Seaborg, though, was equally positive that an "all or nothing" position was indefensible. While eager to make the strongest possible case for the $86.0 million, he believed the Commission should, in the end, be prepared to accept a drastically reduced budget as a last resort to keep the program alive. If it came down to it, something was obviously better

than nothing. The discussion ended with an apparent "sense of the meeting."[64]   If pressed, the Chairman should stoutly defend the $86.0 mil-

lion figure indicating no willingness to bargain a reduction in Rover for

restoration of other items. There was no real consensus, however, on

what Seaborg should do if the President seemed prepared to call the

Commission's hand and did indeed threaten to cancel the whole program.

The Commissioner who was most adamant on the point said rather vaguely

that if this seemed likely, all of the AEC's program priorities would have

to be reviewed. Reading a bit between the lines, one might speculate

that he had in mind trading reductions in the physical research area to

salvage Rover.

FY 1967 continued to be an unusual budgetary year. Norm-

ally Presidential approval or denial of the relatively small number of

items "appealed" to him personally by the agency head signals the end

of a "budget cycle" within the Executive.[65]   This was not the case in

---

[64] An old Quaker phrase which quite nicely captures the
Seaborg style of chairmanship. During the three years in which I
observed the process, even the most sharp disputes among the Commission only very rarely ended in a formal vote.

[65] By all accounts the personal relationship between the
President and the agency head is the critical variable at this stage.
Although I have seen no systematic evidence, there is widely believed
to be great variation across agencies in the proportion of items successfully appealed. Glenn Seaborg's record with Lyndon Johnson in
this regard is generally regarded as extraordinarily impressive.

December, 1965; faced with burgeoning military demands from South
Vietnam, Lyndon Johnson was bearing down especially hard upon his
government. Thus Seaborg returned from Texas with a mixed report
for his colleagues.[66] He had managed to secure the President's approval for all the items listed above. The only conditional provision
was in connection with the 200 BEV accelerator. Johnson had explicitly
noted that his approval of architect-engineering funds was not to be
taken by the Commission to constitute Administration final approval
for the construction of the facility.

After agreeing to the appeal items, however, the President
had unexpectedly directed Seaborg again to reduce the overall Commission budget, this time by $134 million, to be developed from the items
listed in the original Bureau of the Budget "mark-up" as "possible
additional" reductions. The President had specified that the $134 million
was to be prepared in such a way as to maximize reductions in actual
expenditures during fiscal year 1967. Prior to the Chairman's report
to the other Commissioners, the Controller's office developed a set
of recommendations to meet the Presidential requirement. These
are reproduced in Table 7, which for convenience also notes the Bureau
of the Budget's "possible additional" cuts.

---

[66] Minutes of Commission Meeting 2164, December 11, 1965.

TABLE 7

Staff Recommendations
(In $ thousands)

Program	Possible Additional Reductions	Staff Recommendations to meet new Presidential Requirement	Impact on Expenditures
Special Nuclear Materials - Operating (General Cut)	$ 2,000	$ 1,000	$ 1,000
Weapons - On continent	25,000	20,000	20,000
Desalting	1,000	---	---
UHTREX	2,300	---	---
Euratom	2,000	---	---
Merchant Ship - Research and Development	1,500	1,500	1,500
Space - SNAP	2,000	2,000	2,000
Naval Reactors	10,000	10,000	10,000
LAMPRE	4,800	4,800	4,800
ROVER - Operating	86,000	5,000	5,000
- Construction	3,000	1,000	---
FFTF	67,500	65,500	---
Physical Research - Operating	8,000	3,000	3,000
AGS Conversion	45,300	---	---
Biology and Medicine - Operating	2,000	1,000	1,000
Biology Laboratory - PNL	5,000	---	---
Training, Education and Information - Puerto Rico	1,000	---	---
Isotopes Division - Food Preservation	1,870	---	---
Alpha Fuels Facility	2,300	---	---
PLOWSHARE - Excavation	4,850	1,000	1,000
- Scientific	2,350	---	---
GSO	20,030	16,200	---
	$299,900	$134,000	$ 49,300

Source: Memorandum of December 13, 1965, from the Controller to the Commissioners, "Commission Action on Presidential Review of AEC FY 1967 Budget Request."

There was more (or less, depending upon one's perspective) to the staff proposal than meets the eye. To begin, there is the matter of the fast fuels test facility (FFTF). Elimination of all but architect-engineer funds for this facility was plainly the key to the staff recommendations. Again, authorization for this project had emerged as the focal point of negotiations over the Commission's budget; it had obviously, in this sense, become the single most important item among all of AEC's proposed activities. What is perhaps not so obvious is the significance of the series of actions taken on it. At one level the recurring proposals to include only A-E funds in the agency's budget for the coming fiscal year constituted recognized tactical gambits based in part upon the assumption that in future years the sunk costs of preliminary design work can be argued to constitute a de facto commitment to an enterprise. But this is only part of the story. As the director of reactor development and at least one Commissioner argued, the sheer fact of the agency's having twice decided to meet a budget ceiling by deferring a request for full authorization for a project said something about the priority of that project vis-a-vis other activities.[67] In this sense, the Commission's ultimate decision in 1965 to defer for a year the full authorization re-

---

[67] During Commission discussion of the proposed cuts, the chief defender of the FFTF on the Commission was visibly less than delighted with the staff recommendation but chose not to press the point. See Minutes of Commission Meeting 2165, December 13, 1965.

quest is evidence about AEC policy. In the end it was an authorization request for an important project in the civilian power reactor program which was deferred rather than one for a pure research device, the AGS, then regarded as the most likely alternative.

For the moment this is the only point I want to make. Events within the annual budget cycle are part of the process of priority-setting by government. We have nearly completed an almost uniquely full and frank account of a single budget-making process in a particular federal agency, wholly based upon the agency's internal records. What hopefully is now too clear to require emphasis is that this has been an account not only of budget-making, but also of policy-making. Again, this is not to deny that much of what goes on can be accounted for in terms of tactics and strategems. Though it is not self-evident from the figures themselves in Table 7, a second purpose of the December 13, 1965, AEC staff proposal was to reduce programs known to enjoy Congressional support, that is, to reduce areas where chances of restoration later were felt to be good. This was actually the subject of some banter during the Commission's consideration of the recommendations.[68] The proposed $20 million reduction in the weapons program was of this sort, as was the $10 million cut from naval reactors.

---

[68] Minutes of Commission Meeting 2165, December 13, 1965.

On the other hand, the $4.8 million cut from the "LAMPRE"
(an advanced reactor concept) programs was made with no anticipation
of eventual restoration, and, moreover, it signified effective termination of the whole program.[69] This, incidentally, suggests another
general conclusion from the series of events we have reviewed. At
the program level, not all decisions are incremental. And even where
they are, there are important degrees of incrementalism. At various
points during the FY 1967 budget cycle the merchant ship program,
special nuclear materials program, "Rover" and several "SNAP"
projects were seriously threatened by reductions representing substantial fractions of their total respective budgets. The final outcome
can partially be seen in Table 8, to which the Controller directed the
Commission's attention during discussion of the Presidential directive.[70]

The consensual appraisal among the Commissioners and
their staff of the figures reflected in Table 8 was one of optimism. Dr.
Seaborg, for example, stressed what he believed to be the real importance of his successes with the President. As a consequence, the Com-

---

[69] Ibid.

[70] Ibid.

TABLE 8

Operating Expenses by Program
(In $ millions)

	FY 1966	FY 1967 BoB Mark-up	Recommended to Meet Presidential Directive	Change
Raw Materials	$ 210.0	$ 163.0	$ 163.0	$ -47.0
Special Nuclear Materials	376.0	349.7	354.7	-21.3
Weapons	692.4	655.0	639.0	-53.4
Reactors	470.7	486.0	462.7	- 8.0
Physical Research	236.0	260.0	259.9	23.9
Biology and Medicine	83.0	88.0	88.0	5.0
Training, Education and Information	15.8	17.2	17.2	1.4
Isotopes Development	11.6	14.8	14.8	3.2
Plowshare	15.4	17.2	16.2	0.3
Community	8.9	10.1	10.1	1.2
Program Direction	81.5	84.0	84.0	2.5
Security	5.7	5.4	5.4	- 0.3
Total NOA	$2,207.0	---	---	$ -92.0

Source: Minutes of Commission Meeting 2165, December 13, 1965.

mission's plans for the Meson research facility, the Rover program, the AGS, the operations of the weapons laboratories, the 200 BEV accelerator, and the long-term future of the civilian power program were all unaffected by what had been an extraordinarily stringent budget year.[71] The special nuclear materials production program had also fared relatively well, in part, evidently because of the President's personal interest in the Commission's artificial heart program and Dr. Seaborg's success in persuading him of the possible need for substantial quantities of plutonium as fuel.

On this mildly congratulatory note, the internal FY 1967 budget cycle effectively came to an end for the AEC as the Commission approved without substantial additional comment the staff's recommendations for meeting the final Presidential cut (Table 7). The budget as amended by these changes, with a single important exception, became part of the President's FY 1967 budget to Congress.

The exception was Admiral Rickover. He was not pleased with the $10 million cut in his program proposed by the Controller and approved by the Commission at Meeting 2165. In executive session dis-

---

[71] Minutes of Commission Meeting 2165, December 13, 1965. Dr. Seaborg did, however, observe elsewhere in the discussion that the conversation regarding Rover had been very difficult. Dr. Donald Hornig, Presidential Science Advisor, had pointedly and repeatedly questioned the priority of a program with no established requirement and which would not come to fruition until 1985 given the requirements of the war.

cussions during the following week the Commission restored $5 million
of the naval reactors reduction, spreading the balance more or less
evenly among the general operating funds for several programs.

Before leaving FY 1967 for more general matters, a final
thought on the data in Table 8. Calculating each program level as recommended by staff as a proportion of the corresponding level for FY 1966
and comparing each ratio with the equivalent ratio of the totals reinforces
both the Commission's optimistic appraisal of the outcome and our own
interest in disaggregating to the program level. The results of such
calculations are shown in Table 9.

TABLE 9

Per Cent Change in Operating Expenses by
Program

(FY 1966 - FY 1967 Recommendations to Meet Presidential Directive)

Raw Materials	- 20	Training, Education	
Special Nuclear Materials	- 6	and Information	+ 8
Weapons	- 9	Isotopes Development	+20
Reactors	- 2	Plowshare	+ 8
Physical Research	+10	Community	+12
Biology and Medicine	+ 6	Program Direction	+ 3
		Security	- 5

Total New Obligational Authority -4

It appeared, that December afternoon, as if the Commission's total operating budget was going to shrink by about four per cent from its FY 1966 level. This overall contraction obviously concealed, however, striking variation at the program level. The modest two per cent shrinkage in reactor development was a major defensive victory given the preferences of the Bureau of the Budget and probably others within the administration. Meanwhile, most other civilian programs, notably physical research, actually managed to grow. It is precisely this manifest variation in outcomes at the program level to which we now want to turn. Indeed, it will become clear as we both further disaggregate the Commission's activities and extend our discussion across wider time spans that a variety of intriguing things are recorded by the information generated in the federal budget cycles. Many of these things, moreover, have been apparent casualties of the quantitative revolution in American political science.

CHAPTER II

THE POLITICS OF PROGRAM PROSPERITY

1. Politics versus Process

By an impressive margin, the Federal Government spends
more money, does more things, and affects more people than it did
twenty-five, or even ten, years ago. But the record of innovation and
expansion has not been uniform; rather the prosperity of individual programs has varied widely during this period. Some programs have con-
tinuously prospered, grown and evidently become permanent fixtures in
the governmental system: NDEA student loans, research in high-energy
physics, Social Security, and most recently health care. Others seem
to have thrived only temporarily: aircraft nuclear propulsion, manned
space flight, and the "Green Berets"; while still others have an uneven
history of success and failure and are constantly involved in political
turmoil: AID, Model Cities, and the Atomic Energy Commission's
"Plowshare" program.

What is responsible for the success or failure of governmental
programs? Who (or what) determines our national priorities? Traditionally political scientists have regarded the budgetary process as the rich-
est source of evidence on these matters.[1] The assumption has been that

---

[1] The "traditional" literature on the budgetary process is immense. The text and references in either Arthur Smithies, The Budgetary

the budgetary process, the most important "action forcing" mechanism

in government, reflects the aspirations and controversies which cause

some programs to be favored over others.   Within the budgetary process

clashes of interest and priority should be expressed in real dollar terms.

Evidence concerning the goals of program directors and clients, the sup-

port of agency heads, the surveillance of the Bureau of the Budget, the

strategic choices of the President, and the influence of Congress should

all be contained in the data generated annually by the federal budget cycle.

More recent quantitative analyses of the federal budgetary

process do not, however, support these assumptions.   Instead, a younger

generation of political scientists has discovered "striking regularities"

in which what happens in any given year closely resembles what had

happened in the previous year.[2]   Implicit in this approach is the view

---

Process in the United States (New York: McGraw-Hill, 1955), or Jesse
Burkhead, Governmental Budgeting (New York: John Wiley & Sons, 1956),
provide convenient guides. Also of particular interest are: Richard E.
Neustadt, "The Presidency and Legislation: The Growth of Central Clear-
ance," 48, American Political Science Review, (September 1954), pp. 641-
671; Arthur Maass, "In Accord with the President's Program," in C. J.
Friedrich and K. Gailbraith, eds., 4 Public Policy, (Harvard University
Press, Cambridge, Mass., 1954); Fritz Morstein Marx, "The Bureau of
the Budget: Its Evolution and Present Role," I and II, 30 American Political
Science Review, (August and October, 1945, pp. 653-684 and 869-898; and
Lucius Wilmerding, Jr., The Spending Power, (New Haven: Yale University
Press, 1943).

[2] Aaron Wildavsky's highly influential, The Politics of the Budgetary Process, (Boston: Little, Brown & Co., 1964), is the watershed.
The ideas embodied in this analysis were more precisely formulated in

that the events described in the preceding chapter--the strategic and
tactical choices, the interagency disputes and alliances, the battles
with the Bureau of the Budget, and the appeals for Presidential support--
really make very littled difference. In the end what happens during any
given period pretty much determines what will happen in subsequent periods.

There is, of course, an important element of truth in these
findings. As we have seen, budgets are not rewritten from scratch every
year; and hence it is silly to judge the consequences of policy innovations
as if they were. Further, it is probably true that political historians
(and public administrators) have occasionally exaggerated the importance
of particular policies, individual choices, and competing personalities.
After all, they find public administration interesting precisely because
it embodies great controversies between powerful political forces, conflicts which are both inherent in and shed light upon the process of popular government and which have been very much a part of American government from the outset.

Otto A. Davis, M. A. H. Dempster and Aaron Wildavsky, "A Theory of the
Budgetary Process," 60:3 American Political Science Review (September
1966), pp. 529-547. See also, by same authors, "On the Process of
Budgeting: An Empirical Study of Congressional Appropriations," in
Gordon Tullock, ed., Papers on Non-Market Decision Making, (Charlottes-
ville: Thomas Jefferson Center for Political Economy, 1966), pp. 63-133.
This general analytic approach has been importantly extended by John P.
Crecine. See his "A Computer Simulation Model of Municipal Resource
Allocation," (paper delivered at the Midwest Conference of Political
Science, April 1966), as well as Governmental Problem Solving (Chicago,
Ill.: Markham Pub. Co., 1968. See also Ira Sharkensky, The Routines
of Politics (New York: Van Nostrand, 1969).

Still, an important issue remains: what is the relationship between public administration and public policy? The challenge of the quantitative budget studies is their argument that administrators rarely depart very significantly from what they were already doing--they "muddle through" as best they can, making only marginal changes in the established operations of government; and that consequently budgets are massively stable from one year to the next.[3] This theory seems to explain almost everything with a very simple set of principles.

> The most striking fact about the equations /which describe the budgetary process/ is their simplicity. This is perhaps partly because of the possibility that more complicated decision procedures are re-served for special circumstances represented by extreme values of the random variable. However, the fact that the decision rules generally fit the data very well is an indication that these simple equations have considerable explanatory power. Little of the variance is left unexplained.[4]

It may also be the case, however, that these same simple equations ob-scure the relationship between administration and policy. The problem is complicated because budget data presents us with a difficult measure-ment problem. How do we take a yearly government budget and reorder

---

[3] See in this regard Charles Lindblom, "The Science of 'Muddling Through'," 29 Public Administration Review (Spring, 1959), pp. 79-88; and Charles Lindblom, The Intelligence of Democracy: Decision Making Through Mutual Adjustment (New York: Free Press, 1965).

[4] Davis, Dempster and Wildavsky, op. cit., p. 543.

it to provide an indicator of government priorities? This is by no means
an easy question for the budget is simultaneously a yearly process and
a vehicle for deciding among alternative priorities. Obviously, these
are not the same thing even though they are nested within the same data.
The fact that political choices and the budgetary process are so inter-
twined accounts for much of the methodological confusion; conclusions
about the nature of the budgetary process have been generalized to include the policy process as well.

To make these thoughts more concrete, I will continue to
draw upon the activities of the Atomic Energy Commission. Though
now a mature agency with established purposes and programs, the AEC
was created and in many ways has continued to exist in an atmosphere
of uncertainty and conflict regarding the appropriate applications of a
new and poorly understood technology.[5] Was this technology to be applied exclusively to the development of weapons? Or were its applications ultimately to be essentially civilian and peaceful? Could peaceful
applications be carried out with economy and safety? By whom, and
under whose supervision? These and other questions have defined
areas of sharp conflict among philosophies of government and among
programs and personalities. Moreover. the agency's budgetary
records contain massive evidence of these clashes, evidence which is

---

[5] James R. Newman and Byron S. Miller, The Control of
Atomic Energy, (New York: McGraw-Hill Book Co. , 1948).

not at all well handled by the way quantitative techniques have recently been applied to the subject of government budgeting. After first summarizing more fully the conclusions of these studies, I will demonstrate this point narratively by reviewing the government's decision to develop a thermonuclear weapon, drawing largely upon Hewlett and Duncan's comprehensive account of that event. Then, using the Commission's budgetary data, collected over time and across the stages described in the previous chapter, I will suggest how quantitative analysis of public policies can, given the proper theoretical context, assist in answering questions about the establishment and modification of governmental priorities. I will try to test, that is to say, the view that budgetary records can be a source of information about governmental policies as distinct from governmental process.

2. Theories of the Budgetary Process

The budgets of federal agencies are developed over a period which begins as much as eighteen months before appropriations requests are acted upon by Congress. We have seen in the previous chapter how the timing and characteristics of the "stages" in this development may vary from year to year, particularly during the "appeals" process in November and December. The form and to some degree the substance of the constraints on agency behavior are often deliberately varied by the administration to communicate the scarcity of overall financial re-

sources. Our review of the FY 1967 AEC experience strongly suggests
that the effect of this more or less successfully created climate of scarcity
is to render the entire process of budget formulation within an agency
one of explicit competition among alternative "policies. " For those actually involved in budget making each year is "stringent"; there are always
more ways of spending dollars than there are dollars to spend. Programs
compete among themselves for a limited resource with the function of the
"stages" being to facilitate that competition. This competition is largely
obscured when, as in the Davis, Dempster and Wildavsky work, agencies
are taken as the unit of analysis and the histories of their respective requests and subsequent appropriations are regarded as merely replications
of the same event. Thus, variation in the appropriations for sixty-four
non-defense federal agencies from 1947 to 1963 is accounted for by a
"single set of decision rules that are linear and temporally stable. "[6]
In their most sophisticated equation (decision rule), Davis, Dempster and
Wildavsky argue that the Congressional appropriation for any agency is

> . . . a fixed mean percentage of the agency's re-
> quest for a certain year plus a fixed mean percent-
> age of a dummy variable which represents that
> part of the agency's request for the year at issue
> which is not part of the appropriation or request
> of the previous year plus a random variable repre-

---

[6] Davis, Dempster and Wildavsky, op. cit. , p. 529.

> senting the part of the appropriation attributable
> to the special circumstances of the year. [7]

This is to say that appropriations subcommittees normally give an

agency some proportion of what it asked for, adjusted by things in

dispute and special considerations peculiar to a particular year.

The point that Davis, Dempster and Wildavsky most empha-

size is that their decision rules fit the data: ". . . the results are very

good. We leave very little of the variance statistically unexplained. "[8]

In fact, a majority of Congressional decisions (appropriations) have

R^2s exceeding 99 per cent and all but two have R^2s above 90 per cent.

Further, these decision rules seem to square neatly with other re-

search which suggests that the budgetary process in appropriations

subcommittees has become an institutionalized series of actions

sanctioned by an elaborate set of norms and behaviors.[9]

Though we have no quarrel with the statistical validity of

these findings, they are plainly not very helpful as an account of a

governmental decision-making process which often involves sharp

political confrontation. Why is this so? The problem is one of theory.

---

[7] Ibid. , p. 535.

[8] Ibid. , p. 537.

[9] Richard Fenno, "The House Appropriations Committee on
a Political System: The Problem of Integration, " 56, American Political
Science Review (1962), pp. 310-324. See also, Richard Fenno, The Power
of The Purse: Appropriations Politics in Congress (Boston: Little, Brown,
1966.

The essential insights upon which Wildavsky and others have built are

contained in the writings of Herbert Simon and his colleagues.[10] The

theme of this work is that people are quite limited in their ability to

process new information, generate alternatives, anticipate consequences,

and weigh values. The Simon - Lindblom administrator faces a highly

complicated world, a world of multiple values and goals related to each

other in unknown ways. He has no very reliable way of predicting the

consequences of alternative courses of action and little information

pertinent to assessing these consequences even if he had an acceptable

theory. As Crecine has put it,

> (He) is a man with limited knowledge, limited in-
> formation, and limited cognitive ability, making
> a policy choice in an uncertain world by "drastic-
> ally" simplifying the problem and making marginal
> adjustments in past "successful" policies to formu-
> late current policies. [11]

---

[10] Herbert A. Simon, Administrative Behavior, (2d ed.;
New York: 1957); Herbert A. Simon, Models of Man; Herbert A. Simon,
Donald Smithborg and Victor Thompson, Public Administration (New
York: 1950); David Braybrooke and Charles Lindblom, A Strategy of
Decision (New York: 1964); Richard Cyert and James March (eds.)
A Behavioral Theory of the Firm (Englewood Cliffs: Prentice-Hall, 1963).
Allen Newell, J. C. Shaw and H. A. Simon, "Theories of Decision
Making in Economics and Behavioral Science," 49 American Economic
Review, pp. 253-283; C. P. E. Clarkson and H. A. Simon, "Simulation
of Individual and Group Behavior," 50 American Economic Review (1960)
pp. 920-932.

[11] Crecine, 1969, op. cit., p. 11.

Hence, administrators are captives of the past; what they have done yesterday is usually a good predictor of what they will do today. This theory has obvious implications for studying most types of decision-making or problem-solving behavior, and as Crecine, among others, has observed, budget-making in an organizational environment is certainly one of these. It is a complex process in which officials usually under the intense pressure of time and circumstances might be expected to employ whatever decision rules seem to have worked in the past and to make adjustments only at the margins. As a consequence, any given budget request, whether from a department, a bureau, or a program division, can be expected to be some marginal adjustment of either a previous request or a previous appropriation. It can be expected that it is last year's budget with minor changes and can be treated as if most of it had never been reconsidered from year to year. So far as it goes this is quite true. Across aggregations of decision-making units (federal agencies, municipal administrations, or individual budget makers), behavior at time "T" can be shown to be a robust function of comparable behavior at time "T-1." The trouble is that the budgetary process is also a battlefield for conflicting priorities and alternative policies. The categories of analysis established by Wildavsky, Crecine and others help us understand the behavior of the pertinent decision-maker viewed as a problem-solver. They do not, however, shed much light upon the events which over time cause some activities to prosper and grow while others wither and die. It is this variation in the competitive success of alternative and often explicitly competitive programs, rather than the cognitive processes of the decision-making units, which are central to the politics of public administration. The "problem solving" perspective is inherently unable to account for the differential success of alternative policies; indeed it cannot describe what public policy means at all.

A different level of explanation and a different unit of analysis are required, ones which focus on the policies themselves and their fate over time. In the context of the budgetary process, programs are the operational units of public policy. They describe what government is actually doing. They provide "categories that are close to being /the/ true outputs of government. "[12]

Agencies can be considered decision-making entities; they are not, however, the descriptive unit for what government is actually doing. They merely reflect how it happens to be organized. Also--unlike programs--agencies do not usually succeed or fail. Agencies can, moreover, be both organizations and institutions. When they are both, they are likely to be hardy as well as inert.

---

[12] Roland N. McKean and Melvin Awshen, "Limitations, Risks and Problems," in David Novick (ed.), Program Budgeting: Program Analysis and the Federal Government (Cambridge, Mass.: Harvard University Press, 1965), p. 286.

By comparison the use of programs as units of analysis is helpful in a number of ways. Programs exhibit lively variance; in contrast to agencies, their recent history is likely to be a less useful guide to their present condition or their future behavior. More to the point, programs reflect what government is doing; in the fashionable jargon, they are output rather than input categories--a behavioral rather than an administrative classification. [13]

Programs have histories in which we can see evidence of support and opposition from a variety of competing interests at different levels of government. Agencies (or bureaus), except in their first years of operation, do not have such histories. They are normally accepted as part of the fixed institutional landscape subject to change only rarely and during periods of crisis and rapid change in political ideology. An important lesson of the Eisenhower Administration is that changing the party in power does not usually open up an already established agency (e.g., Social Security Administration) to attack. Such a change does, however, usually affect the relative priorities of programs within an agency.

---

[13] For a thoughtful discussion which complements many of these points, see: Charles L. Schultze, The Politics and Economics of Public Spending, (Washington, D.C.: The Brookings Institution, 1968). Indirect, but I believe vivid, support for many of the same arguments can be found in Charles L. Schultze, Edward R. Fried, Alice M. Rivlin and Nancy H. Teeters, Setting National Priorities: The 1972 Budget, (Washington, D.C.: The Brookings Institution, 1971). See especially Chapters 8-11.

Thus the salient characteristic of established agencies is stability--

organizational and budgetary. It is this underlying stability that

Wildavsky and others have captured. Naturally there is not much mean-

ingful conflict at this level of government. The budgetary process tradi-

tion strongly suggests that when all the programs for a given agency are

considered together, there will be a great deal of similarity between

what happens at any given stage of the budget cycle and what happened

at a previous stage. This is precisely what is reflected in Table 10.[14]

TABLE 10

Correlations Among Budgetary Stages of 23 AEC
Programs Pooled Across FY 1958 - FY 1972

	Division	Gen'l Mgr.	AEC	BoB	Appeal	Presidential
Division	1.000					
Gen'l Mgr.	.996	1.000				
AEC	.997	.999	1.000			
BoB	.995	.998	.997	1.000		
Appeal	.996	.997	.997	.998	1.000	
Final	.995	.996	.997	.998	.999	1.000

[14] The data from which Table 10 was calculated was drawn
from the AEC's internal financial records between 1956 and 1972. These

The requests or allocations for all stages of the process have been correlated with the other stages across the fifteen fiscal cycles for which we have data. For these fifteen observations, the funds requested at a given stage correlate almost perfectly with that requested at a previous stage and that granted at a subsequent stage. The perfection of these correlations is powerful support for Wildavsky's basic argument about the regularities of the budgetary process, but, it suggests very little about the political conflicts which we know were taking place during the period spanned by this data. For, within this apparently stable framework five substantial AEC programs were cancelled altogether, two major activities experienced a sharp monotonic decline in their fortunes, three grew impressively, and most others fluctuated widely. Morevoer, the picture is not very much different at the program rather than the agency level.

---

records provide information on fifteen agency "budget cycles,"--FY 1958 - FY 1972, inclusive. Within each cycle it was possible to isolate at least six discrete stages beginning with the program divisions' requests to the Commission's General Manager and ending with the official Presidential budget for a given year. These stages are the columns of Table 10. The intermediate stages represent the General Manager's recommendation to the Commission; the Commission's "September" submission to the administration; the Bureau of the Budget's "mark-up" of that submission; and the "appeal" of the "mark-up," either to the Bureau or the President. This fifth "appeal" stage is the only one not strictly comparable across all fifteen years. Records of this process are often difficult to locate and for FY 1959 and FY 1960 there is no evidence that an "appeal" as such was allowed at all. All of these data are reproduced in Appendix A.

When requests and allocations are correlated at the program
level there is on the whole less close association across stages but the
average magnitude of the correlation coefficients is still quite high. Most
are in the .80 - .90 range, and out of twenty-three programs, for only
four is any pair of stages associated at a level less than .70.[15] So, even
at places where conflict is <u>known</u> to have occurred, the budgetary process
perspective merely uncovers "striking regularities." A mere change in
the unit of analysis, that is to say, is insufficient to get at the underlying
process of policy formulation; we apparently need a more profound change
in perspective.

There are at least two issues here. First, as we have already
noted, there is the measurement problem: how do we take a yearly government budget and reorder it to produce information about government priorities. This is a matter of finding among the budget records the differences
as well as the regularities over time and among programs which are meaningful in terms of public policy as distinct from explaining the process of
budget formation itself. If we can successfully do this, the causal problem

---

[15] It was possible to identify and trace the histories in whole
or in part of twenty-three AEC programs over the period 1956 - 1972.
As noted in Chapter 1, the twenty-three programs selected represent a
compromise between an exhaustive categorization of all AEC activities
into mutually exclusive headings that the people involved would agree
represent "real" programs as distinct from mere projects on the one
hand or "accounting categories" on the other. The twenty-three identified
programs are mutually exclusive but are not exhaustive of all Commission
activities.

becomes clearer. For the second issue is a causal one, namely, once we have measured priorities how do we account for their variance across time. On a priori grounds we may suspect that this variation is caused by the joint effects of internal bureaucratic interests, Presidential prefer- ences, clientele group activities, or even the "technical" failure of experi- ments. The relative impact of these factors is, we might suppose, sensi- tive to the personalities and skills, say at "bureaucratic gamesmanship," of the various participants, the degree to which they believe in their ideas, and the simultaneous policies and priorities of other agencies.

The budgetary records themselves can hardly be expected to provide unambiguous evidence about these matters or to help us sort out the complicated causal relationships among such factors. But neither is it completely useless for these purposes. In reviewing the experience of the Atomic Energy Commission in the FY 1967 cycle, we saw that differ- ences regarding what the government should be doing and what it should be doing first do exist among the participants represented by the succes- sive stages of the budgetary process. It was clear that the AEC's General Manager favored the Commission's power reactor programs over pure research in high energy physics. This perference did not in the end pre- vail as the Commission itself, at the prodding of the Chairman, settled upon a different ordering of the agency's priorities. We also saw that obvious differences existed between the Commission as a whole and the

Bureau of the Budget regarding the Rover program and the AEC's plutonium production activities, among others. Again, the Commission's priorities prevailed.

The point is, we know these differences about priorities have causal impact on what government does and when it does it. Success at one level of government does not <u>necessarily</u> imply success at another. What is important to an agency's chief executive officer may or may not be important to a politically appointed senior administrator. In either case, those priorities are unlikely to correspond exactly to those of the Bureau of the Budget, the President, or the Congress.

So far the only empirical support for these arguments is the narrative case study of the Atomic Energy Commission's FY 1967 budget cycle, material not immune to the criticism that such studies are merely isolated occurrences unrepresentative of any general principles. Eventually we want to test the proposition that by examining the comparative fates of programs as they move together through the budget cycle we can recover more systematic evidence about the differing priorities of the interests represented at various stages. With this evidence in hand, we may be in a position to discover whose priorities count. For, my fundamental interest in all of this is to shed some light on the reasons why some programs prosper while others stagnate. Do variations in attention and support within an operating agency explain these differences, or do they more nearly reflect the effects of support or opposition elsewhere in government? How much causal impact do the preferences of agency

heads have by comparison with those of the Bureau of the Budget? Plainly,

such questions are central to an understanding of the behavior of govern-

ment as "a persuasive process where (those) lacking absolute power (seek)

to get something done through others who have the power to resist."[16]

   It has often been noted that as a scholar one can develop theories

of why and how things happened which are convincing to oneself and which

may even be valid in some sense, but which those who participated in the

events would neither recognize nor accept. For this reason it will be

helpful as a preliminary to addressing these theoretical problems to

flesh out our views about the histories of programs and the way they re-

flect conflict and consensus about public policy in terms of another brief

"case study, " this time of the events leading to the AEC's development,

testing, and production of thermonuclear weapons.

3. The Great Thermonuclear Debate

   To the casual observer, few post-World War II policy decisions

now seem to have been so inevitable as President Truman's action in

February of 1950 authorizing development of thermonuclear weapons.

---

[16] R. E. Neustadt, Presidential Power (New York: Signet
Books, 1964), p. 41.

Of course, the fact of the matter is that the issue was bitterly contested over several months, and that, for a short time, it appeared the program would not be undertaken. The Presidential decision was contrary to the unanimous recommendation of a committee of the nation's premier scientists and to the advice of the Chairman of the Atomic Energy Commission.

These events affected the future role of the Atomic Energy Commission in shaping of nuclear weapons policy, and in turn had consequences for all of the Commission's programs, both military and civilian. In relation to the military, the AEC was reduced to a passive role as a mere supplier of hardware to meet military requirements. The impact of this reduction in status upon all other AEC activities was profound and pervasive. Yet, the facts now available strongly suggest that these developments were not inevitable.

On September 3, 1949 the American government learned that the USSR had successfully detonated a nuclear device. Early in February, 1950 the White House announced a Presidential decision to develop a thermonuclear weapon--the "Super" bomb. The decision itself was apparently not especially agonizing. President Truman reportedly felt that he "had no choice but to go ahead."[17] A senior advisory group meeting a few days previously felt similarly constrained, believing its function merely to be "to prepare a record to support the only

---

[17] Richard G. Hewlett and Francis Duncan, op. cit. , p. 408.

decision possible under the circumstances. . . . The months of debate and the course of events had all but settled the issue. "[18]

The situation in February contrasted dramatically with that four months earlier. The initial consensus within the AEC had been to take the Soviet development in stride and to respond "with nothing more than speeding up existing programs. "[19] For the Commission this would primarily have involved expansion of its nuclear material production facilities, a matter which had already been under consideration for some time. A feature of this discussion significant for the forthcoming debate over the "Super" was the assumed ground rules regarding the appropriate division of labor between the Atomic Energy Commission and the Defense Department. These rules permitted the AEC to consider only whether existing production facilities were sufficient to satisfy projected military "needs, " in the establishment of which the civilian commission was allowed no material role.

> Secretary Johnson clearly had no intention of admitting
> State Department or Commission officials to the inner
> circles of military planning. He had told Webster
> (chairman of a "liaison" committee) that he would not
> permit the Commission, as the "producer" of nuclear
> weapons, to participate with the military, as the "con-
> sumer, " in determining weapon needs for the same

---

[18] Ibid. , p. 406.

[19] Ibid. , p. 371.

reason that he was opposed to having the Department
of Defense certify the need for additional Commission
facilities.[20]

The successful establishment of such domains of competence
is, of course, a central tactic of bureaucratic politics.[21] These domains
do not accidentally develop; they result from the actions of administrators
attempting to protect a set of interests. A key element in the evolving
thermonuclear controversy was the position which David Lilienthal chose
to adopt on these matters. For there was by no means unanimous agreement with the initial low-key actions proposed by the Atomic Energy Commission as a response to the Soviet detonation. The Joint Committee
was particularly restive. Senator Brian McMahon's typically blunt
position was that the United States "could never have enough atomic
bombs." The JCAE Chairman was exuberantly supported by the young
Staff Director of the Joint Committee, a Yale Law School graduate and
self-appointed strategist who had a generous view of his talents as a
military and political analyst. It all seemed quite simple to Borden:
". . . the facts led inexorably to the conclusion that there should be a
substantial increase in the requirements for nuclear weapons and a
new, concerted effort to develop the ultimate weapon system--the

---

[20] Ibid. , p. 370.

[21] Anthony Downs, Inside Bureaucracy (Boston: Little,
Brown, 1968), pp. 264 ff.

thermonuclear weapon carried by a nuclear-powered airplane. "[22]

Another important participant was Lewis Strauss, a member of the Atomic Energy Commission. By the end of September he had become convinced that the Commission should consult the General Advisory Committee of the Atomic Energy Commission on the matter of the Super, which now appeared to him to be the "only" way for the United States to "regain the absolute advantage" over the Soviet Union. Otherwise, the nation's present "relative advantage" would "surely diminish. "[23]

Meanwhile, other developments were taking place outside Washington. The possibility that recent international developments might revive the thermonuclear bomb idea were not lost on its most committed proponent, Edward Teller. The possibility of a fusion-based weapon had been Teller's driving intellectual passion since before the end of the war. The weapons community in general, however, had been unwilling to divert to an effort whose ultimate success seemed so problematic the immense intellectual and physical resources needed to work seriously on the problem. Teller's imaginative notions had consequently languished for several years as a "study" rather than as a research and development program.

---

[22] Hewlett and Duncan, op. cit., p. 372.

[23] Ibid., p. 373.

It was not long before weapons scientists interested in the Super got together with the Joint Committee. "The outcome was predictable: the legislators and the scientists were more than ever convinced that the superweapon might well save the nation from the Soviet threat." A subsequent meeting between the scientists and the Atomic Energy Commissioners was less auspicious. Lilienthal in particular seemed to the weaponeers "uninterested and almost repelled by the proposal."[24]

This was roughly the situation when, toward the end of October, the matter came to the enormously prestigious General Advisory Committee (GAC) of the Atomic Energy Commission, the institutional locus of J. Robert Oppenheimer's then formidable authority. Hewlett and Duncan's description of Oppenheimer's initial assessment of the situation is worth quoting at length:

> The Super, Oppenheimer wrote, /to James B. Conant/ was fast becoming a relevant alternative as a response to the Soviet threat. The technical prospects for the Super were not much better than they had been seven years earlier, but "two experienced promoters" like Lawrence and Teller were bound to change the climate of opinion. They had already had some effect on competent scientists, but they had made the greatest impact on members of the Joint Committee and the Joint Chiefs. The Joint Committee, "having tried to find something tangible to chew on ever since September 23rd has at last found its answer. We must have a

---

[24] Ibid. , p. 377.

super and we must have it fast. " . . . Oppenheimer
confided to Conant that he was not concerned about
the technical problems because he was not sure "the
miserable thing" would work, nor that it could "be
gotten to the target except by ox cart. " He was
worried that "this thing appears to have caught the
imagination, both of congressional and of military
people, as <u>the answer</u> to the problem posed by the
Russian advance. "[25]

It was in this atmosphere that the General Advisory Committee wrote

its famous negative report. The Committee concluded that "it could

not endorse high priority development of the super weapon, mostly

for technical reasons.[26]   Moreover, for most (but not all) of the

Committee, even if the weapon could be built, it was not clear that

it should be. Oppenheimer, Conant, Rowe, Smith, DuBridge and

Buckley advocated complete and unconditional renunciation of the

weapon. Fermi and Rabi, in even stronger language, passionately

rejected the whole concept of the bomb, arguing that its construction

could not be justified on any ethical grounds. Because of his absence

from the country, Glenn T. Seaborg's position was somewhat ambig-

uous.[26a]

The General Advisory Committee report "pleased Lilienthal, "

but by his own estimate "did not by itself seem a convincing response to

the tremendous pressure which had built up for the weapon.[27]   Oppen-

---

[25] Ibid. , pp. 378-9.

[26] Ibid. , p. 384.

26a Ibid.

[27] Ibid. , p. 385.

heimer, too, had doubts; doubts which, curiously, focused on Lilienthal, the one senior administrator who fully shared his own views about the folly of the proposed program. "Oppenheimer was no longer sure that Lilienthal had the necessary energy and resiliency to carry a tough de- cision through the Commission."[28] Oppenheimer was correct.

Strauss carried the battle to the other Commissioners. His arguments were finely adjusted to minimize the controversial, non- technical and political aspects of an essentially political and ethical controversy.

First, according to Strauss, the Commission simply had to get the facts straight. How much talent and material were necessary? These estimates would then have to be compared with a purely technical judgment on the chances for success. (Even the GAC had concluded that successful development was probable, given sufficient resources.) Next, "the military services would have to determine the value of the weapon."[29] Finally, the State Department would have to judge the effect on Western Europe.

> On the purely technical and economic questions which
> were within the Commission's competence, Strauss...
> failed to see the consistency in a position which advo-
> cated developing more efficient and more powerful
> fission weapons but rejected the Super.[30]

---

[28] Ibid., p. 387.

[29] Ibid., p. 387. (My italics)

[30] Ibid., p. 391.

Obviously the only way to confront this powerful position was by attacking its principal assumption: that the Atomic Energy Commission, or any civilian authority for that matter, had to accept the military's own estimate of the military value of the device. Strauss, one would expect, was far too astute a man to believe that the military's judgment on this matter could be entirely disinterested and objective. Lilienthal, however, did not choose to attack it. By this time he was faced with a split Commission--Gordon Dean having joined Strauss in support of the Super. Still, the great power and prestige of the General Advisory Committee was available for adroit deployment on the other side. Instead, the important strategy session between the Commission and the General Advisory Committee was poorly managed and apparently accomplished little more than to irritate Commissioner Dean.

Consequently, on November 9, Lilienthal carried a report to the President in which the members of the divided Commission, in effect, each presented his own view. Lilienthal himself "took a broad view,"[31] focusing on the global implications of American development of a weapon of mass destruction which had no apparent peaceful applications. Such arguments were bound to be less than telling in an increasingly charged atmosphere in which "several scientists had be-

---

[31] Ibid., p. 390.

come missionaries for the project. "[32] Lilienthal, though, "was convinced the report struck the right note. "[33] Interestingly, Oppenheimer
had anticipated the weakness of the Lilienthal position and had requested
permission to take the matter independently to the President. Lilienthal
however decided he personally could make a stronger case, and chose to
make it on moral grounds. Oppenheimer's more technically based reservations were ignored.

It now seems clear that these events were a watershed regarding the civilian commission's role in nuclear weapons matters. In subsequent years the Atomic Energy Commission's role in policy issues relating to the military applications of atomic energy would become increasingly
narrow despite its prevailing near monopoly of technical expertise. The
pattern established after the H-bomb decision was one in which the
Commission's contractor operated and staffed weapons laboratories
were the source of "bright ideas" which they communicated directly
with pertinent military personnel and institutions through channels which
more or less completely by-passed policy levels within the AEC.[34] Once
the military had determined there was a "requirement" for a particular

---

[32] Ibid., p. 391.

[33] Ibid., p. 394.

[34] The Commission staff within the Division of Military
Applications was (and is) "wired into" this communication process, but

concept or device, the Commission became a mere developer, tester and producer. Administration of this process of development, testing and fabrication is the responsibility of the Commission's Division of Military Application. As defined, this is a responsibility which generates very few "policy" issues.

Returning to the events of 1949, pressure continued to mount throughout November; indeed the whole issue almost became public during the middle of the month.[35] The Joint Chiefs formally declared that Soviet development of a thermonuclear bomb without equivalent United States capability would be "intolerable,"[36] and the President asked a special committee of the National Security Council to evaluate all relevant political, military and technical factors.

This was another critical period. It is evident from Hewlett and Duncan's account of the activities of this review group that only the Atomic Energy Commission possessed the technical knowledge pertinent to a decision on the military value of the weapon.[37] Thus, the information on this central point was developed within the Atomic Energy Com-

---

this Division had traditionally been manned and directed by military officers or personnel with a strong military background.

[35] Hewlett and Duncan, op. cit., p. 395.

[36] Ibid., pp. 396-7.

[37] Ibid., pp. 396-7. "In succeeding weeks the question of military value became the principal concern of the Commission members

mission by the Commission staff. This was precisely the effective

monopoly of information which might have served as the basis for an

effort by the AEC to secure for itself a far more substantive role in

weapons matters.

Clearly any Commission attempt to challenge the Department

of Defense or the Joint Chiefs supremacy on these matters would have led

to a major confrontation. Moreover, the outcome of such a battle was by

no means certain. Lilienthal's position would have been weakened by

several structural factors. First, the Atomic Energy Commission

under Lilienthal had continued the "contracting-out" policy initiated by

the Army when it administered the Manhattan Engineer District. Under

this policy, private concerns were hired by the government to operate

atomic energy facilities. The entrepreneurial activities of the weapons

scientists who favored the Super were a direct consequence of this admin-

---

of the working group. Paul Fine, from the Commission's Division of
Military Applications, analyzed this question in a lengthy study paper.
. . . He summarized the probable effects . . . (and) appraised the technical problems including the ignition of the light elements, the production
of tritium, and ordnance engineering. Fine was most helpful in his estimates of costs of an all-out effort on the Super. . . . Fine concluded that
unless the superweapons were very large, the damage area resulting
from their explosion would scarcely exceed that of fission weapons
which could have been produced with the same materials and facilities.
And were there, he asked, enough targets for weapons of that size?
This was the sort of question that preoccupied Manley, whom Lilienthal
had asked to serve as a member of the working group. . . . The Defense
members . . . were still saying that they did not know what the military
value of the Super would be, but Manley thought Fine's analysis made
that position untenable. "

istrative arrangement. Since the scientists were technically employees
of a contractor rather than the government they felt free to promote their
ideas at various levels of government. It is unlikely that scientists employed by an executive agency would have considered themselves so free.[39]
Two time-honored principles of liberal government would also have limited
Lilienthal's ability to carry the fight to the Joint Chiefs: the principles
of legislative supremacy and administrative pluralism. Both were basic
to the 1947 Atomic Energy Act. In the context of the circumstances surrounding the debate over the Super, the sentiments of the Joint Committee
combined with diversity of opinion among the Commissioners would obviously have multiplied Lilienthal's leadership problems.

Yet even when allowance is made for the inherent weakness of
Lilienthal's hand, the fact remains that he made no serious effort to ex-
ploit the potential leverage on these events with the Atomic Energy Commission did possess as a result of its monopoly of technical information.
Rather, and somewhat sadly, during the critical period in the beginning
of December when "Defense representatives were...using evasive tactics"

---

[39] Hewlett and Duncan, op. cit., p. 399. The "contracting-
out" system has become the AEC's standard management device. For
analysis of its origins and effects, see Harold K. Orlans, Contracting
for Atoms (Washington, D. C.: The Brookings Institution, 1967).

and the State Department "had shown no inclination to take any part in
the study, " Lilienthal's attention had to be "snapped back to the Super. "[40]

Lilienthal's curious ineffectiveness as Chairman of the Atomic Energy

Commission, a muted but important theme of the entire Hewlett and

Duncan volume, is nowhere more evident than in their description of

his role in the thermonuclear debate. In a very real sense the tragic

figure of this period is not Oppenheimer so much as Lilienthal. Had he

possessed Strauss' drive, commitment, and sense of tactics the story

might have had a quite different ending.   Even the usually cautious

Hewlett and Duncan conclude:

> Lilienthal's insistence upon seeing development of
> the Super largely as a moral issue had destroyed
> the very climate for decision-making he had set out
> to create in 1947. By opposing the Super on other
> than technical grounds, some of the Commissioners
> and members of the GAC had sacrificed their immun-
> ities as technical advisors in the policy debate and
> were now subject to political attack. [41]

And attack is precisely what the other side did.   In a series

of hearings during January the Joint Committee, the weapons scientists,

and the senior military were able to lay the foundation of a technical and

military case strong enough to neutralize the position of the General Ad-

visory Committee.   By the end of January "the General Advisory Committee

---

[40] Ibid. , p. 397-398, op. cit.

[41] Ibid. , p. 399.

was effectively removed from further consideration of the Super. "[42]
The Commission itself capitulated soon thereafter. The Joint Committee
and its allies, "dismissing the moral twinges as simply an emotional reaction to a difficult problem" had successfully established a record which
would support only one Presidential "decision"--build the Super. The
President himself, as we have already noted, believed in the end that
'he had no choice but to go ahead. "[43]

4. Program Prosperity

These events highlight at least two important features of the
process through which programs develop and prosper within the American
governmental system. Ideas, first of all, do not automatically become
programs. The one resource which is seldom in short supply in government is ideas; they are the great administrative surplus product--as
Presidents quickly learn when they ask for suggestions for State of the
Union speeches. But, most ideas never become programs, and among
those which do there is considerable variation in their prosperity,
longevity, and hardiness. Hewlett and Duncan's fine narrative describes
how the transformation of the thermonuclear idea into the thermonuclear
program was brought about. In the first instance, it was due to the ener-

---

[42] Ibid., p. 403.
[43] Ibid., p. 408.

getic entrepreneurial activity of Teller and his fellow weapon scientists.
They imaginatively and effectively seized upon an exogenous event (the
USSR's acquisition of nuclear weapons capability) and turned it into the
investment capital for their idea. They became "missionaries for the
project. "[44]

Second, the circumstances surrounding the establishment
of the thermonuclear weapons program left the Atomic Energy Commission in an oddly passive position regarding the program's future development. Politically the program owed its existence to the strong support
of the Joint Committee and the Joint Chiefs. These institutions succeeded,
perhaps with the aid of Lilienthal's administrative maladroitness, in
establishing their priorities independently of AEC views. As a result,
the future course of the thermonuclear program was in large measure
independent of developments within other Atomic Energy Commission
programs. Just as ideas do not automatically become programs, pro-

---

[44] Ibid. , p. 390. At this stage of the program development
process the critical causal elements are probably psychological and situational rather than institutional or programmatic. It is true that the Cold
War was upon Washington. It is also true that Edward Teller was (and is)
particularly hostile to the Soviet Union. Yet, there is no structural reason
why Edward Teller did not apply his genius to nuclear power reactors instead of explosives. For the political scientist as distinct from the psychologist, the novelist, or the historian, "analysis" of Teller's behavior
strikes us as an unproductive enterprise. The point is that whatever its
causes, the behavior did have important structural consequences.

grams do not automatically or "naturally" grow and prosper. They do
so as a result of the relative strengths of the forces supporting or op-
posing their continuation or expansion. The important question is where
a program finds the political resources to provide for its continued prosperity. To answer this question, we must first define precisely the statistical meaning of "prosperity" which we will be using.

The raw data from which we must develop an index of prosperity is in the form of absolute dollar levels of programs from year to
year. An index based upon this data will have to meet two different
problems of comparability.[45]

---

[45] Fred Bookstein makes several pertinent points on the
practice of index formation. An index has something to do with combin-
ing observations. It is a new number computed from sets of observations according to some algebraic rule; this number is then used in analyses where the old data would create only confusion. In one familiar application, the index is an adding-up of "indicators" each measuring (with unknown biases) an underlying "variable." While the indicators are measuring aspects of one underlying thing, the index estimates the thing itself.
The additive combination, often called a "scale," is a single value allowing comparison across units which responded to the measurement process
in different but "equivalent" ways. This general practice is usually called
"reducing the dimensions" of the data. There is another sort of index,
however, which does not have this reductive feature. Each datum may be
accurate by itself as the expression of some stable measurement, yet still
be unsuitable for comparison with other data. We may wish to extract a
meaning determined by its context. How much is a particular measurement
above some average? What percentage is it of the total? How much does
it deviate from what we might have predicted? If we want to compare the
numerical answers to those questions across the units of analysis, we must
normalize our observations, without decreasing their number.

The first has to do with the variation in the total AEC operating budget between FY 1958 and FY 1972, which was, of course, by no
means constant over that period. In Table 11, below, we have calculated
the sum at each stage of the twenty-three programs on which we have calculated data. It varies from year to year, ranging from a low of $2006. 3 bil-
lion in FY 1967 to a high of $2568. 5 billion in FY 1963.[46]

It seems reasonable to argue that programs are equally prosperous only if each preserves its proportion of the total even as the total
changes both from year to year and across the stages of budgetary process.
A first step, then, toward operationalizing the notion of "prosperity" is to
divide all program allocations at all stages by the total for that stage.
This, however, leads to a second problem of comparability.

There is great variation in the absolute magnitude of program
budgets. Among the twenty-three AEC programs for which we have data,
there are several with budgets in the $5 - $10 million range, and a few

---

In transforming our budget data to measure "prosperity, " we are trying to
construct an index of the second sort. We are interested, that is, not in
reducing the "dimensionality" or number of our data, but rather in increasing their commensurability. (Private communication with the author.)

[46] For any given year or stage, the totals reflected in Table 11
are equal to about 90 per cent of the comparable total operating budget, the
remaining 10 per cent being that portion of the AEC budget which we were
unable to allocate to meaningful or interesting output categories. Since we
are explicitly interested in competition among programs, the aggregated
totals shown have been used as the basis for the transformation described
in the text.

TABLE 11

Total at Each Budget Stage for 23 AEC Programs
(In $ billions)

Fiscal Year	Division Request	General Manager	Commission	BoB	Appeal	Final
1958	$2170.9	$2059.1	$2199.1	$2081.2	$2083.2	$2076.6
1959	2414.9	2235.4	2267.9	2253.9	2253.9	2252.3
1960	2575.7	2501.7	2510.9	2447.5	2472.7	2451.0
1961	2494.3	2409.6	2368.8	2206.6	2310.3	2296.4
1962	2538.7	2499.2	2491.1	2285.3	2306.5	2343.0
1963	2586.2	2428.7	2447.5	2389.8	2592.3	2568.5
1964	2781.2	2468.5	2586.6	2366.7	2546.3	2381.4
1965	2505.1	2428.1	2447.0	2294.5	2283.1	2239.6
1966	2323.8	2251.4	2257.4	2104.0	2195.3	2129.1
1967	2213.6	2098.1	2118.2	1986.0	2034.4	2006.3
1968	2399.9	1999.1	2110.1	2005.8	2053.6	2026.4
1969	2438.2	2272.8	2269.8	2151.7	2225.3	2180.5
1970	2376.0	2238.9	2274.4	2104.8	2169.9	2037.4
1971	2469.4	2285.1	2303.9	2024.4	2121.0	2013.7
1972	2420.7	2179.5	2150.7	1962.6	1990.2	1980.5

which often were greater than $400 million. The obvious consequence
is that each of the smaller programs is a tiny proportion of the total
agency budget and is thus "lost" for analytical purposes. For example,
one of the most politically controversial AEC programs is "Plowshare,"
a project to develop non-weapons applications for nuclear explosives.
This program has never commanded more than one per cent of the total
Commission budget.

We need to normalize the percentages obtained by dividing
each program budget by the appropriate total so that these small programs are not made to seem insignificant out of sheer tininess. To
adjust for this problem we have first calculated for each budget stage
a program's mean proportion of the total for that stage across either
(a) all the years spanned by our data; or (b) when a program began or
was cancelled within that period, the years during which the program
existed. We have then divided a program proportion of the total for
each stage/year by this mean and multiplied the quotient by 100, hence
converting to a percentage. The effect is to normalize these percentages
so that they average 100 for the period FY 1958 - FY 1972, or, when appropriate, for the years a program existed. We believe the characteristics of this index and its behavior over time to be highly suggestive of
the process of competitive growth, i. e. , "prosperity" in which we are
interested. Eventually we shall want to use "prosperity change scores. "

This is the numerical difference of the prosperity scores across years

for a given stage and will be zero when a program's proportion of the

stage total does not change over the years.

Meanwhile, consider the following sample program histories

as reflected in the series of prosperity scores shown in Table 12.

TABLE 12

Four AEC Program Histories Expressed as
"Prosperity Scores"

Fiscal Year	Rover	High Energy Physics	Sherwood	Weapons
1958	25	20	87	69
1959	19	25	95	75
1960	28	34	130	67
1961	34	36	95	68
1962	56	51	88	80
1963	128	82	86	94
1964	187	118	83	92
1965	165	107	80	109
1966	174	122	92	105
1967	173	144	103	104
1968	131	149	108	110
1969	145	147	109	122
1970	103	156	114	129
1971	94	154	123	133
*1972	33	150	97	136

All programs show striking variance in prosperity. We see

quite vividly the growth, decay and fluctuation of which we have spoken--

all within the context of a roughly constant total budget. These variations

were caused by political events, not the operation of a budgetary process.

The sudden reversals in the fortunes of "Rover" were caused by various officials of three administrations having attached sharply different priorities to the undertaking. The competitive success of high energy physics resulted in part from the constant attention of the Atomic Energy Commission Chairman with a strong interest in pure research. High energy physics did not grow "accidentally" or "naturally"--indeed none of these curves represents any sort of "natural process. " On the contrary, each is the record of a sequence of priority settings made within a political system. Programs do not naturally grow, decline, or remain constant, or anything else. They are caused to do all of these by politicians and administrators making often difficult choices among competing claims upon scarce resources. This is precisely the "authoritative allocation of values" which is the very essence of the political process. It is this authoritative allocation of values which is captured by the variations in prosperity portrayed in these plots of competitive growth and decay. The relative stability of "Sherwood" (controlled thermonuclear research) is not an illustration of organizational process in Lindblom terms.[47] Sherwood has remained constant, has resisted competing claims upon its share of the Commission budget, only because it has been supported by the Commission, the Bureau of the Budget, and the President. Its

---

[47] cf. Charles E. Lindblom, "The Science of 'Muddling Through,'" 10 Public Administration Review (Spring, 1959). Op. cit.

constant level of prosperity is an indicator of stable political support,
not the operation of some "budgetary constant" which could have evaporated completely, or even ballooned to the high priority briefly attached
to the Rover program in the early Kennedy years.

Alternatively, consider the history of weapons. This has
been a truly prosperous enterprise. We have seen how the circumstances
surrounding the decision to build thermonuclear bombs left the Atomic
Energy Commission with little influence over the future of this program.
We have also noted how the function of the Commission came to be one
of merely fulfilling requirements for nuclear explosives in the establishment of which it played no role. The AEC, that is to say, played no role
in setting the priority of weapons relative to other nuclear activities or
among types of weapons. The competition for resources among the
latter took place with the relative priority of weapons already set by
forces external to the Commission. The weapons program record of
continuous prosperity is, therefore, the story of the consequences of the
actions taken in 1950. The program emerged from the thermonuclear
debate with a very real competitive advantage over other AEC programs.
Weapons was a "stronger" program. This notion of comparative program
strength is one to which we shall shortly return. First, though, we should
use the ability to measure prosperity to summarize what the Atomic Energy
Commission has actually done since 1956.

We could, of course, just subtract a given program's prosperity in FY 1958 from its score in FY 1972 and rank the programs according to the numerical value of the result. The "net prosperity change" is not, however, an especially helpful number. Now, we can recover exactly the same rank ordering by working instead with "prosperity change scores." For any program, the mean of the distribution of these change scores across all fifteen yearly intervals is also an indicator of how that program has prospered during the period for which we have data. The numerical value of these indicators, moreover, has an instantly appealing interpretation. At glance at Table 13 shows that since FY 1958 fifteen programs have prospered and eight have not.

TABLE 13

Arithmetic Mean of Prosperity Change Scores, FY 1958 - FY 1972
23 AEC Programs
(Presidential Budget)

Rank	Program	Mean	Rank	Program	Mean
1	High Energy Phy.	9.0	13	Sherwood	.57
2	Nuclear Safety	8.1	14	Rover	.43
3	Prog. Dir. & Adm.	7.1	15	Euratom	.08
4	Gen. Reactor Tech.	6.1	16	Training, Edu. & Information	-2.2
5	Biol. & Med.	5.4	17	Advanced Systems	-2.8
6	Cooperative Power	5.1	18	Spec. Nuc. Mats.	-3.5
7	Weapons	4.5	19	Pluto	-4.0
8	Naval Reactors	4.5	20	Army Reactors	-7.0
9	Civilian Power	4.3	21	Merchant Ship	-7.7
10	SNAP	4.1	22	Raw Materials	-13.6
11	Plowshare	3.5	23	Aircraft Nuclear Propulsion	-25.6
12	Isotopes	3.3			

As a record of the AEC's activities for the past fifteen years, however,
Table 13 is partly misleading. We know from examining the raw prosperity scores that some programs like weapons, high energy physics or
program direction and administration have grown essentially monotonic-
ally; while others like Plowshare or Rover have experienced sharp reversals in their fortunes. Likewise, among the eight unsuccessful programs, two--raw materials and special nuclear materials--would be
considered by those familiar with the AEC activities as different from
the others. It makes very little sense to think of these two as unsuccessful, or "unprosperous" in any sense which implied competitive weakness.
Both are important, even basic, AEC programs, whose decline as a proportion of the total program was due to outside pressures, not to weakness in the competition for a share of the total Commission budget.
Both are pre-eminent examples of what the professional administrator
regards as _strong_ but substantially fulfilled programs. This brings us
once more to the concept of program strength. For the administrator
it is a separate dimension from the notion of prosperity with which we
have so far been preoccupied.

The distinction between a "strong" and a "weak" program
is intuitively clear to the professional administrator. Within both the
Atomic Energy Commission and the Bureau of the Budget there is nearly
universal agreement about which have been the strong programs over the

past several years. In addition to raw materials, special nuclear mater-

ials and weapons, officials cite naval reactors, biology and medicine,

and high energy physics. The existence of two distinct dimensions, with

the consequent four logical possibilities, suggests a compact way of sum-

marizing the actual history of governmental activity.

The administrator's intuitive measure of program strength-

seems to turn on resistance to change, a resistance which he is willing

to attribute to any of a number of causes--a preponderance of political

support over hostility; superior internal program administration (i. e.,

"a tight ship"); a particularly talented or "strong" program director; or

a general "acceptance" of the program and its projected growth levels.

(The biomedical program is perhaps the best AEC example of this last

category.) These intuitive measures hint that in the bureaucrat's lexi-

con a "strong" program is a "predictable" program.

We have used the mean of the distribution of prosperity

change to summarize the competitive growth of all AEC programs since

1956. Another statistical parameter of the distribution of change scores

should summarize relative program strength, if strength is indeed "pre-

dictability." Table 14 reports the standard deviations of each program's

fifteen prosperity change scores between FY 1958 and FY 1972. A low

standard deviation indicates a small amount of scatter around the mean

change score, which is to say, a predictable change score. In fact, the rank ordering of programs reflected in Table 14 corresponds almost exactly with a priori notions of program strength. [48]

TABLE 14

Rank Order of Program Strength
(Standard Deviations of Prosperity Change Scores
Across 15 Fiscal Cycles: FY 1958 - FY 1972)
(Presidential Budget)

Rank	Program	Standard Deviation of Prosperity Change Score
1	Biomedical Research	6.1
2	Naval Reactors	6.2
3	Special Nuclear Materials	6.4
4	Program Direction and Administration	6.7
5	Weapons	7.1
6	Raw Materials	11.4
7	Training, Education and Information	11.9
8	High Energy Physics	13.3
9	Civilian Power Reactors	15.4
10	Sherwood	16.6
11	Nuclear Safety	17.1
12	General Reactor Technology	27.5
13	Aircraft Nuclear Propulsion	31.3
14	Isotopes	34.8
15	Rover	36.2
16	Army Reactors	37.4
17	SNAP	38.8
18	Plowshare	39.6
19	Cooperative Power Reactors	44.9
20	Advanced Reactor Systems	51.2
21	Euratom	55.8
22	Merchant Ship Reactors	57.4
23	Pluto	83.5

[48] Except for "program direction" and "training, education and information" the top eight programs in Table 14 are those consistently cited by AEC officials as "strong."

Let us now combine our evident ability to measure strength with our previous summary of prosperity. A cross-tabulation or plot of the two rank orderings should suggest four distinct categories or programs. There first will be a cluster of programs which have been both prosperous and strong. These are the high priority programs which, one might suppose, have controlled or dominated the agency's other activities. In contrast, there will be a group of programs low on both dimensions, many of which may have succumbed in the struggle for scarce resources. The "off-diagonal cells" will contain two even more interesting sets of programs. This should be a group whose members were strong but not especially prosperous. One is tempted to term these an agency's "dinosaurs" since, given our assumptions, their low prosperity can only be due to forces operating in the external environment rather than any "competitive weakness." Anticipating a bit, the two Atomic Energy Commission programs which unambiguously fall in this category are raw materials and special nuclear materials. In both instances, changes in the external environment caused the respective declines. Finally, perhaps the most interesting category are the weak but prosperous programs. It is among these that most of the intra- and inter-agency disputes over priorities have occurred. These are the programs whose histories reflect clashes of interest and preferences within the AEC and between the Commission and the administration.

Table 15 presents this four-fold categorization of the twenty-three Atomic Energy Commission programs. The "dinosaur" metaphor suggests an analogous "animal" label for the other three categories. Those also appear in Table 15.

TABLE 15

Four-fold Categorization of AEC Program Histories
FY 1958 - FY 1972
Rank Order of Mean Prosperity Change Scores by Rank Order of
Strength Scores

Lions	Bears
Strong (Rank Order 1-8) and Prosperous (Rank Order 1-14)	Less Strong (Rank Order 9-23) but Prosperous (Rank Order 1-14)
High Energy Physics Biomedical Research Program Direction and Administration Weapons Naval Reactors	Nuclear Safety General Reactor Technology Civilian Power Reactors Cooperative Power Reactors SNAP Plowshare Sherwood Isotopes
Dinosaurs	Turkeys
Strong (Rank Order 1-8) not Prosperous (Rank Order 15-23)	Neither Strong (Rank Order 9-23 nor Prosperous (Rank Order 15-23)
Raw Materials Special Nuclear Materials Training, Education and Information*	Euratom Advanced Systems Pluto Merchant Ship Reactors Aircraft Nuclear Propulsion Army Reactors

*This is the only obvious anomaly in this crude classification scheme and is almost certainly attributable to measurement error. Training, Education and Information is, as the name suggests, not a homogeneous output category.

Given the crudeness of our measuring instruments, these categories (along with their obviously fanciful labels) should, perhaps, not be asked to bear too much weight. For one thing, in any causal sense, they clearly ask more questions than they answer. Why, for instance, even assuming we can satisfactorily account for the "dinosaurs," are some programs "lions" rather than "bears"? Do "lions" become "dinosaurs" and "bears" become "turkeys"? (Plainly, the metaphors very quickly get out of hand.)

Still, at a minimum, the four categories do order a universe of programs and suggest some fruitful causal questions. They also suggest some non-trivial conclusions about what the Atomic Energy Commission has been up to since the mid-fifties. The distribution of the programs within the categories confirms the belief within the Commission that for many years pure research programs have fared a great deal better than applied research programs. On the other hand, the military reactor programs (with the notable exception of Rickover's naval reactors) have been an especially sad lot. Half of the "turkeys" were military reactor projects. And the programs included in the "bears" quadrant are, in fact, those where debates about priorities have been sharpest. There has been disagreement within the agency and between the Commission and the Bureau of the Budget about the future of each; the fact that half of its programs in this group are civilian power reactor programs says

a great deal about where intra-administrative debates over priorities
have been centered for the past decade and a half.

4. Conclusion

What else have we accomplished? There is apparently
growing interest in examining federal budgets to determine how the
nation is allocating its resources and exercising its spending priorities.
The authors of one of the most recent and best of such studies correctly
point out that in order to understand what a budget for any one year says
about the priorities of those responsible for it, one must pay attention
to past trends.

> In determining priorities and formulating the federal
> budget, the President and his advisors do not start
> with a clean slate, deciding de novo how . . . the ex-
> penditures for fiscal 1972 should be allocated in
> meeting national goals. Recent history, prior commit-
> ments, current political realities, relations with Con-
> gress, economic and social events beyond the control
> of budget makers--all play a major role in limiting
> their ability to change radically the current shape of
> the budget. What they consider desirable must be
> tempered by what they consider feasible. . . . the
> margin of truly free choice is surprisingly small. [49]

Still, obligational and expenditure patterns do change even at the aggregated federal level. Schultze and his colleagues, too, find impressive

---

[49] Charles L. Schultze, E. R. Fried, A. M. Rivlin, N. H.
Teeters, Setting National Priorities, The 1972 Budget (Washington, D. C.:
The Brookings Institution, 1971), pp. 12-13.

variation in the objects of government expenditure over time. They proceed to infer changing priorities from changing absolute outlays.[50] But
we have seen in reviewing the circumstances of one fiscal year how programs are in explicit competition with each other as they move jointly
through the budget formulation process. A measure of relative priority
levels must take account of this competition. The prosperity index developed in the preceding pages does so; it extracts from each individual
budgetary observation a meaning determined by its context. The essential
idea here is that the individual budgetary figures must be seen as the
product of two quite different processes. One is the budgetary process ,
the public accounting that organizations give for the dollars that they receive. The stress here is on organization, the continuing complex hier-
archy of government--bureaus, divisions, agencies and departments.
And the key to understanding administrative behavior in these terms is
in the incremental nature of the process. The other is the policy process.
Here emphasis is on the competition among programs for scarce resources which are needed to expand, or to continue, or even to begin.
The terms of this struggle are policy choices and political priorities;
the spokesmen are tough-minded policy entrepreneurs and sophisticated
politicians.

---

[50] Ibid. , pp. 19-21.

The great difficulty in untangling these two aspects of the budgetary process is that they occur simultaneously. The methodological problem this poses can be handled by a series of transformations which in general affect different observations in different numerical ways but whose result is a set of numbers which now may be compared freely among themselves. Inspection of these numbers confirms the fundamental proposition of this preliminary analysis: in the context of the "massively stable" processes cited by other scholars, there is considerable variation in the fortunes of federal activities at the program level. We believe that the explanation of this variance constitutes the real challenge for further empirical analysis of budgetary data. We have been able also to measure separate characteristics of programs; their "strength" or "acceptance." The combination of these two dimensions--prosperity and strength--produced some non-obvious organizing principles summarizing the historical competition within the AEC's programs between FY 1958 and FY 1972.

What has been the nature of this competition? Has it been a "war of all against all" or are certain activities capable of causing other less strong programs to "pay" for their prosperity either by exercising first claim upon newly available resources--the decline of the "dinosaurs"-- or by actually growing at the expense of lower priority activities. Bruce Russett has suggested that we may be able to recover some evidence about the extent of such "benefits" or "payments" by examining the patterns of covariation among yearly changes in program levels.[52] Since

we now have strong a priori reason to believe the Atomic Energy Com-

mission's weapons program to have been independent of other Commis-

sion activities for the past twenty years, the intercorrelation of changes

in weapons prosperity with that of the other twenty-two programs seems

especially pertinent. They are reported in Table 16.

TABLE 16

Product-Moment Correlations
Prosperity Change Scores, Presidential Budgets
FY 1958 - FY 1972 With Weapons Program

Raw Materials	-.47	SNAP	-.26
Special Nuclear Materials	-.25	General Reactor Technology	-.44
Civilian Power Reactors	-.13	Advanced Systems	-.10
Cooperative Power Reactors	-.32	High Energy Physics	-.29
Euratom	-.19	Sherwood	-.37
Merchant Ship Reactors	-.28	Biology and Medicine	-.24
Army Reactors	--	Training, Education and	
Naval Reactors	--	Information	--
Aircraft Nuclear Propulsion	--	Isotopes	-.17
Pluto	--	Plowshare	-.25
Rover	--	Program Direction	-.23

[52] Bruce Russett, "Who Pays for Defense?" 32:2 American
Political Science Review (June, 1969), pp. 412-426. See also, Bruce
Russett, What Price Vigilance: The Burdens of National Defense (New
Haven: Yale University Press, 1970), especially Chaps. 5 and 6.

Everyone pays for defense! With the exception of the Commission's various military reactor enterprises (the largest group among those with insignificant correlations), all AEC programs change scores are negatively associated with changes in the weapons program. As anticipated, the relationship between prosperity changes in raw materials and weapons is high and negative. Decay in the prosperity of the former has been strongly associated with the growth of weapons. But the latter has evidently not only benefitted from the decline of this "dinosaur," it has also in Russett's sense been able to make other programs, notably general reactor technology and controlled thermonuclear research, "pay" for its prosperity.

The difficulty with patterns of covariation such as this is that, though fascinating, they may also be wholly spurious. Certainly they do not in themselves illuminate the real causal processes which produce variation in the prosperity of programs. At most, the sign of the associational measure, particularly when it is negative, may provide some clue about the right questions to be asked. Thus in the case of the AEC weapons program there is no reason not to accept the overall pattern of inverse association as empirical confirmation of what we would suspect on independent grounds. But positive correlations among prosperity change scores have no obvious causal interpretation and the meaning of differences in magnitude between any pair of negative coefficients is totally obscure. More importantly, the covariation patterns cannot tell us why some programs are stronger than others. Assuming the competitive struggle for limited funds is not exactly a war of all against all, what is it that makes some more equal than others? It is strong directors who make for strong programs by "running a tight ship" and by "effectively generating support at the agency and Congressional levels."[53] Directors generating such support are able to neutralize opposition by the most potent natural enemy, the Bureau of the Budget. Programs which are supported at the Commission, Bureau of the Budget, Presidential and Congressional levels are prosperous; programs which are not supported soon fall victim to the exigencies of the budgetary process.

This widely accepted professional wisdom, then, contains a clear theory of the governmental process. National priorities are not set by administrators with national constituencies; they are set at the operating levels of federal bureaus--by program directors sensitive to their own clienteles. National priorities are established by bureaucratic entrepreneurship in a process which settles priorities without anyone being aware of them. In this regard, Davis, Dempster and Wildavsky's stochastic models perpetuate a fundamental error about the way govern-

---

[53] These observations are based on a number of interviews with officials in AEC and the Bureau of the Budget. In the AEC case, these interviews are complemented by several close personal associations with program staff.

ment operates. The whole metaphor of an inert bureaucratic machine doing the same thing this year that it did last year misses the basic point. Priority setting in the federal bureaucracy resembles Nineteenth Century capitalism: priorities are established by aggressive entrepreneurs at the operating levels of government. Programs prosper because energetic division directors successfully build political support to withstand continuous attacks upon a program's resource base by competing claims. As a consequence, the only matters which reach the President are those already in dispute. At the Presidential level the administrative process is less one of "policy-making" than "dispute-settling." It is at this level where things are accepted simply because they have been accepted, where the desirable has to be adjusted to the feasible. On the whole, the differences which count, the actions which produce the patterns of relative prosperity and strength we have discussed occur at lower levels of the administrative process.

All of this is missed by taking the Wildavsky and Lindblom perspective. By concentrating on the underlying regularities of the administrative process, these scholars are obliged to argue (in effect) that except for learning adjustments, no changes of any significance occur. We have seen that real change does occur within this "massive stability," reflecting real conflicts over purpose and priority. The more telling point about the process as such is that it is one which establishes the program director, the operating-level bureaucrat, as a central figure in the determination of public policy. The history of the Atomic Energy Commission's weapons program is far more typical of the way public values are allocated than the dramatic termination of the aircraft nuclear propulsion program.[54]

This is a strong theory and we must be careful to stress that our discussion is limited to the single agency on which we have data. But if this fact makes us somewhat cautious in the end, it should be said also that it is our feeling that the concepts we have specified and the theory which underlies them are probably more--not less--applicable to other areas of government. The Atomic Energy Commission has been a fairly stable agency both in administrative organization and actual spending levels for the last ten years. That we find such great variation in the relative prosperity of programs here seems to suggest that we can expect greater fluctuations elsewhere, particularly in the controversial areas of social policy.[55] Do program directors occupy the same crucial position throughout the government? Is there more or less Presidential

---

[54] W. Henry Lambright, "Shooting Down the Nuclear Plane," Inter-University Case Program, ICP Case Series No. 104, (Indianapolis: Bobbs-Merrill, 1967).

[55] Congress appears to be much more active in the area of social policy. An excellent account of administrative policy in this area refers again and again to Congressional intervention in specific programs. CF. Gilbert Y. Steiner, The State of Welfare, (Washington, D. C.: The Brookings Institution, 1971). Or in a different area, Arthur Maass, Muddy Waters: The Army Engineers and the Nation's Rivers (Cambridge, Mass.: Harvard University Press, 1951).

leadership in other policy areas? For what programs is Congressional intervention truly a significant factor?

These are the type of questions that need to be asked. By translating budgetary data into the actual operating units of government programs, students of public administration should be able to provide more than speculative answers. Prosperity scores are by themselves an important first step, for they establish a measure of a program's success or failure. Further, there is in our prosperity scores the hint of additional information relating to the level at which policy is actually made, i. e. , whose policy preferences at which level of government determine budgetary outcomes.

CHAPTER III

THE AEC's CIVILIAN POWER REACTOR PROGRAM

1. Historical Context, 1946 - 1963

In 1946, President Truman considered atomic energy to be "too important a development to be made the subject of profit-seeking."[1] This view, widely shared among the post-war political and scientific establishment, was a principal reason for the government's retention under the original Atomic Energy Act of an historically unprecedented monopoly of nuclear science and technology.[1a] At this time predictions of vast practical benefits easily to be realized from "the peaceful atom" were common. Commission policy during the first years of AEC operation, however, was squarely based upon the premise that scientific talent and resources had to be conserved for immediately essential activities such as weapon design and

---

[1] Harry S. Truman, Memoirs (Garden City, N. Y.: Doubleday & Co., 1955), Vol. 1, p. 529. Also quoted by Harold Orlans, Contracting for Atoms (Washington, D. C.: The Brookings Institution, 1967), p. 195.

[1a] Newman and Miller, op. cit. The authors, however, do make the point that national security considerations were the most important factor in the establishment of "an island of socialism" in the private economy. See especially Introduction, pp. 1-26.

testing, improvements in production reactors (to manufacture plutonium for bombs), and development of the "Redox" process to re-process reactor fuel.[2]

A certain restiveness on the part of Oppenheimer's General Advisory Committee notwithstanding, the activities of the Commission throughout the late 1940's fully reflected these priorities. As a consequence the only significant development of nuclear energy for non-explosive purposes during this period was the submarine propulsion reactor. For a time following the first Russian nuclear weapon test in 1949, the AEC's programs became, if anything, more geared to national defense.[3]

By the end of the Truman administration, though, a number of industrial interests, particularly a few large firms associated with the Commission's weapons production and naval propulsion programs were becoming visibly unhappy with the relatively stagnant commercial situation. After a series of unsatisfactory interim arrangements, the Atomic Energy Act was substantially amended in 1954 to permit private industry under heavy regulation to pursue the commercial development of nuclear technology. The Atomic Energy Commission retained sole

---

[2] Hewlett and Duncan, op. cit., p. 79. See also Chapter VII, passim. Hewlett and Duncan's account, incidentally, strongly hints that the persistence of these priorities was due more to the beliefs of the staff than to those of the Commissioners and the Chairman.

[3] Ibid., pp. 219-221.

right to own all fissionable materials, important patent rights and pre-

rogatives, the right of determining the specific terms under which

private owners might be licensed to operate nuclear facilities, and an

all-embracing responsibility for encouraging "basic research and de-

velopment."[4]

The 1954 legislation effectively ended the government

monopoly of nuclear technology and provided the Atomic Energy Com-

mission its charter to encourage the development of what was still

universally thought to be the immense and immediate "promise of the

peaceful atom." Among the possible practical realizations of this

promise, the most important was universally agreed to be the use of

the energy produced by the controlled fissioning of U-235 as a new

heat source for central station electrical generating plants.

Since its spectacular success over Hiroshima, atomic

energy has been suggested, with varying amounts of enthusiasm, as

a better way of doing any number of things: propelling both the under-

water and surface navy, excavating canals and harbors, powering

---

[4] Philip Mullenbach, Civilian Nuclear Power (New York: The Twentieth Century Fund, 1963), pp. 4-6. See also, Paul W. MacAvoy, Economic Strategy for Developing Nuclear Breeder Reactors (Cambridge, Mass.: MIT Press, 1969), Appendix A, "Strategies for Nuclear Reactor Development," which is, in part, a concise summary of technical developments during the late 1940's and early 1950's. See also, Richard G. Hewlett, "Man Harnesses the Atom." in M. Kranzberg and C. W. Pursell, Jr., eds., Technology in Western Civilization, (Madison, Wisc.: Univ. of Wisconsin, 1967), pp. 256-275.

artificial hearts, preserving citrus crops, flying aircraft, missiles

and space rockets, and retorting metals. None of these potential ap-

plications, however, has ever rivalled in economic and social impact

the use of controlled fission energy as a heat source for the generation

of electrical power. [4a]   Because of this, the Atomic Energy Commis-

sion's power reactor development program has generally been regarded

as the government's most important effort in support of applied nuclear

technology. And from its inception this program has been surrounded,

if not overrun, by political controversy. The history of these disputes

during the period 1954 - 1960 has been competently recounted elsewhere

and need not long detain us here. [5]

[4a] It has also seemed from the outset to be the industrial
application closest to realization on technical grounds. See Newman
and Miller, op. cit., p. 125. For a thorough but reasonably accessible
discussion of the physical and engineering principles of nuclear reactors,
see Loftness, op. cit. This book, incidentally, includes technical de-
scriptions of many, if not all, of the specific reactor projects, both power
and propulsion, referred to in this and other chapters.
    Richard Hewlett notes that when nuclear fission was dis-
covered in the 1930's scientists who saw its energy implications generally
believed the most likely application would be in power plants, not weapons.
The potential significance of the fast-neutron reaction for weapons was
not seen until the summer of 1941. See Richard G. Hewlett, "The Advent
of Nuclear Power in the U.S., 1945-1968." (Paper delivered at meeting
of the American Association for the Advancement of Science, Dallas,
Texas, December 26-31, 1968, p. 3.)

[5] Mullenbach, op. cit., Chap. 1.   See also, U. M. Staebler,
"Objectives and Summary of USAEC Civilian Power Reactor Programs,"
in J. Gueran, et al., eds., The Economics of Nuclear Power (New York:
McGraw-Hill Book Co., Inc., 1957).

Three related issues controlled the formulation of civilian

nuclear power policy during the Eisenhower years: the amount and kind

of federal support that should be given to commercial interests, espec-

ially the potential reactor manufacturers; how to proceed with reactor

development in the face of the then bitter controversies over publicly

owned utility systems; and the respective federal and commerical re-

sponsibilities for the construction of prototype or full-scale plants that

could not at current levels of technology hope to make a profit.[6] In the

latter regard, a major political battle before the 1954 revision to the

Atomic Energy Act had resulted in the establishment of a precedent for

government construction of full-scale demonstration plants. The Atomic

Energy Commission had built a 60-thousand kilowatt reactor in a private

utility system at Shippingport, Pennsylvania.

During most of the 1950's it was policy, therefore, not lack

of legal authority, which prevented the government from doing so again

elsewhere. Under the leadership of Lewis Strauss, the AEC chose, as

a matter of executive policy, to take a fairly narrow construction of its

role in developing power reactor technology. The Democratic members

---

[6] Mullenbach, op. cit., p. 7. See also: Herbert S. Marks,
"Public Power and Atomic Power Development," Law and Contempor-
ary Problems, Winter 1956, Duke University School of Law, Durham,
N. C., pp. 132-147. And, John G. Palfrey, "Atomic Energy: A New
Experiment in Government-Industry Relations," Columbia Law Review,
March, 1956.

of the Joint Committee on Atomic Energy, especially Clinton Anderson

of New Mexico, were not pleased by this stance and were constantly

prodding the Commission toward a more aggressive role.[7] The JCAE

Democrats were enthusiastically supported in these efforts by one of

the five Commissioners, Thomas Murray, whose policy differences

with Chairman Strauss were approaching the character of a personal

feud.[8] Hence in early 1957 Commissioner Murray found a sympathetic

audience on the JCAE when he expressed grave concern over the inade-

quacy of current AEC civilian power reactor policy.[9]

Many of the arguments Murray used in 1957 have now be-

come part of the official ideology supporting the AEC's power reactor

development program. Perhaps the most important of these was the

contention that private industry was financially incapable of assuming

a major share of the fiscal burden of developing the technology for

---

[7] Congressional hearings during the period contain abundant evidence of these disputes. See especially, Development, Growth, and State of the Atomic Energy Industry, Hearings before the Joint Commit- tee on Atomic Energy, Congress of the United States, 85th Cong., First Session, February 1957, (U.S. Gov't Printing Office, Washington, D.C., 1957), pp. 41 ff.

[8] For more background on Strauss' opposition to government construction and operation of plants whose purpose was not advancement of the technology see Lewis L. Strauss, Men and Decisions, (New York: Doubleday & Co., Inc., 1962), p. 319.

[9] Development, Growth, and State of the Atomic Energy In- dustry, op. cit., pp. 56-65.

commercial use. The most popular analogy was to the air transport industry. Officials like Murray and Senators Jackson and Gore often cited Congressional determination during the early thirties that civilian air transportation should be developed by private industry with substantial direct government assistance.[11] Representatives of the then "infant" nuclear industry of course found the analogy congenial. The capital requirements of power reactor technology were argued to be such that private funds could not possibly hope to supply the needs for development. Thus, Dr. Chauncy Starr, at the time the general manager of the Atomic International Division of North American Aviation, was able to urge the appropriateness of such direct support "in spite of the hesitance of industry to accept the concept of direct or indirect subsidy of industrial effort by the government."[12]

The position of the utilities was more complicated than that of the potential reactor manufacturers. The private utilities were extremely nervous about the evolving AEC power reactor development program. They were inclined to see it as potential camouflage for federal support of publicly owned utilities which in concert with the government would eventually "squeeze" private utilities out of the power business

---

[11] Ibid., p. 208.

[12] Ibid. For background on the analogy to air transport, see Frederick C. Thayer, Jr., Air Transport Policy and National Security, (Chapel Hill: University of North Carolina Press, 1965).

with massive "atomic TVA's. "[13]

The extent to which these fears have shaped the civilian
power reactor programs remains uncertain, yet within the Commission
one often hears speculation that many investor-owned utilities have in
effect been "coerced" by the industry's peak associations into buying
nuclear generating plants. MacAvoy's unemotional assessment lends
some support to these speculations:

> The buyer of electricity generating facilities is a
> corporation of great complexity with objectives so
> diverse that no monocausal explanation of patterns
> of demand is appropriate. . . . Yet the companies
> have departed from an exclusive interest in adding
> the largest and lowest cost plant. The non-breeder
> nuclear reactors purchased in the early and mid-
> 1960's at the demonstration or postdemonstration
> stage required net expenditures per kilowatt far
> greater than those in alternative fossil fueled
> facilities. The companies have not only purchased
> "high cost" advanced systems, but have engaged in
> outright research where the specific company re-
> search gains were not obvious and where the public
> explanation was couched in terms of "the good of the
> industry. "[14]

The effect of the political forces dominant during the Eisen-
hower-Strauss years is less controversial so far as government programs are concerned. Under Strauss' chairmanship the Commission's

---

[13] The point was made by various AEC officials during
interviews with the author.

[14] MacAvoy, op. cit., p. 53.

civilian reactor development program was based on the premise that the government should carefully restrict its activities in exploring new technological concepts by constructing and operating only small experimental reactors while leaving essentially full responsibility for designing and constructing large reactors to private industry. As a method of providing federal assistance in these efforts, while avoiding the spectre of federal nuclear power, the AEC invented its controversial "cooperative power reactor demonstration program" to supplement in-house research and development efforts.

This program represented the principal AEC response to the Joint Committee's pressure upon the administration to get on with the job of lending government help in the form of construction and operating subsidies for "experimental" power plants which were, nonetheless, actually part of a utility's generating system.[15] As the cooperative power program evolved, however, small publicly-owned power companies became increasingly concerned that their interests were being by-passed by the government's reactor development policies. In response to these pressures the cooperative program was soon modified and came to be seen by AEC as a convenient means of pursuing

---

[15] Mullenbach, op. cit., pp. 136 ff. In general, and simplifying a complex story, AEC tried two subsidy approaches under the cooperative power reactor demonstrator program. In its "first round," announced in 1955, the AEC provided direct funding assistance for re-

the development of a variety of reactor concepts in small projects at relatively low cost to the government, while at the same time assuaging the criticisms of the public power interests that AEC policy favored private power companies.[16]

In retrospect however many of the early cooperative projects seem to have been marred by weak engineering which led to some embarrassing white elephants.[17] How much of this may have been avoidable is, again, a matter of some controversy, although there tends to

---

search and development costs and waived "use charges" for the nuclear fuel in the initial years of plant operation. These conditions were conceived primarily to encourage private utilities to build light water plants. Later, to meet the criticisms from public utilities which we have noted, the Commission announced a "second round" to encourage public power companies to build smaller reactors, preferably incorporating advanced technology. Here the AEC actually ended up owning the reactor while bearing all research and development costs and the costs of fabricating the core. The utility owned the electrical portion of the plant and had operating responsibility for the whole facility. Finally, a "third round" was devised in 1957, again aimed at private utilities. The object was construction of advanced concepts but AEC assistance was limited to essentially "first round" terms.

[16] To get some feeling for the differences between a reactor "concept" and a working machine, as well as the immense difficulty of turning the former into the latter, see MacAvoy, op. cit., Chapter 2. For more amusing material on the same theme, see FY 1971 Authorization Hearings, pp. 1702-1703. Hewlett, op. cit. (1967), also treats this issue.

[17] Perhaps the most notable of these was the reactor built in cooperation with the Consumer's Public Power District of Nebraska, known as the Hallam reactor. For details on this unhappy enterprise, see FY 1967 Authorization Hearings, pp. 798-820.

be general consensus among informed observers that virtually all of
the Commission's early reactor development efforts were characterized by indecisiveness and lack of direction. In Harold Orlans' words,
"The manifold purposes the $\overline{/reactor/}$ program has striven to serve, the
political crossfires in which it has been caught, and the periodic reversal
or modification of staff technical judgments to comport with broader
policy objectives have not facilitated decisive management."[18]

The Joint Committee on Atomic Energy continued to be dissatisfied with the reactor development policies represented by the cooperative program well into the Kennedy Administration. Committee
Democrats, especially Gore, Anderson and Holifield, saw these policies
as an abdication of crucial technical leadership on the part of an agency
which was continuing to base its most important applied research and
development effort "on the hope that somebody else will come in and do
the job of development at their expense rather than at government expense."[19] Holifield and others would plainly have preferred the AEC

---

[18] Harold Orlans, op. cit., p. 141. As Orlans observes, the
consensus on this point extends to present AEC management itself. The
author's own conversations fully support Orlans' conclusions regarding
the widespread impression that the civilian power program in the fifties
"lacked a clear and coherent objective and effective management."

[19] The words are Chet Holifield's. See FY 1965 Authorization
Hearings, p. 367.

to orient its program around the "Shippingport pattern," i.e., with the government assuming full responsibility for constructing prototype plants for "demonstration purposes." At the time Holifield expressed this dissatisfaction, he and other critics could reasonably argue that government assumption of this sort of responsibility with regard to the "light water" reactors was the reason that particular technology was then on the verge of allowing utilities to decide to build nuclear generating plants on the basis of lower costs over the life of the facility compared with conventionally fuelled alternatives.[20]

In making these arguments, Holifield knew that there was at least one highly sympathetic ear within the AEC. In 1962 President Kennedy had appointed James T. Ramey to the Commission. As the Joint Committee's staff director throughout much of the Strauss chairmanship, Ramey had been one of the leading critics of the AEC reactor development policies. Under his direction the technical staff of the JCAE (Ramey himself is a lawyer) had been anything but reluctant to question the Commission's own technical judgments on civilian power research and development.[21] As a member of the Commission, Ramey

---

[20] Ibid., p. 368. In fact, just such a decision was made for the first time later in 1963 by a New Jersey utility. Light water reactor technology had become commercially competitive in high cost energy areas "where electricity from fossil fuel systems was estimated to be available at 7 mills per kilowatt hour." MacAvoy, op. cit., p. 113.

[21] Such disagreements were perhaps most apparent in connection with the development of "gas-cooled" reactors and an ill-fated project at Oak Ridge known as the "Experimental Gas Cooled Reactor."

soon found himself in disagreement with its senior staff on reactor development policy issues. Both Alvin R. Leudecke, General Manager,
and Frank K. Pittman, the director of reactor development, were closely
identified with the previous administration's policy of placing heavy reliance upon commercial interests to bear the financial burden of building
working prototypes to demonstrate advanced reactor concepts.

It was not until late 1964 that officials with views more congenial to Ramey's were given responsibility for directing the Commission's programs. In November of 1964 the Atomic Energy Commission
announced a major reorganization of its reactor development activities.
A new senior staff position, an assistant general manager for reactors,
was created, and John A. Swartout, the deputy director of the Oak Ridge
National Laboratory, was appointed to fill the position.[22] Simultaneously,
the responsibilities and functions of the division of reactor development
were divided among two new divisions and a new "office." The naval
reactors "branch" of the old division of reactor development became
the division of naval reactors, ending the fiction that Rickover operated
as subordinate to a division director. An office of space nuclear propulsion was created with responsibilities for all programatic activities

---

[22] USAEC Headquarters Announcement #150, November 18,
1964. Swartout held the job for only a year. His place was taken by
George M. Kavanagh, a senior AEC staff aide whose most recent previous responsibilities had been in the disarmament field.

in that area, including Rover, and most of the SNAP projects. Finally, the division of reactor development became the division of reactor development and technology, retaining program responsibility for the civilian power program. Milton Shaw, who had been Technical Assistant to the Assistant Secretary of the Navy for Research and Development since 1961, was made director of the new reactor division. Prior to his assignment to the Pentagon, Shaw had been an engineer in the Shippingport nuclear power plant and had served as Rickover's principal assistant in the design and development of the nuclear propulsion plants for the Enterprise and the Long Beach. Shaw came to the Commission with the reputation of being a forceful personality and a very strong manager.

As events in the reactor development area during the following year were of quite fundamental significance for all Commission priorities, it will be helpful to review their background in some detail.

2. Advanced Converters

In 1958 the Joint Committee on Atomic Energy had published a long-range plan for the development of civilian nuclear power establishing a ten-year goal of achieving "competitive nuclear power in high cost energy areas. As 1964 began, the Atomic Energy Commission could claim that two reactor concepts had already met this goal.[23] The "pressurized water" reactor, shown to be operable at Shippingport, had displayed rapid and impressive improvement in cost and operating performance. The Yankee Atomic Electric Plant, put into operation at Rowe, Massachusetts in 1961, had shown wholly reliable production of electricity from the start. Not coincidentally, the pressurized water concept was the technology on which Rickover's naval reactors program was based. Progress on the other concept--"boiling water" reactors--was not, however, so directly based upon the research and development experience of a military program.

Such achievements notwithstanding, it was evident to the Commission that "light water" technology (i. e. , pressurized and boiling water reactors) was highly unsatisfactory in the long run from both an engineering and a resource conservation perspective. These first generation commercial power reactors are grossly inefficient consumers of fissionable material. For the AEC these unfavorable fuel utilization characteristics coupled with the economics of uranium supply and demand

---

[23] Proposed Expanded Civilian Nuclear Power Program, (U. S. Gov't Printing Office, Washington, D. C. , 1958). On the second point see John F. Hogerton, "The Arrival of Nuclear Power, " Scientific American, Vol. 218, No. 2, February 1968. Loftness, op. cit. , provides additional technical material on these matters. Also useful, especially with regard to the economics of reactor operation, is V. Lawrence Parsegian, Industrial Management in the Atomic Age (Reading, Mass.: Addison-Wesley, 1965), see esp. pp. 108-117.

were seen by many, particularly Commissioner Ramey, as justification for an accelerated effort to develop more advanced (efficient) systems. But it was equally obvious that such a program would be very expensive, and once again the issue was who should accept primary responsibility. Ramey, for his part, was quite clear on this point; government could not rely upon private industry to accept major responsibility for the large financial outlays that were going to be required to develop advanced reactors. The "third round" terms of the cooperative program were inadequate and would have to be substantially modified.[24] Pittman, as the director of reactor development, however, was reluctant to see the Atomic Energy Commission repeat its earlier unhappy experiences in cooperating with utilities to build plants incorporating advanced technologies.[25]

A combination of technical and commerical circumstances complicated matters. Five different reactor concepts, each identified with a particular manufacturer, seemed to offer roughly equal promise as the basis for a second and more efficient generation of nuclear power plants. Faced with this situation, the AEC reactor staff was strongly inclined toward a position of _laissez faire_, arguing that utilities would have to select on their own from this menu the concept or concepts

---

[24] Minutes of Commission Meeting 1984, January 9, 1964.
[25] _Ibid._

which seemed worthy of prototype construction. The Atomic Energy

Commission, according to staff, was as a matter of technical fact

simply unable to guide the utilities in this choice. [26] In February, 1964

the Commission issued two public announcements inviting industry (i. e. ,

manufacturer - utility partnerships) to propose cooperative arrangements

for prototype projects involving one of five advanced concepts. In issu-

ing the announcements the Commission did not indicate any superiority

of one concept over the others. However, funds and legislative author-

ization specifically for one of the five known as "spectral shift" were at

the time already available, while for the others it was the AEC's an-

nounced intent to seek administration approval during the FY 1966 budget

cycle for such proposed projects as were of interest. [27]

On one point there was consensus among both the staff and

the Commissioners: successful development of one or more of these

---

[26] Minutes of Commission Meeting 1991, February 6, 1964.
See also, AEC 711/104, "Encouragement for Industry Proposals to Build
Prototype Nuclear Power Plants," February 7, 1964; and AEC 1058/2,
"Spectral Shift Control Reactor," February 3, 1964.   The five reactors
concepts were: spectral shift, high temperature gas-cooled, sodium-
graphite, heavy water organic-cooled, and "seed and blanket. " See
Loftness, op. cit. , for technical details on each.

[27] The Commission had first requested funds to cover construction of an advanced prototype in its FY 1964 budget submission.
At that time the plan had been to select a particular reactor concept in
late 1963 and invite utility bids in early 1964. The administration, however, had apparently insisted upon identification of a specific concept as
a condition for authorizing prototype funds and only the "spectral shift"

concepts (now generically beginning to be called "advanced converters")
was a necessary technical bridge between current light water technology
and true breeder reactors.

 The first response to the Commission invitation was received
in April. It involved the "spectral shift," and this was to become a
source of some embarrassment, for reactor development staff now saw
this concept as markedly less attractive on technical grounds than the
four specifically cited in the other February invitation. Yet not only
had money already been appropriated for a spectral shift prototype,
but the manufacturer was also known to be rather desperate to maintain
a foothold in the nuclear industry. By the end of June the issue was unresolved and the coolness of reactor development staff toward spectral
shift had visibly deepened.[28] Two additional proposals, each involving
one of the remaining four concepts, were in hand, and staff approached
the Commission for authority "to proceed to negotiate the bases of arrangement" for each of the three proposals, the idea obviously being

concept, an engineering modification of the pressurized water system,
could be identified as being in a position where prototype construction
could begin within a year and a half.

[28] Minutes of Commission Meeting 2022, June 22, 1964.
The competitive structure of the reactor manufacturing industry has
been a muted theme of AEC reactor development policy since the early
1960's. Two companies, General Electric and Westinghouse, have
dominated the field from the beginning through command of light water
technology.

to throw spectral shift into the pot with the other two and stir to see
which manufacturer/utility came up with the arrangement most financially favorable to the Commission.[29]

Both the Commissioners and reactor development staff were
reluctant summarily to reject the spectral shift proposal even in light of
its increasingly apparent technical disadvantages. Technical considerations were not the only factors shaping the Commission's advanced
converter policy. These had to be balanced against the sensitive matter
of government responsibility for the competitive structure of the reactor
manufacturing industry. In the spectral shift case, continuation of the
manufacturer in the reactor business seemed to depend upon the construction of this plant. Direct influence had already been brought to
bear at high levels of the administration to move ahead with a project
whose funding was already assured.[30] Overt pressure aside, the charge
that the domination of the light water market by two manufacturers was
a direct consequence of AEC policy had just enough prima facie plaus-
ibility to sting. Both General Electric and Westinghouse had been
heavily involved in AEC military programs, the former as the prime
operating contractor for the Hanford plutonium production works and the
latter in the naval propulsion program. That the expertise gained through

---

[29] Minutes of Commission Meeting 2029, July 23, 1964. And
AEC 777/105, "Advanced Converter Reactor Concepts," July 21, 1964.

[30] Ibid.

this experience had direct commercial implications was too obvious

to deny. A number of other companies anxious to capture part of the

reactor market had been generally unsuccessful in competing with

General Electric and Westinghouse. There was no disagreement

within the Commission that this situation was undesirable and con-

sequently an important, though tacit, objective of the advanced con-

verter program was to provide these other firms a toe hold in the

reactor market.[30a]

Both the political and technical situations were complicated

by yet another contender for inclusion in the advanced converter pro-

gram. Admiral Rickover's naval reactor staff was working on an ex-

tension of light water technology dubbed "seed and blanket." They too

had found an interested utility and were advancing a strong claim for

financial support. During the summer various technical analyses were

undertaken, perhaps most notably by the General Advisory Committee,

and eventually reactor development staff was prepared formally to recom-

ment rejection of the spectral shift proposal and acceptance of the high

---

[30a] Commission sensitivity to the competition issue is understandable. As Newman and Miller, op. cit., observed in 1948: "Throughout the [Atomic Energy] Act there are exhortations and admonitions directed to the Commission 'to strengthen free competition in private enterprise' . . . ; to encourage 'the entry of new, freely competitive enterprises'
. . . ; 'to insure the broadest possible exploitation of the fields' . . . ; 'to
discourage the growth of monopoly' . . . ; etc." p. 72.

temperature gas-cooled reactor (HTGR) as the basis for definitive

negotiations.[31]

The staff also recommended that AEC support for research

and development on the other concept, sodium graphite, should be con-

verted into support for research on sodium-cooled fast breeder reactors.

Under these terms the Commission could continue to support research

at the parent company at about $5 million per year over the next three

years with an orderly decrease in annual funding. Such a program was

argued to leave the manufacturer in the position of being able to sell a

reactor of the type involved in the proposed cooperative. These recom-

mendations were approved and the Commission turned its attention to

the non-trivial problem of securing the approval of a skeptical Bureau

of the Budget to proceed with both the "high temperature gas-cooled

reactor" and "seed and blanket."

The former was to be supported on a "modified third round"

basis, and the proposed financial arrangements were immensely com-

plicated.[32] The overall AEC liability for the project was estimated at

---

[31] AEC 777/106, "Implementation of Advanced Converter Program," August 25, 1964. See also, Report of the Reactor Subcommittee
of the General Advisory Committee on Advanced Converter Reactors,
August 18, 1964. The GAC report. incidentally, was particularly unfavorable to the Rickover approach. For discussion of these matters see Minutes
of Commission Meeting 2041, August 25, 1964.

[32] Both now discarded proposals, the spectral shift and the
sodium graphite, had involved "second round" arrangements. Whether

about $80 million, of which $38 million was a direct funding commitment

for research and development and "first of a kind specialized equipment. "

Though there was some feeling on the Commission that this represented

a lot of money for a single project, staff was authorized to proceed with

negotiations.[33] One thing on which the Commission was adamant was

that the responsibilities and obligations of the reactor manufacturer must

be explicit in the final contractual instrument.[34]

    With these decisions, the Commission, after two years' de-

liberation, had settled upon an advanced converter program.

    The important point about this program, however, was the

degree to which it duplicated the management and development philosophy

which had guided the AEC's reactor efforts since the days of Strauss.

The advanced concerter program as it stood in the early fall of 1964

was not really an AEC program. It was an industrial program receiv-

ing government support. The series of events which we have partially

reviewed was one in which the Commission played an essentially passive

role attempting to balance competing technical claims and political pres-

---

this fact was one of the considerations in their rejection is not clear from
the Commission's records. Staff, remember, was frankly cool toward
further "second round" ventures.

[33] Minutes of Commission Meeting 2044, August 27, 1964.

[34] Ibid.

sures against its own programatic goals and financial constraints. With

one highly significant exception, it was a program which evolved in re-

sponse to external events. The exception was Rickover's seed and blanket

project which was based on a wholly different conception of government's

role and responsibilities in these types of enterprises.

The cornerstone of the naval reactors approach (and therefore,

some would contend, the key to the success of the water reactors) was

tight control of contractor activities by government engineers and adminis-

trators. The naval reactors program has always been pre-eminently a

government program in the sense that government administrators, sup-

ported by thorough technical expertise, have exercised daily control of

research and development activities and have never been in the least re-

luctant to confront contractors with their views on all engineering and

development details.[35] This is not the role which the Commission's

reactor development staff conceived for itself in the advanced converter

program. The basis of the civilian power program had traditionally been

the more diffident assumption that government was in no position to

question the technical judgment of private manufacturers. Government

---

[35] Hewlett (1968) op. cit. , pp. 10-11. Dr. Hewlett and his
associate, Francis Duncan, are currently writing a complete history of
the naval propulsion program in which this point will be developed in detail. Publication is anticipated in early 1973.

merely should maintain general oversight of industrial efforts and offer "guidance" where appropriate. This philosophy is the key to the events of 1964 which we have just sketched. As we are about to see, however, this issue of the proper role of government in areas where public funds were underwriting the (eventually profit-making) activities of industry was soon to be sharply drawn at the policy level within the Commission. Milton Shaw, appointed director of reactor development in November of 1964, ardently believed in the Rickover philosophy.

3. New Priorities in Reactor Development

The utility and the reactor manufacturer involved in the high temperature gas-cooled reactor project were unable to agree on contract terms between themselves and the former withdrew from the venture early in 1965.[36] The reactor manufacturer, however, soon returned to the Commission with a new partner and plans for an even more advanced facility.[37] Unfortunately from the manufacturer's standpoint the Commission's new director of reactor development was less than enthusiastic about the HTGR project. From the first, Shaw had shown every indication of wanting to assign top priority to the fast

---

[36] FY 1966 Authorization Hearings, p. 1378 and pp. 1540-1541.

[37] Summary Notes of Commissioners meeting with representatives of the Public Service Company of Colorado, February 20, 1965.

breeder program which he clearly intended to turn into a real government program in the Rickover sense.[38]

Not only did the HTGR represent a continuation of the old management approach, but it also involved some highly novel design features on the successful development of which the Commission, in Shaw's eyes, would be gambling substantial amounts of money that were needed elsewhere. Shaw obviously believed that commitment of such funds without corresponding technical control would be a serious mistake given the requirements of the breeder program. Other senior staff and some of the Commissioners had some reservations about these views. During the discussions of the high temperature gas-cooled reactor project there were repeated expressions by various members of the Commission and its senior staff of the belief that in cases where the ultimate customer for a technology resulting from a hardware development program was a commercial interest (as opposed to the government itself in the case of naval reactors or Rover), it was AEC's responsibility to carry the development program through the initial experimental phases and then to turn it over to private industry. The government it was argued should not accept responsibility for guaranteeing the ultimate success of a particular development project. Shaw agreed with the validity of this distinction, especially to the degree it implied that the

---

[38] Minutes of Commission Meeting 2088, February 23, 1965.

proposed $40 million in direct research and development assistance pro-
posed for the HTGR was a "hard ceiling," that AEC was not going to
"bail out" the project if difficulties were encountered. The problem as
Shaw saw it was the manufacturers' evident reluctance to accept the necessary final responsibility. Projects such as this should not, indeed, be
government programs; but they had to be someone's program.[39] Shaw
saw the HTGR as a seriously underfunded enterprise over whose eventual
success the AEC would in fact have little control and which in the end
would divert management, financial, and technical resources from the
fast breeder. In an area involving difficult and novel research and development, he thought the Commission would be proceeding with little
definite information on the technical uncertainties involved and no definitive outline of the program which would address these uncertainties.[40]

Among the Commissioners, however, there was a plain
desire to see this arrangement proceed. In fact, the staff was mildly
chided at one point about being overly "officious" and driving the manufacturer to the wall.[41] This concern was, at least for some of the
Commissioners, based upon a more general concern about the current

---

[39] Minutes of Commission Meeting 2091, March 12, 1965.

[40] Minutes of Commission Meeting 2098, April 6, 1965.

[41] Ibid.

technical status of the whole civilian power reactor program. As
Seaborg put it, after ten years the whole program was still firmly
rooted in water reactors with the distinct possibility the advanced
converter effort would itself become a water reactor program.[42]
The Commission proved sensitive to this point and hence on these
grounds alone was inclined to be generous toward the manufacturer
of the high temperature gas-cooled reactor.

Additionally, though, it seemed to most of the Commissioners that given known administration and Budget Bureau attitudes
the reactor development program would increasingly have to be based
upon cooperative arrangements in which the industrial partner accepted
the open end of the deal and assumed final responsibility for technical
control of the undertaking. Naturally Shaw was decidedly skeptical that
programs could proceed on this basis and he was strongly supported by
at least one Commissioner. The argument that the self-interests of
the private firm gave them the strongest possible incentive to assure
the technical success of development seemed to them flawed. Even in
extreme cases where such success was a matter of commercial life or
death to a company, the tendency of private industry was to cut corners
as the magnitude and complexity of development problems became apparent.

---

[42] Ibid. Rickover's "seed and blanket" was an extension
of light water technology.

Though these reservations were the subject of several discussions, they ultimately did not prove persuasive to a majority of the Commission, and staff was authorized to negotiate a definitive contract to build an HTGR prototype.[43] But the terms of debate had been set and the basic issue soon resurfaced in a series of discussions regarding the role of the Argonne National Laboratory (ANL) in the breeder program. The FFTF which, as we have already seen, played so prominent a role in the FY 1967 budget deliberations was the key to Shaw's strategy for assuring that the fast breeder would be a government program. As such it was not a universally popular project, particularly among institutions with competitive efforts. ANL was such an institution; faced like most other Commission laboratories with a need to define a role for itself, its management had for some time been endeavoring to place the laboratory in a position of technical leadership on breeders. As a practical matter the vehicle for these ambitions in 1965 was a proposed facility (known as FARET) which was directly competitive with the FFTF. While ANL's reasons for considering the FFTF an error were therefore perhaps obvious, similar concerns were

---

[43] Minutes of Commission Meeting 2099, April 15, 1965.
The reactor is now under construction at Fort Saint Vrain, Colorado.
A recent (5/1/70) GAO review has concluded that the project is progressing "satisfactorily" and has the potential of being completed on schedule.
AEC financial assistance consists in a waiver of fuel inventory use charges up to $6.4 million plus direct research and development aid of $40.9 million.

expressed in the fall of 1965 from segments of the commercial reactor industry. Industry evidently viewed the FFTF as the beginning of a new AEC "power center" which would dominate all future reactor development.[44] From their point of view, the effect of the FFTF would be to divert funds from government-industry cooperative arrangements for the construction of breeder prototypes. The manufacturers were interested in pressing the Commission to use its limited reactor development funds to move toward a breeder prototype at the earliest opportunity. If the Commission secured funds for a cooperative breeder prototype in its FY 1967 budget, a plant could be built by 1971. Giving priority to the FFTF, however, would delay such a reactor by several years. Those making this case, moreover, apparently believed the FFTF to presage a future AEC decision to build a breeder prototype as a government project at its Idaho reactor testing grounds.[45]

MacAvoy's analysis of the Atomic Energy Commission breeder program cites the nuclear engineer's maxim: "Provide me with a fuel element and I'll build you an efficient reactor."[46] The author goes on to discuss the formidable technical hurdles which must be overcome in the development of breeders.[47] Such considerations

[44] Minutes of Commission Meeting 2156, November 17, 1965.

[45] Ibid.

[46] MacAvoy, op. cit., p. 22.

[47] Ibid.

were the basis of Shaw's position in the fall of 1965. He argued first

that a fuel test facility was an absolutely necessary precondition to

resolution of many of the uncertainties of breeder technology. These

questions, moreover, had to be answered before any utilities would be

prepared to make the enormous financial commitments involved in

prototype construction, regardless of what the reactor vendors might

think. In these circumstances the clear AEC obligation was to provide

the required technical base--as a government program. These argu-

ments proved decisive. FARET was cancelled and the division of re-

actor development authorized to proceed with preliminary design work

on FFTF.[48] The fast breeder program was going to be a government

program; Shaw had managed the first significant reorientation of the

civilian power program since its creation.[49] The effect was that for

the first time in its history the civilian power program had become

what the Joint Committee had wanted for ten years, a top priority

---

[48] Minutes of Commission Meetings 2156, 2158, November 30, 1965.

[49] Coincidentally, the Rickover "seed and blanket" project
began to experience some unanticipated technical problems which eventually led to its cancellation--by Rickover himself. (See Rickover's
memorandum to General Manager, December 20, 1965.) The division
of naval reactors, however, has continued to press for a priority program to develop "light water breeders" as an alternative to the Shaw
"liquid metal" effort. Rickover's testimony at the FY 1967 Authorization Hearings (pp. 1692-1709) makes a powerful case in support of his
long-held belief that the sensible way to develop breeders is by building
upon light water technology. Though the continuing controversy over

Commission activity. Philip Mullenbach could argue in 1963 that in
this area the federal government had "assumed the necessity of, though
not full responsibility for, shepherding a new technology through to competitive commercial feasibility."[50]

In a real sense, the Commission with these actions had now
assumed full responsibility for developing more efficient power reactors,
and, as we shall see, it has been increasingly willing to sacrifice other
programmatic goals to meet this commitment. Before turning to such
matters, however, several points should be made about the breeder program itself.

The official justification for the priority assigned to the program has remained quite consistent since the policy changes of the mid-
1960's. Breeder reactors are being developed because they provide the
most efficient means of exploiting the energy available in uranium; they
minimize the quantity of uranium consumed per unit of electricity generated, and hold promise of yielding potential fuel costs of less than one
mill per kilowatt-hour (7 - 8 mills is now common). They will (in sharp

---

the proper technical orientation for the breeder program is well beyond
the scope of this study, my own instincts are that the Rickover case is
enormously persuasive. The substantive point of the MacAvoy book, incidentally, is that gas reactors are marginally more attractive economically and technically than the liquid metal concept for which Shaw has opted
so heavily.

[50] Mullenbach, op. cit., p. 319 (emphasis added).

contrast to current reactor technology) permit very high utilization (per-

haps 90 per cent) of the uranium processed from ore, thereby extending

known energy reserves by several orders of magnitude; and finally they

will provide a market for the plutonium produced from the water reactors.[51]

This last is the most clearly political consideration behind

the breeder program. The AEC has steadily maintained that the need

to provide such a market is not a principal or controlling cause of the

priority being given to the development of breeder technology. Some of

the Commission's critics would probably be skeptical, pointing out that

the economic urgency of this matter is far greater than the more remote

engineering and conservation considerations. That is, the strictly finan-

cial pressure to develop a use for the plutonium being produced by pres-

ent reactors is of far more immediate concern to the nuclear industry

and the utilities than the question of efficient fuel utilization stressed by

AEC.

---

[51] Hewlett, op. cit. (1967), provides the following explanation of the concept of "breeding": "If, on the average, slightly more
than two neutrons were emitted from each fissioning uranium nucleus,
one neutron could be used to continue the chain reaction. A second could
be captured by a U-238 nucleus to produce an atom of plutonium, this replacing the original atom of fissionable U-235. The occasional third neutron by the same process could produce an additional atom of plutonium.
If a reactor could be built to achieve this kind of neutron economy, it
might be possible to use the chain reaction to generate power and at the
same time to produce more fissionable material than was consumed. "
(p. 262.)

An exchange during the FY 1968 hearings captures all of

these issues nicely:

Rep. Hosmer: "You mentioned this morning the burning of
plutonium in thermal reactors. If you do so,
it is not going to be worth any $8 to $10 a gram
as it would be under the assumption we have
been going on in the breeders. So, if you
don't bring in the breeders before you get a
lot of plutonium piled up, (1) the utilities
who haven't made arrangements to dispose
of it are going to be in rather bad shape,
and (2) the (reactor) manufacturers who
have agreed to buy back or dispose of the
plutonium are going to be in bad shape.
. . . Certainly many of the decisions relative to going nuclear (i. e. , decisions by
utilities to purchase reactors) today are
made on a rather firm assumption that this
$8 to $10 plutonium price is going to continue,
and that these breeding technologies will be
available at a time when the plutonium supply
starts coming in. If we don't have this type
of use for it, we are going to have a panic in
this industry, are we not?"

AEC Commissioner Ramey: "I think a part of this . . . will depend on how they (the utilities) account for the
plutonium in terms of interest charges. If (it)
is going to be charged as an inventory item and
sitting there, then there will be a financial incentive probably for them to utilize it rather
than to hold it for 10 years to stick into a
breeder. "

Dr. Kavanagh, AEC Senior Staff: "We feel a commitment to be
concerned about the plutonium. . . . We have encouraged the industry to work on plutonium
recycle (i. e. , use of plutonium to fuel water
reactors). We do not feel that we have to, or
should appropriately, solve their problem all
by ourselves, . . . we are working very hard

on fast breeders. They may turn a (plutonium)
surplus into a scarcity, but that is not our purpose in working on them. Our purpose is to
provide a technology which will make useful
power available. There may be problems with
plutonium in the next decade . . . the components of the problem. . . are so complex that
we have not really figured them out. We are
trying to do that.

"But the rationale for our (breeder) program
is not just what happens to plutonium. "

Rep. Hosmer: "I understand that. I really feel what you are
doing is re-enunciating the continuous policy
that the AEC has . . . responsibility for a considerable amount of expenditure in both research
and development. "[52]

I find little reason not to take the AEC more or less at its

word on these issues. By doing so we side-step the frustrating business

of untangling motivations while getting to what is for our purposes the

really essential point. AEC reactor development policy continues to

reflect commercial interests in ways which are far more fundamental

than the mere creation of a market for plutonium. From its beginnings

reactor development policy has been based upon the potential and actual

comparative advantages of reactors in terms of unit power costs. This

is a case designed to appeal primarily to reactor customers; those simply

purchasing electricity (perhaps on highly inelastic demand curves) may

---

[52] FY 1968 Authorization Hearings, pp. 805-809.

find it quite beside the point. Moreover, because official justifications
of government support for reactor development have traditionally been
aimed at potential buyers of reactors, calculations of unit power costs
have followed the standard commercial practice of ignoring externalities.
Many contemporary critics of the Atomic Energy Commission's reactor
policy are perceptive enough to grasp this fact. From their point of
view it does not seem unreasonable to demand that a public agency pur-
porting to ground its priorities in the interests of all the people--in
sharp contrast to commercial enterprises which make no such claim--
ought to be sensitive to external or social costs.

But the AEC reactor program has remained an engineer's
program. As we have seen, its stated sole objective has been the
achievement of more efficient reactors--reactors with better fuel
utilization characteristics. This however is an "obvious" or "natural"
frontier only from a very narrow technical perspective. More than
anything it is a case of the solution defining the problem. Commission
research and development objectives, that is, have been defined in
terms of available technical skills: given a hammer, the world becomes
a nail. The fuel utilization characteristics of power reactors are after
all only one of many system parameters on which official priorities
might be based. (An altogether obvious alternative are safety characteristics.)

This situation has compounded the political problems of the
civilian power program. Consider Admiral Rickover's statement: "In
my view, the sole purpose of breeding is to get more energy out of your
uranium and thorium reserves and thus insure a long term source of
electrical energy for future generations."[53] But the civilian power
program above all now needs political support and "future generations"
are not especially potent political allies while the utilities already have
a machine which by their standards is remarkably efficient and tractable.[54] The Atomic Energy Commission is well aware that its present
policies are generating more controversy than consensus and are eager
to be told what they are "doing wrong." The difficulty is they tend to
answer the question themselves by assuming that they have a "market-
ing" rather than a political problem; a problem of information, not
power. By assuming the self-evidence of the problem as they have defined it, i. e., the need for more efficient reactors, the Commission
has tended to believe that if only the "nuclear community" could manage
to do a better job of making assorted technical "facts" known, present

---

[53] FY 1971 Authorization Hearings, p. 1674. Rickover continued: "The proponents of the introduction of a coolant other than light
water will have to convince the utilities that the benefits of the new reactor system warrant the effort, expense, and risk of developing a new
industrial base to support the new concept.

[54] The author's interview with the superintendent of a large
pressurized water reactor.

opposition to the breeder program would diminish. But public policies

prosper or falter because of their political consequences, and the "facts"

as the Atomic Energy Commission conceives them are largely irrelevant

to the politics of the situation: virtually no one aside from the AEC's own

staff and that of its laboratories and contractors is interested in reactors

with better fuel utilization characteristics, especially when it involves

development of an entire new technology at a time when "the utilities

have already committed themselves to about $50 billion in long-term in-

vestment and operating costs for light water reactors."[55]

Hence, the breeder program is in more ways than one a

"government program." From this vantage point it seems more than

anything to be a program whose evolution illustrates our earlier argu-

ments about the way priorities become established in the federal govern-

ment. Without questioning the wisdom of Milton Shaw's far-reaching

technical and managerial judgments, it seems clear that he has succeeded

in establishing his values largely independent of external political forces.

The prosperity of the breeder program within the Atomic Energy Commis-

sion since 1965 is the consequence of the same sort of aggressive entre-

preneurial activity at the operating levels of government which led to the

establishment of the thermonuclear weapons program. The difference is

---

[55] Admiral Rickover, FY 1967 Authorization Hearings, p. 1674.

that in the latter case the program evolved with the support of a powerful external ally--the military establishment. Within the executive the civilian power program has never had such an ally and its prosperity as a consequence has been a much more uncertain matter. For in the absence of strong external support the program, as we have seen, has been repeatedly affected by the ongoing debate over how big government should be and what it should do. In connection with reactor development policy the debate has turned on the degree to which government should restrict its activities in exploring new technical concepts.

On the premise that the government should do only the things which industry cannot do for itself, the AEC for several years allowed essentially full responsibility for designing and constructing large reactors to remain in the commercial sector. This policy however stumbled over the fact that commercially viable reactors posed a host of technical problems which in a very real sense were beyond the financial, administrative and technical competence of private industry. Eventually, Milton Shaw was able to give effect to the alternative position that important public goals require public programs.

The technical and economic facts of the power reactor development business seem to support the new AEC policy. If breeders are going to be built, the government in some sense is probably going to have to build them--as a public program. The issue of whether such machines ought to be developed is well beyond my interests (and com-

petence). What does interest me is the way priorities are set when

government chooses to bring about public ends by public means. To

pursue this issue I now want to review yet another AEC program, peace-

ful uses for nuclear explosives.

CHAPTER IV

PLOWSHARE

1. Background: Atmospheric Nuclear Testing and the AEC Weapons
   Community

        Just how tenuous is the connection between public politics
and public policy? The author of a recent attack on the AEC's Plowshare program flatly states: "There is no mechanism by which the
wishes of the people can shape the plans of the AEC."[1] At the same
time Dr. Edward Teller, one of the program's most enthusiastic proponents, was confessing to me his own reluctant conclusion that in
spite of obvious technological promise Plowshare could never succeed
because "people believe nuclear explosives to be wicked."

        Each observation is partly to the point. On the one hand,
Plowshare has been characterized by a remarkable amount of self-
initiated and self-directed activity on the part of its government sponsors. The efforts on behalf of Plowshare by the Lawrence Radiation
Laboratory (LRL), the Commission's San Francisco operations office,
and the division of peaceful nuclear explosives do not fit the image of

---

[1] Peter Metzger, "Project Gasbuggy and Catch-85,"
New York Times Magazine, February 22, 1970, p. 79.

a government passively responding to the demands of an external clientele. Indeed both the Commission and the laboratory have assiduously (though some might argue, ineptly) tried to develop a clientele for their program and are not in the least reluctant to acknowledge it.[2]

Hence in a very direct sense, Plowshare's history can be seen as a paradigm instance of priorities being established by the entrepreneurial activity of public administrators at the operating levels of the federal system; can be seen, that is, as an illustration of the extent to which public policy can be controlled by political forces originating within government rather than the electorate. From such a perspective, Plowshare is essentially a story of governmental, as distinct from public, politics.

But this is at best a fragmentary picture, for as Dr. Teller implied, Plowshare has also been affected, perhaps decisively, by a series of extra-governmental events and circumstances. In fact, the program's history can also be seen as the record of the impact of what

---

[2] Scholars have of course long since given up the notion that executive agencies exist simply to carry out popular or legislative mandates. In 1940, Professor Friedrich wrote: "Public policy, to put it flatly, is a continuous process, the formation of which is inseparable from its execution. Public policy is being formed as it is being executed, and it is likewise being executed as it is being formed." See C. J. Friedrich, "Public Policy and the Nature of Administrative Responsibility," in C. J. Friedrich and E. S. Mason, eds., Public Policy, (Cambridge: Harvard University Press, 1940).

Peter B. Natchez would call an "issue public" upon public policy.[3]
Whether "the people" as an undifferentiated unit consider nuclear
explosives inherently wicked is an open question; that a vocal and informed though perhaps small subset does is undeniable. The political
activities of this group has significantly influenced the program's
fortunes from its beginning in 1957, a time when nuclear testing was
a major national issue. An intense and often acrimonious debate continued over weapons testing both inside and outside government during
the program's formative years at the end of the Eisenhower Administration. The positions taken by the Atomic Energy Commission in these
debates set the frame of reference within which Plowshare itself was
debated during the Kennedy and Johnson Administrations. Thus, the
history of Plowshare is intimately associated with the development and
testing of nuclear weapons, though in ways far more complicated than
those commonly cited.[4] As a background to a review of Plowshare,

---

[3] Peter B. Natchez, The Reasonable Voter, unpublished
Ph. D. Dissertation, Harvard University, 1969. See also, Peter B.
Natchez and Irvin C. Bupp, "Candidates, Issues, and Voters," in
John P. Montgomery and Albert O. Hirschman, eds., Public Policy,
Vol. XVIII, (Cambridge, Mass.: Harvard University Press, 1968),
pp. 409-439.

[4] Perhaps the crudest claim was that of the Soviet Union
that the whole program was merely a camouflage for clandestine weapons
development. Only slightly more subtle is the charge it is a "WPA project" for under-employed nuclear weaponeers. A related matter: Plowshare remains sharply controversial and I had better make my own
position explicit from the outset, even though an assessment of the

it will therefore be helpful to recall some of the main themes of the test

ban controversies of the second Eisenhower Administration.

It is something of an irony that what today would be considered a decisive argument against atmospheric testing was dismissed
as irrelevant in the fifties and within the government probably weakened
the case of its opponents. For it is quite clear that the position of the
early critics of atmosphere nuclear testing was not at all helped by their
insistence upon posing the issue in what we would now consider "ecological" terms. Most of the high nuclear policy-makers of the second Eisenhower Administration were preoccupied with "deterrence," not "ecology."
The concern over the consequences of introducing radioactive material
into the atmosphere was a positive handicap to those questioning testing
policy as they were unable convincingly to relate their position to the
strategy of deterrence. The magnitude of this handicap is evident in the
AEC records of the matter.[5] AEC Chairman Lewis Strauss, for example, simply was unable to accept the relevance of ecological concerns,

---

program's value is not part of my purpose here. The development of
peaceful uses for nuclear explosives seems to me to be a marginally
good idea, but one to which I would attach rather low priority in the context of other needs even within the AEC.

[5] The public literature on these matters is large. I have
found Harold K. Jacobson and Eric Stein, Diplomats, Scientists and
Politicians, (Ann Arbor, Mich.: University of Michigan Press, 1966)
to be particularly reliable.

in part apparently because he was quite persuaded that the biological
dangers of fallout were trivial. Though the amounts of radioactive
debris routinely injected into the atmosphere during the fifties would
now be viewed with positive horror, Strauss' disinterest was not considered outrageous at the time, and in fact drew upon respectable if
not entirely unanimous technical support. The Cold War was accepted
as the "real issue" and Strauss was able continually to argue that in
this context nuclear testing was a "spurious" issue because it did not
in itself constitute "true disarmament." Officials who demurred were
inclined to argue either that (a) fallout might be dangerous, or (b) even
if it were not, a lot of people were convinced it was and the government
ought to take them seriously. In either case, there was strong consensus
at the highest levels of the administration about the validity of a Strauss
frame of reference and these doubts were not persuasive.

It was not until the post-Sputnik creation of the Office of
Presidential Science Advisor and the appointment of James Killian to
that position that the Eisenhower Administration began gradually to
move away from consensus on the Strauss position. As Stein and
Jacobson document, this appointment and the concomitant reconstitution
of the Scientific Advisory Committee to the Office of Defense Mobilization
as the President's Science Advisory Council was an institutional change

of some importance.[6]   For the first time since Oppenheimer's departure,

the university scientific community had access to high policy matters in

the nuclear security area, and from the outset Killian was an uninhibited

advocate of "greater flexibility. " His continuing presence in policy meet-

ings had an immediate impact on the quality of the internal discussions of

disarmament matters, though, at first, with little concrete effect.

In December of 1957, Soviet Premier Bulganin initiated the

first of what was to be a long series of correspondence with the United

States Government on the cessation of nuclear tests. The exchange,

however, was treated by the administration as primarily an exercise in

communication.[7]   The "President's" replies were drafted at the oper-

ating level of the State Department and subject to the standard (and, of

course, stultifying) review and concurrence of all interested agencies.

The principal criterion of review seems to have been the estimated im-

pact of the documents on public opinion; Jacobson and Stein conclude

that there is no evidence that anyone at policy levels thought the whole

exercise to be especially significant.

In March of 1958, Senator Humphrey's Disarmament Sub-

committee of the Senate Foreign Relations Committee held a series of

---

[6] Harold K. Jacobson and Eric Stein, op. cit., pp. 32 ff.

[7] Ibid., pp. 39 ff.

hearings on the testing matter.[8]　　These hearings were dominated by
pessimistic AEC assessments of the disarmament picture reflecting
the current Commission policy line that weapons testing was unimport-
ant in itself and was only relevant to disarmament as an adjunct to a
cut-off of weapons production.　However, an acceptable agreement to
this end probably was infeasible since it would require several thousand
resident inspectors in the USSR and the disclosure by Russia of substantial highly sensitive information.　This position can hardly have come as
a surprise to Senator Humphrey and his colleagues; it had been the un-
varying AEC position since 1956 and was widely known as the "theory of
the link" (i.e., the link between cessation of testing and "real" disarmament).　Its formal abandonment within the year would signal an important shift in administration policy.

　　　　For, meanwhile the Soviet Union had concluded a test series
and with much fanfare proclaimed their intent forever to eschew further
testing.　This development provoked a flurry of high-level conclaves in
which John Foster Dulles took the position that the world was beginning
to look upon the United States as a militarist and a warmonger because
of its intransigence on nuclear testing.　Dulles received Killian's eager

---

　　　　[8] U.S. Congress, Senate, Hearing before the Committee on
Foreign Relations Subcommittee on Disarmament Hearings: Control and
Reduction of Armaments, 85th Cong., 2nd Sess. (1958).

support. The upshot was another exchange of correspondence between the President and the Soviet leadership. This time the United States' contributions were in large measure personally prepared by Dulles and eventually led to agreement on a "technical conference" between United States scientists and Soviet scientists to be held over the summer in Geneva.

The internal record is fairly clear on the reasoning behind the administration's tactics. Dulles had won reserved acceptance of the point that the United States somehow had to get off the defensive on the testing issue. A consensus then developed that a technical forum would offer an ideal opportunity to refurbish the United States image since the Soviets could be counted upon to stall and prevaricate. The "world" would see that the United States alone was truly interested in peace. No one within the administration suspected that the Russians might turn up in Geneva actually prepared for substantive discussions.

The denouement of the 1958 Technical Conference,[9] caught the administration, and especially the AEC, off-guard. Unhappily, having given negotiating authority to a group of independent scientists, without fully appreciating the sublety of the line between technical and political exchanges, the administration found itself faced with a set of sharply

---

[9] Harold K. Jacobson and Eric Stein, op. cit., pp. 53 ff.

limited options. Short of disavowing its own experts and thereby play-
ing havoc with the initial public relations intent of the exercise, it
had little choice but to go along with some kind of test moratorium. The
ultimate official response, however, was yet another example of this administration's abiding disinclination to question old assumptions. Though
the Soviet behavior in Geneva had quite obviously confounded the premises
of their previous tactics, the Eisenhower policy-makers, strongly influenced by the AEC, reacted to the challenge by precisely repeating their
earlier error. While there was consensus that the United States was now
obliged to go along with a testing "moratorium, " its acceptance would be
publicly linked to "real progress" in disarmament. Insistence upon this
link was thought to insure that the moratorium would be of short duration.
Events during the fall and winter of 1958 enormously complicated the
situation.

First, it became evident that irrespective of further developments in Geneva, where the negotiations had become bogged down in disputes over the agenda, the President's assiduously cultivated "Prince of
Peace" image was hardly compatible with a unilateral United States re-
sumption of testing regardless of whether "real progress in disarmament"
had been made.

Of more long-term significance, though, was the emergence
during the period of the weapons scientists as an independent and influen-

tial participant in the broadening policy debate. During the fall of 1958 the weapons laboratories began to provide the administration, through AEC channels, with technical data which threw doubt upon the basis of the current United States negotiating position. At issue was the degree of assurance that could be had with regard to using long-range seismic measurement techniques to detect nuclear explosions. Since this administration was positively obsessed with the notion that the ability to detect Soviet "cheating" was the keystone to any agreement, the consternation provoked by the laboratories' "decoupling" hypothesis was immense.[10]

These matters were debated without resolution throughout the fall. By December, however, John Foster Dulles had become persuaded that the AEC-backed "theory of the link" was clouding the diplomatic waters and acutely damaging the United States "world image" (something he took quite seriously) by making it more difficult to prove to public opinion that the Soviet Union was really unwilling to accept adequate control (i.e., inspection) measures. The old position was revised and for the first time it became United States policy to seek an "adequately controlled" test ban as an end in itself.[11]

---

[10] Jacobson and Stein, op. cit., pp. 223-224. Basically the weapons scientists were suggesting that it might be technically possible quite thoroughly to mask the seismic effects of underground nuclear explosions.

[11] Ibid., p. 154.

In early 1959 yet another influence began to make itself felt. The British Government had become increasingly restive with the United States disarmament policy. The public literature suggests, but does not fully develop, the importance of British activity during the last two years of the Eisenhower Administration.[12] In February of 1959, British Prime Minister Harold Macmillan visited Moscow, and without the prior consent of the American Government, proposed to Krushchev the idea of an annual "quota" of inspections of suspected violations of a test ban treaty. The notion of such a "quota" instantly became the focal point of a three-cornered dispute. First, the three governments were never able to agree on the precise way Macmillan had actually framed his presentation of the idea. The British subsequently maintained that Krushchev had been left with the understanding that a "reasonable" quota would probably be around twenty-five inspections per year. The Russians, however, claimed that Macmillan had actually implied a much lower figure, perhaps five inspections per year. The Eisenhower Administration tended to believe the Russian accounts of the British-Soviet discussions.

Meanwhile, there was a round consensus among Atomic Energy Commission and Department of Defense scientists that the larger

[12] Much of the pertinent internal record remains classified. The following summary draws heavily upon the author's interviews with former AEC Commissioner John G. Palfrey.

figure was at best the lower limit of a "useful" quota. The AEC

technical staff appear to have felt that if the Soviets would agree

to a quota of between seventy-five and twenty-five inspections per

year, a comprehensive test ban might be enforceable. The Russians,

for their part, however, never gave anyone the slightest indication

that they would even consider a number greater than ten.

By late spring, President Eisenhower was becoming

personally annoyed over what he was coming to see as the major

embarrassment to his administration being caused by the now quite

complicated test ban imbroglio. He apparently made his feelings

rather unmistakably known at a cabinet meeting. He instructed his

administration to forget the idea that the Soviets would ever agree

to an airtight inspection system and to concentrate instead on work-

ing toward some compromise which would give the United States

simply "reasonable assurance" that the Russians were not system-

atically violating a treaty. Even such limited assurance would be

preferable to the present situation in which the Russians were both

enjoying the public relations advantage of an anti-testing posture,

and for all the American government knew, simultaneously gaining

the military benefits of a wholly unpoliced de facto test ban. (The

moratorium was still in effect and was likely to remain so since the

Eisenhower Administration had to all intents decided that the American government would not unilaterally break it.)

The President directed the establishment of a scientific committee to determine what number of inspections would give the United States the "reasonable assurance" he sought.[13]

The results of this technical panel's review were both unexpected and highly discouraging. The scientists concluded, in effect, that with present technology, even a "reasonably" guaranteed comprehensive treaty was hopeless. Something like "several hundred" inspections per year would be necessary to reasonably assure the United States that the Soviets were not systematically violating such a treaty. Even the Atomic Energy Commission recognized that the Russians could never be expected to take this idea seriously. The scientists concluded by suggesting that the only way to reduce the number of inspections was to undertake an extensive research program to augment present seismic knowledge. (This recommendation eventually led to the establishment of the "VELA" program and hence an increase in the AEC weapons budget.)

On the heels of this technical report, the administration was jolted from another quarter. One of the AEC weapons laboratories

---

[13] Jacobson and Stein, op. cit., pp. 154-174, confirms the main outlines of this account, but again the foregoing is based principally upon my research for and discussions with former Commissioner Palfrey.

had developed some data which appeared to indicate a potential safety problem with some of the nuclear weapons then in the strategic stockpiles. Though the problem was later resolved, its appearance at this juncture of the test ban issue had at least one important consequence. For several weeks in the fall of 1959 the administration was preoccupied with an issue the existence of which the negotiating team was not informed.

December 1959 saw yet another reassessment of United States testing policy. In response to the findings of the technical panel, the administration, in another important policy change, adopted the notion of a "phased" test ban treaty.[14] The essential idea was to propose as an initial step a treaty whose prohibitions extended only to technically defined limits of "feasible control. " (Defined, that is, in terms of resultant seismic shocks.) Within the Executive the threshold concept was accepted with great reluctance, especially by the Department of Defense and the Atomic Energy Commission which now began to urge the acute need for a major program of seismic research.

The Soviet Union, on March 19, responded by proposing a treaty prohibiting all nuclear tests in the atmosphere, the oceans, in outer space, and all underground tests which produced seismic oscillations of magnitude 4. 75 or greater.[15] In retrospect, this Russian

---

[14] Jacobson and Stein, op. cit. , Chap. 7, pp. 231-261.

[15] Jacobson and Stein, op. cit. , p. 240.

proposal appears as something of a high-water mark in the efforts of
the Eisenhower Administration to resolve the nuclear testing issue.
It did not, of course, lead to a treaty; eighteen months later the administration was endeavoring to devise a satisfactory system of safeguards
under which a program of joint United States - USSR seismic research
could be initiated as a first step toward a "threshold" treaty.

It is well beyond the scope of our interests to sort out
the various causes of this performance. The point I have wanted to
make should now be very clear. The impact of the nuclear weapons
community upon policy was both profound and pervasive throughout
these events. Although by 1960 the Atomic Energy Commission because of its intransigence had become virtually isolated from the
rest of the Executive Branch, the non-technical assumptions upon
which AEC positions were based were in greater or lesser degree
shared by the entire governing establishment. In essence, the Commission and its weapons scientists were wholly persuaded that the
Soviet Government's sole objective was at best to embarrass and at
worst to deceive the Americans. Whether the Russians might actually
have wanted some sort of test ban treaty for any other combination of
purposes was not seriously asked.

By basing their own recommendations squarely upon
"worst case" assumptions and conscientiously marshaling technical
data to demonstrate the relative ease with which the Soviets could

deceive the West, the Commission's weapons scientists forced the
rest of the administration into the impossible position of proving a
negative. Among a group of men whose basic instincts were intensely
conservative, this was a position of almost impregnable strength.
Hence, the positions taken by the Eisenhower "disarmament principals"
strongly reflected the priority assigned by the Atomic Energy Commission to the continuing technical superiority of the U.S. nuclear stockpile.

Perhaps two related points are worth recording as personal observations. First, the literature on these events does not
reflect the truly formidable degree to which John McCone as Atomic
Energy Commission Chairman was able to dominate policy sessions
of which he was a participant. On the basis of the superior staff work
of General Alfred D. Starbird, the AEC's director of military applications, McCone's presentations were invariably supported by solid ar-
rays of technical data and developed with surpassing logic and cogency.

Second, it is now conventional to picture Eisenhower himself as a rather vague administrator who often stressed procedure
above substance. Whatever its relevance to other areas, the internal
record does not support this view in the nuclear weapons testing area.
The President seems to have known very well what he wanted, to have
had a firm grasp on the basic issues, and to have often been exasperated

by the rigidity of his principal advisors.   Ultimately, however, he was dominated by these advisors because he was unwilling in any fundamental way to come to grips with the assumptions upon which their advice was based.   Thus repeated technical assurances on the problems of seismic detection seem to have sincerely disappointed him, but the experts, having spoken, had to be listened to.

The more general point is the administration's failure to use its potential organizational and procedural resources to develop sources of technical expertise with a different perspective than the AEC weapons scientists.   Because of this failure dissenting interests were unable to marshal the expertise necessary to challenge the AEC experts.   This insulation of AEC technical expertise from effective challenge is a major theme of the Plowshare program to which, against this background, we can now turn.

2. Plowshare: From Idea to Program

The relevance of the foregoing events to the Plowshare program was vividly captured by the director of the division of peaceful nuclear explosives: "The public furor over fallout had reached a peak when the moratorium came along and left the test ban people mounted on their white chargers without a windmill to tilt at.   They had become crusaders without a cause.   But then along comes the

AEC with some damn fool scheme to use atom bombs to blast a harbor
in Alaska and desecrate the wilderness. We were an obvious target."[16]

The most important events leading to the establishment
of the Plowshare program are already a matter of essentially accurate
public record.[17] Briefly, concerns generated by the 1956 Suez crisis
caused a group of scientists at the Lawrence Radiation Laboratory (LRL),
notably Dr. Harold Brown, to consider the use of nuclear explosives to
excavate a sea-level canal through Israel. At Dr. Brown's initiative a
classified symposium was held at Livermore in February of 1957.[18]
Representatives of all three Atomic Energy Commission weapons
laboratories, Lawrence Radiation Laboratory, Los Alamos Scientific
Laboratory, and the Sandia Corporation, discussed a series of technical
papers proposing a wide variety of possible applications of nuclear explosives. In addition to the possibility of nuclear excavation for such
projects as the removal of earth to expose ore for open pit mining,

---

[16] John A. Kelly, in an interview with the author. Kelly
has been the principal AEC headquarters staff officer responsible for
Plowshare since the program's inception.

[17] Hearings on Peaceful Applications of Nuclear Explosives,
1965, pp. 61-64; Hearings on Nuclear Explosion Services, 1969, pp.
317-323.

[18] Dr. Herbert F. York, Director of Livermore, requested
permission to hold the conference by letter dated October 15, 1956, to
General Starbird, Director of the Division of Military Applications. The
request was approved by the Commission at Meeting 1251 on December 4,
1956. The Commission's only comment was that the peaceful applications
work "must not interfere with the weapons program."

water storage basins, and the digging of canals and harbors, such ideas

as the production of power by repeated explosions in large underground

cavities; stimulating oil production through fracturing; and crushing

ores underground for in-site leaching all received attention.[19] The

written report of the symposium formed the basis of a subsequent re-

quest to the AEC in Washington to establish, with already available

funds, a modest exploratory program. The Commission routinely

granted permission asking its San Francisco Operations Office (SAN)

to assume administrative responsibility, and assigning internal re-

sponsibility to the division of military applications.[20] The important

point here is that Plowshare began as an LRL as opposed to an AEC

program. This fact had profound effects upon both the technical

choices which were made as the program developed and upon the

political and administrative conflicts to which these choices gave rise.

---

[19] Hearings on Peaceful Applications of Nuclear Explosives, op. cit., p. 62.

[20] AEC 811/6, "Non-military Uses of Explosive Nuclear Devices," and Minutes of Commission Meeting 1293, June 27, 1957. Again the stipulation was that the new program should not interfere with "normal weapons activity." The assignment of headquarters responsibility to the division of military applications, quite natural at the time, later became the subject of some controversy. On March 11, 1959, Senator Clinton Anderson wrote to Chairman McCone (in part): "It has come to my attention that queries concerning Project Plowshare have been answered by AEC's division of military applications.

"It has been suggested that such a title for the division servicing the peaceful applications of the atom is unfortunate. The

Established in 1954 as the second nuclear weapons laboratory, Lawrence Radiation Laboratory grew in an atmosphere of sharp technical rivalry with Los Alamos. Scientists who have been with the laboratory from the beginning recall its collective attempts to adopt bold, imaginative and brash postures in contrast to the more staid Los Alamos.[21] In early 1957, LRL was congratulating itself upon its first major weapons design success; an LRL "device" had been chosen as the basis for the warhead of the Polaris missile system.

In this atmosphere, Plowshare represented an effort of the laboratory scientists to "spread their wings" by working on an idea which had been the subject of casual discussion for some time. When Brown decided to push the notion, circumstances were extremely congenial. The other scientists were eager, funds were more than plentiful, and an apparent "need" was at hand. It should also be noted

---

Russian allegation has been that our proposed peaceful applications are really weapons tests in disguise. When the director of military applications answers letters dealing with Project Plowshare, . . . it does not tend to refute the Russian claim. " In 1961 a new Division of Peaceful Nuclear Explosives was created.

[21] Most of the following background is drawn from interviews with Dr. Roger Batzel, an assistant director of the laboratory, and a member of his staff, Dr. Edward H. Fleming. On the rivalry between Los Alamos and Lawrence Radiation Laboratory, see Transcript of Hearings before Personnel Security Board, 1954, In the Matter of J. Robert Oppenheimer, (Washington, D.C.: U.S. Atomic Energy Commission.

that knowledge about nuclear explosive phenomenology was extremely

narrow at this time. In retrospect, several of the applications dis-

cussed in 1957 would probably strike many scientists as highly dubious

at best. But at the time even such a "far-out" notion as using nuclear

explosives to produce stored energy apparently seemed plausible to

some very well-informed people. [22]

Hence, while ideas do not automatically become programs,

the transition for some is plainly less arduous than for others, and I

have found no evidence that Harold Brown encountered any opposition

whatever in securing approval for his idea. Indeed, while Atomic

Energy Commission officials now remember the late fifties as some-

thing of a golden age when it was not especially difficult to get almost

all promising ideas funded, they cite Plowshare as having been some-

what exceptional even in this easy environment. It was one of the

most "sensible" and most "obvious" concepts proposed for research

and development support. [23] As one senior administrator put it:

---

[22] For example, Commissioner Willard F. Libby, as
reported in the Washington Post on December 3, 1957. This story,
incidentally, was the first official public comment on Plowshare.

[23] All the senior AEC officials with whom I spoke agree
on this point. An example of one of the wilder schemes briefly funded
during this period was "Orion," the idea here being to use "directed"
nuclear explosions to propel spacecraft.

"Plowshare instantly appealed to everyone because of its obvious promise of practicality. "[24]

There is also widespread consensus that one of the most important policy choices made in the very early months of the program's formal existence was the Lawrence Radiation Laboratory decision to concentrate their efforts upon the development of excavation technology. For Gerald Johnson, to whom Brown had delegated administrative responsibility for Plowshare, excavation seemed easily the most straightforward and practical of the various potential applications of nuclear explosive technology. [25] There appeared to be an objective basis for supposing that nuclear explosives could be used as highly efficient earth movers. [26] Or, as Roger Batzel puts it: "All of the other appli-

---

[24] John Philip, San Francisco Operations Office. For several years Philip, as chief of SAN's special projects office, bore responsibility for Plowshare.

[25] In an extremely candid interview in May, 1970 Johnson readily acknowledged the importance of his early decision to concentrate upon excavation technology. In fact, on the grounds of simple technical feasibility he still considers it a good idea. The problem in his view is that "political constraints" have grown much faster than the technology to deal with them. Nuclear excavation seems to him less feasible today than in 1957 only because "the growth of constraints has outpaced technical progress. "

[26] A glance at the photograph facing page 495 in Hewlett and Duncan, op. cit., perhaps explains this belief. The photograph, captioned "A Pacific Island Disappears, " shows the replacement of the island of the Eulagelb by a crater "more than a mile in diameter" following the detonation of a 10. 4 MT thermonuclear device.

cations were speculation in greater or lesser degree. We all <u>knew</u>
nuclear explosives would burn very large holes in the ground. " But
Johnson and others also agree that the apparent presence of a real
need for excavation technology was an equally important consideration.
The Suez crisis had only stimulated an interest, extant for some time
within a number of agencies and bureaus, in the construction of sea-
level canals both for the Middle East and the Central American isthmus.
As Johnson and his associates saw it, the existence of this interest
meant that Plowshare could be directed toward an objective which
did not need justification by the sponsoring agency; neither LRL nor
AEC would be called upon to justify the need for sea-level canals.
The need for such projects could be treated as a "requirement. "

Note how Plowshare from its earliest moments reflected
the basic institutional interests of its laboratory sponsors. In this
sense, it is strikingly similar to the breeder reactor program; again
in a peculiar way the solution was defining the problem. In comparison
with other potential applications of explosive technology, the objective
of a program focused upon excavation was clear and uncomplicated,
presented the fewest technical uncertainties, and was glamorous.
There seemed to be abundant gross empirical evidence that the objective was attainable. (Not at all the common situation in nuclear
research and development.) Only engineering "details" seemed to

stand between concept and accomplishment. Still, the rapid transformation of Plowshare into a nuclear excavation program was "natural"
or "inevitable" only from the perspective of the laboratory. It might
well have been a far different program had it originated and been
guided by an institution other than one with the combination of interests
and skills represented by the Lawrence Radiation Laboratory. Plowshare was a program invented by scientists working for government
and looking to government for support. It is only in this very special
framework that excavation represented an "ideal" program.

The relationships among the Atomic Energy Commission,
its university contractor, the Lawrence Radiation Laboratory, and the
rest of the government were the key to the evolution of Plowshare. Administered on the basis of the needs and interests of government agencies
and their contractor, Plowshare is an almost pure case of an attempt to
achieve public ends by public means. But the public means defined their
own ends, ends which by the most generous interpretation were not set
by any meaningful non-governmental interests.[27] Indeed, the immediate

---

[27] One might of course argue that all new technologies
pushed by their inventors are means in search of ends. The problem
remains the same: to insure that such searches are carried out in the
broadest possible context and with maximum opportunity for internal
criticism. For a thoughtful discussion of this point see: Dean Schooler,
Jr., Science, Scientists and Public Policy (New York: The Free Press,
1971).

consequences of the concentration upon excavation technology was to cause the entire program to collide with the demands of an energetic and resourceful issue public. While an excavation program may have been close to ideal for the laboratory's purposes, it was to prove a very porous foundation on which to build non-governmental support for a potentially controversial enterprise.

3. Excavation: Plowshare as a Public Issue

Within months of the program's formal establishment in the spring of 1957 the Lawrence Radiation Laboratory, on the recommendation of an industrial consultant, had decided upon the Pt. Hope region of Alaska's north shore as the site for a project (soon to be known as "Chariot") to demonstrate the feasibility of using nuclear explosives to construct a harbor. Though the laboratory wanted to push forward with dispatch, various officials in Washington and the San Francisco Operations Office urged caution on the need to thoroughly evaluate the effects of the planned explosions on the local ecology. The idea of a bioenvironmental survey was not a popular one; the laboratory for one was strongly opposed.[28] The laboratory was in something of a novel position. Its administrators and scientists were accustomed to operating under

---

[28] The point was made by John Kelly, Director of AEC's Division of Peaceful Explosives, in an interview with the author.

groundrules which permitted them essentially complete freedom of
action, and in particular they had been encouraged in the view that
technical programs were wholly their responsibility. The effect was
a system which, in the words of one official, had by the late fifties
evolved into a "caricature of responsible public administration. "
The laboratories were closed communities possessing unique skills
and knowledge; they looked upon the AEC simply as a source of money.
Among the laboratory scientists a strong "esprit" had developed; a
sense of identity as scientists working for the University of California
and a sense of differentiation from government "bureaucrats. "

With regard to Plowshare, the "bureaucrats'" insistence
upon a time-consuming environmental survey conflicted sharply with
the practical freedom from administrative control under which the
laboratories had been accustomed to operate. The basis of this freedom
was the fact that in the end no one knew anything about the nuclear weapons program except the laboratories. There was literally no one inside or outside government able in any serious way to challenge the
technical judgment of the laboratories on weapons matters. There
were no weapons experts as such within the Commission. No administrator in Washington, civilian or military, had ever been able independently to determine whether a particular weapons test was necessary.

Hence the laboratories, which in principle were merely
government contractors, were in fact completely immune to criticism

and were able wholly to manage their own affairs, limited only by the total amount of money available to them. But even this constraint was far more theoretical than actual for there were few, if any, real incentives in the weapons administration system to question the need or priority of a particular weapons development project. The laboratories had been given an explicit charter to design anything they considered useful. The Atomic Energy Commission's administrators had traditionally encouraged them to pursue any and all "exciting" concepts. Consequently, at any given time the laboratories had a "shopping list" of concepts and designs in various stages of development. This "shopping list" was constantly under discussion with military research and development officials in Washington.

In practice the laboratories throughout the fifties were able to approach the pertinent service with an idea for, say, a nuclear land-mine. Any expression of interest by the military in the development of such a device was more or less automatically transformed into a "military requirement" which the laboratory could then cash in with the AEC for funds to support further research and development. Indeed, according to one AEC official intimately familiar with the process, the system was often even more perverse. Even if the military initially declined interest in the gadget, the laboratories were perfectly capable of taking the position that the demurral was based on ignorance or misinformation and that research should proceed with a view toward building a working model to demonstrate the advantages of the device. As the AEC official put it, "What is the general going to do? Write his Congressman?"

The overall effect was that virtually all items on the laboratories' catalogues of partially tested and untested ideas eventually ended up being "required" by the military. The Commission, which was then called upon to fund such "requirements" was in no position to question either their validity or their priority.

At the time Plowshare was born the AEC's San Francisco operations office served as Livermore's administrative agent. In the weapons area, however, SAN's practical power was negligible.[29] SAN performed administrative housekeeping chores, with the laboratory saying in effect: "Just give us our money, do the arithmetic, and keep out of our way, thank you." This apparently is more or less exactly what SAN did; programs were initiated and controlled by the contractor who possessed a monopoly of the pertinent prestige and expertise.

One of the Commission's first administrative acts in connection with Plowshare, however, had been to delegate to SAN operational responsibility for this program. SAN was given a much broader mandate for Plowshare than it had ever exercised for the weapons pro-

---

[29] The following is based upon an interview with John Philip.

gram. The strains inherent in this situation converged around the Pt. Hope excavation project and the AEC insistence upon an environmental study. Since all of the program dollars came to SAN and not LRL, the operations office was able to prevail upon the weapons scientists to proceed with caution. SAN formed a committee chaired by Dr. John N. Wolfe, a member of the Atomic Energy Commission's division of biology and medicine, to develop a program of environmental studies. The committee undertook over forty separate scientific investigations between 1958 and 1960, ranging from "the caribou of Northwestern Alaska" to "adsorption equilibria between earth materials and radionuclides." The studies were performed by university, private and governmental research organizations under contract to, or by agreement with, the Atomic Energy Commission.[30]

In a sense, though, the laboratory's fears turned out to be justified, for the bioenvironmental study did prove to be the vehicle by which public opposition to nuclear weapons testing made its impact upon the weapons scientists' plans.

---

[30] All of these studies have been published by the AEC. See Norman J. Wilimovsky and John N. Wolfe, eds., Environment of the Cape Thompson Region, Alaska, (Oak Ridge: USAEC Division of Tech. Information, 1966). The volume is available as PNE-481 from the Clearinghouse for Federal Scientific and Technical Information, National Bureau of Standards, Springfield, Virginia.

The laboratory's initial promotional efforts for project

Chariot were anything but temperate. The industrial consultant had

proposed the Alaskan north shore as an excavation site principally

on the grounds that the area was likely to become a major new source

of petroleum (an accurate forecast) and that consequently a harbor

would be needed.[31] The subsequent public relations statements of

the Lawrence Radiation Laboratory scientists stressed the economic

benefits to the Pt. Hope area of a new deep water harbor. Chariot

was ballyhooed in a series of flashy statements as a positive bonanza

for a blighted area. Unfortunately the laboratory was unable to de-

velop any independent support for its claims about the value of a new

harbor in the Alaskan north shore. Even the military, again approached

as a consumer of last resort, was uninterested.[32] Eventually the

laboratory had to back down and was soon issuing statements to the

effect that the project would not result in a fully usable harbor, but

---

[31] Internal records suggest that the actual need for a
harbor was an important consideration for the Commission in approving
LRL's plans for Chariot. See Minutes of Commission Meeting 1353,
April 9, 1958. The Commission instructed General Starbird to caution
the laboratory that "there should be a reasonable need for having a harbor at Pt. Barrow." Subsequently, in informing the Secretary of the
Interior about the project, Acting Chairman Floberg wrote: "We would
not, however, feel justified in doing this excavation without reasonable
assurance that the harbor will be useful . . . " (Letter dated May 22,
1958.)

[32] Letter from Deputy Secretary of Defense Quarles to
Chairman Strauss, dated June 23, 1958.

was merely a feasibility demonstration which probably would not yield any direct benefits for the local residents, specially the Eskimos.[33] Meanwhile the allegations that Chariot represented a substantial risk to these people had become the focus of intense public opposition.

Whether the 1958 - 1961 testing moratorium was actually a cause of this situation in the sense implied by John Kelly's reference to the critics of the project as "crusaders without a mission" is, of course, an open question. It may, though, have been the case that the moratorium did cause the environmental study to become protracted and that this facilitated the activities of the project critics, two of the most prominent of whom were participants in the study.

In fact the study itself quickly became the object of further controversy as Chariot's critics claimed that objective analysis could hardly be expected when the AEC was, in effect, acting simultaneously as investigator, judge and jury. John Kelly's account of the ensuing developments bears repeating: "We ended up with these two guys--William Pruitt and Don Charles Foote. We hired Pruitt to count reindeer; he was a reindeer tracker. Pretty soon he and Foote (an anthropologist who had been employed to investigate "human ecological relations" in the Pt. Hope area) had become buddies and were spending

---

[33] AEC 811/37, "Proposed Revisions to the Program for Peaceful Uses of Nuclear Explosives."

all their time agitating the Eskimos against Chariot. The Eskimos went to their ministers and then we had those New England missionaries on our necks. And then of course the St. Louis bunch got into the act."[34]

The "St. Louis bunch" was "The St. Louis Committee for Nuclear Information," formed in the mid-1950's to inform the public about the hazards of fallout. But, Don Charles Foote does seem to have been the key personality in the public controversy over Chariot. His research required him to spend considerable time in the Pt. Hope area, far longer than the other project scientists, most of whom spent no more than a few weeks in Alaska and to become familiar with its local Eskimo culture.

SAN evidently initially became aware of the impending controversy when Foote informed them that he had arranged a "town meeting" of the Pt. Hope Eskimos. Foote soon began to ask SAN about the effects of the experiment on the Eskimo culture and to question its value in that light. Apparently dissatisfied with the official position on the matter, he contacted the St. Louis Committee who in turn began to press the AEC. John Kelly made several trips to St. Louis to discuss the project with the committee members but to no avail as they flatly refused to accept the validity of AEC's technical judgments.

---

[34] Interview with John Kelly.

At the time, the Lawrence Radiation Laboratory was proposing to use four relatively small nuclear devices each of which would have produced approximately 20 kt of fission energy, and one larger device designed for 100 kt of fission energy. Since exact fission/fusion ratios were classified, Kelly took with him to St. Louis calculations based upon the assumption that the four small devices were all fission and the larger one would contribute 20 kt of fission energy. The laboratory believed that 80-90 per cent of the gross fission products would be trapped underground, but Kelly's figures took the more conservative lower limit. The St. Louis Committee for Nuclear Information would not admit the accuracy of the Atomic Energy Commission estimates, and instead published their own calculations reporting that the radiation picture was substantially more hazardous.[35]

By the spring of 1961 a new group, the Alaskan Con- servation Society, had been formed. Leslie Vierak, a botanist from the University of Alaska who had also made some field studies in

---

[35] AEC 811/82, "The St. Louis Committee for Nuclear Information Bulletin on Project Chariot." An attempt to assess the relative factual merits of this controversy is something I will avoid. Kelly insists that the St. Louis study stated that about 250 per cent more strontium-90 would be distributed than could have been the case even if the whole experiment had been fission. He further believes such exaggeration to represent a "recurrent pattern."

connection with the bioenvironmental survey, was named as president

of the group. By that time pressure upon Congress, the Commission,

and other interested executive agencies had mounted strikingly. Nearly

all of the objections, however, came from a small group of individuals

and the two organizations already cited.[36]

The most immediate effect of this controversy was that

the Alaskan political and economic "establishment" began noticeably

to cool toward the project. The University of Alaska had originally

been interested and receptive as had the state government. In the

face of the activities of the individuals and groups questioning the

project, however, communications broke down between the Atomic

Energy Commission and interested officials in Alaska, particularly

---

[36] Memorandum from the director of Military Applications to the Commissioners dated May 15, 1961, identified the following as critics who "did not seem satisfied with any reasonable answer":

1. Mr. Don Charles Foote
2. Reverend Keith Lawtin, Manchester, N. H.,
   an Episcopal Missioner at Pt. Hope, Alaska.
3. Reverend Beadford Young, Manchester, N. H.,
   substitute Episcopal Missioner for Pt. Hope,
   and wife.
4. Mr. James A. Maddock and wife, Ipswich, Mass.
5. Mr. Vincent Foster, Ipswich, Mass.
6. Mr. Maxwell Foster, Ipswich, Mass.
7. Mr. Leslie Vierak, University of Alaska.
8. Dr. William Pruitt, Sociologist, University
   of Alaska, who had made some carbon studies
   for the Chariot project.
9. Alaska Conservation Society.
10. The St. Louis Committee for Nuclear Information.

at the local level. The trouble seems to have been that neither the Commission nor the laboratory knew how to proceed when it was unable to justify an undertaking on grounds of national security. All prior Commission experience with opposition to its nuclear testing activities had been conducted in the tacit understanding that opposition could, in the end, simply be ignored.[37]

Interestingly, Harold Brown had seen the problem from the start. In summarizing the results of the original technical symposium for Herbert York, the Lawrence Radiation Laboratory director, he wrote:

> It is plain that many of the difficulties involved in the non-military uses are not technical but have to do with questions of public opinion or with such nuisances as broken windows. The government faces such nuisance problems in other activities also, but the situation is greatly complicated by the public fear of nuclear and thermonuclear bombs (quite justified) and of tests (less justified). The suggestion that such explosions may have non-military uses may not encounter as much of the public hostility produced by fear, and in fact such programs if successful might produce a change in attitude.
>
> In order to bring about such a change, however, an altered public relations program would have to be

---

[37] As one AEC official told me, "The AEC knows perfectly well that with any weapons program you can try to be nice, you can be courteous and explain how necessary a project is, and how risks are being minimized, but if it doesn't work you also know you can just tell the people, 'Go away. National security is at stake.' And that's that."

adopted. This would involve the disclosure of
some of the ideas being worked on and some of
the problems connected with them, somewhat
in the manner which has been used for Project
Sherwood. Of course detailed weapons characteristics and design features would have to be
withheld, but for public relations purposes this
would prove little hardship. [38]

Both the Commission and the laboratory were slow, how-

ever, to recognize that the old rules under which dissent could be ig-

nored did not apply with a project like Chariot. Consequently Chariot's

sponsors never took seriously the need to convincingly demonstrate to

those willing to give the project's critics the benefit of the doubt that

its risks were clearly out-weighed by its benefits.

Meanwhile, costs had also become an issue. An impos-

ing array of technical problems had developed; working on the north

coast of Alaska had turned out to be a nightmare, and attempts at deep

drilling in permafrost had shown that the costs of executing Chariot

would far exceed initial estimates. This situation worsened in the

months following the 1961 change of administrations and the Commis-

sion for the first time began to express serious doubts about Chariot. [39]

This was a period which John Kelly recalls as a low point for his pro-

---

[38] Memorandum from Harold Brown to Herbert York
dated February 26, 1957.

[39] Minutes of Commission Meeting 1742, May 31, 1961.

gram. Not only were technical problems combined with the political furor to cast serious doubts on the feasibility of Chariot, but the whole Plowshare program was now faced with a new Presidential Science Advisor (Jerome Weisner) for whom, in Kelly's words, "all atoms were bad atoms."

Plowshare had never been especially popular at the State Department. As early as October, 1958 the State Department had communicated to the Commission its restiveness with a program which at the very best seemed to them just a gratuitous complication to disarmament progress.[40] The new Kennedy Administration soon proved particularly receptive to this position. (Even under Eisenhower the Commission had been instructed not to give Chariot "national publicity.")

Chariot was quietly put on the shelf in the summer of 1961.

4. The Failure of a Public Program

A highly regarded study of the petroleum industry develops the argument that a complex corporate system resembling a political

---

[40] Letter from Undersecretary Herter to Chairman McCone dated October 28, 1958.

[41] Chariot's demise was not publicly acknowledged until the following spring when LRL formally told the Commission it "now believed Chariot no longer justified on technical grounds." Letter from John Foster to John Kelly dated April 30, 1962.

more than an economic institution 'has harnessed public law, govern-

mental machinery, and opinion to ends that directly challenge public

rule. "[42]

A similar perspective can hardly begin to account for the

early history of Plowshare. In fact, one could argue with some justice

that in this instance a complex administrative system buttressed by a

monopoly of pertinent technical expertise was able to harness public

policy to ends that, if they did not directly challenge, at least tempor-

arily ignored other public goals. [43]

Strangely, this divergence not only continued, it actually

widened following Chariot's cancellation, even though, as Kelly saw

at the time, the new administration was obviously intensely committed

to just those ends which seemed incompatible with Plowshare. The

Chariot debacle did not materially affect the relationship between

Plowshare and the government's concern with the troublesome Panama

Canal situation. At an early date the program had attracted the atten-

tion of the American Governor of the Panama Canal Zone. [44] Governor

---

[42] Robert Engler, The Politics of Oil, (Chicago, Ill.: Univ. of Chicago Press, 1967), p. 9.

[43] Again I want to make clear my own belief that such defiance may be justified if one accepts the arguments about Plow-share's technical promise and the putative implications of that promise for national priorities.

[44] Letter from George H. Roderick, Assistant Secretary of the Army, to Chairman McCone dated May 29, 1959.

Potter subsequently brought his influence to bear at high levels of the
Eisenhower Administration and succeeded in commissioning a National
Security Council paper on the possibilities of a sea-level canal exca-
vated with thermonuclear explosives. Though nothing apparently came
of this study under the Eisenhower Administration, the idea re-surfaced
within the Kennedy Administration when in September of 1961 the President was confronted with a Panamanian demand to re-negotiate the canal
treaty. A high level working group was convened from which the Atomic
Energy Commission was pointedly excluded. General Potter, Panama
Canal Zone Governor, had not lost interest in Plowshare however and
at his express urging prominence was given to the argument that the
only way to build a new canal under financial conditions that would
eventually permit Panama to run it was nuclear excavation.

The working group eventually developed a series of recommendations regarding United States policy toward Panama and the Canal
Zone. For Plowshare, the most pertinent of these was a directive to
AEC to establish a formal research goal to determine within five years
the feasibility, costs, and other factors involved in nuclear methods of
excavating a new sea-level canal.

Plowshare's sponsors had perhaps learned from Chariot
that the anticipation of an external requirement may not be especially
helpful in obtaining support for a development program. A requirement no longer had to be anticipated; it had become established. But

even the establishment as distinct from anticipation of a requirement

does not automatically lead to prosperous development programs.

Plowshare's problems were far from over. While the immediate

effect of these events was to put the floundering excavation program

back in gear and to provide the impetus for the first nuclear cratering

experiment, "Sedan," executed at 100 kt on July 6, 1962, the technical

ingenuity of the Lawrence Radiation Laboratory scientists continued to

out-distance the Commission's ability to sustain requests for develop-

ment funds.[45]

The reason was that the basic problem remained; the

administration's commitment to a test ban treaty, a goal which was of

course met in the summer of 1963 with the signing of the Limited Test

Ban Treaty.

As part of a highly orchestrated effort to manage the

Limited Test Ban Treaty through what was thought be be a potentially

hostile Senate, various administration witnesses testified to the effect

that the treaty would not inhibit the Plowshare program.[45a] This turned

out to be untrue; the next excavation experiment, "Schooner," origin-

ally scheduled for October, 1963, was temporarily abandoned when

---

[45]"Sedan" was a thorough technical success, producing
a crater approximately 320 feet deep and 1200 feet in diameter. See
Hearings on Peaceful Applications of Nuclear Explosives, 1965, pp. 155-156.

[45a]U.S. Congress, Senate, Hearings before the Committee
on Foreign Relations, Nuclear Test Ban Treaty, 88th Cong. 1st Sess.
(1963) see esp. pp. 205-215, pp. 433-442, and pp. 829-865.

its execution was held by many within the administration to be incompatible with the provisions of the treaty regarding the deposition of radioactive debris beyond United States borders. By late 1963 Plowshare appeared to be about where it had been two years before. Then, in January of 1964, a sensational series of riots in the Canal Zone led to yet another high level review of the Panama situation, and once more the argument was heard that nuclear explosives represented the only way to build a canal which Panama could eventually own.

Following these deliberations, President Johnson appointed a five-man panel, "The Atlantic-Pacific Interoceanic Canal Study Commission," to develop firm recommendations based on definitive technical studies of all the alternatives for improving or replacing the Panama Canal.[46] Nuclear excavation was explicitly cited as one of these alternatives. Plowshare once more had a "requirement." It had also for the first time acquired an ally. Canal Commission Chairman Robert Anderson was personally interested in the program, and one of the Commission members, General Kenneth E. Fields (Ret.) was a former AEC general manager.

---

[46] U. S. Congress, Underground Uses of Nuclear Energy, Hearings before the Subcommittee on Air and Water Pollution of the Committee on Public Works, U. S. Senate, 91st Cong., 2nd Session, Pt. 2, August 5, 1970. In support of his testimony, AEC Commissioner Clarence E. Larson submitted voluminous official material on the background and activities of the Atlantic-Pacific Interoceanic Canal Study Commission. Of particular relevance is the historical material reprinted on pp. 973-983.

Appointment of the Canal Study Commission, however, did not lessen the frank schism within the administration over excavation experiments. The State Department remained highly skeptical and ACDA was flatly hostile. Because of this disagreement each proposed excavation experiment was accompanied by a series of delays and postponements as the Commission was continually called upon to guarantee that these operations would not jeopardize the Limited Test Ban Treaty. There is consensus within the Atomic Energy Commission that without the prodigious advocacy efforts of John Kelly during endless review sessions even the few experiments which were eventually authorized would not have been undertaken.[47] In recalling the period, Kelly notes (with some understandable cynicism, but also some justice) that the Limited Test Ban Treaty has in effect been merely a Plowshare Ban Treaty; it is not clear that it has inhibited weapons testing at all.[48]

The story of the intra-executive debates caused by the divergence of interests between the Canal Study Commission and the Atomic Energy Commission on the one hand and ACDA on the other

---

[47] Ibid. See pp. 720-729 for a complete chronology of Plowshare's "administrative and technical milestones," including a catalogue of all nuclear and non-nuclear experiments.

[48] It has of course effectively halted atmospheric testing. Since 1963, though, underground weapons testing has established itself as a thriving industry.

is in itself a fascinating study in governmental decision-making to which this cursory review hardly does justice.[49]   For our purposes it simply underlines the salient point about Plowshare: that it has survived as long as it has in an almost completely hostile political environment.   First, as we saw, it began and continued under the worst possible circumstances.   The moratorium and attendant treaty hassles had Eisenhower's Administration confused and defensive.   Kennedy's people almost uniformly considered it simply a nuisance.   Until at least 1960 the Lawrence Radiation Laboratory was entirely preoccupied with excavation technology, in part because such projects were believed to be the most "feasible," but also because the orientation and tempo of the program had been established by nuclear weapons physicists.   (LRL had no geologists and little engineering capability of the type required for progress in non-excavation technology.)   For the weapon physicists the most salient consideration with regard to nuclear explosives was that the comparative advantages of thermonuclear explosives were realized by very large devices.   This implied large projects, which in turn seemed to argue for excavations.   This caused Plowshare to be identified with burning big holes in the ground, with fallout--with

---

[49] A forthcoming book by John G. Palfrey will treat the matter in detail.

disaster. Excavation means big projects, harbors, dams, highways, or canals. But such projects are almost always motivated by the needs of governments, not industry. Preoccupation with excavation technology meant that the program would have to look to government for allies. Such allies were slow to materialize and when they did they proved less than imposing. As John Kelly admits, most of the Johnson Administration was "very unimpressed by the whole canal business."[50]

Most AEC officials are now inclined to believe that the concentration upon excavation to the exclusion of other applications inhibited the growth of the one ingredient which could have been the key to truly a prosperous program--real industrial interest. The laboratory's initial efforts to secure such interest led to nothing.

The Athabaska Tar Sands are a peculiar geological formation in remote northern Alberta which have long been known to contain the world's largest known hydrocarbon reserve. Between 300 - 600 billion barrels of oil are estimated to be suspended in permanently frozen sand. (Compared to the known 300 billion barrels of liquid oil reserve.) The oil, however, has completely defied at-

---

[50] The LRL scientists were also probably too optimistic about the possibility of rapidly developing cratering technology. Progress on this front is now seen to require a more complicated blend of experimentation and basic research than was initially thought. The point was made by Gerald Johnson during my interview with him.

temps at extraction. In 1959 Edward Teller suggested that thermonuclear explosives might be the solution and he approached personal
acquaintances in the management of Richfield Oil Company with the
idea. Richfield expressed interest and agreed to underwrite the cost
of preliminary geological surveys and to pay for the necessary thermonuclear devices. Approaches were made to the Canadian Government
which unfortunately proved quite sensitive to contemporary Russian
claims that the whole Plowshare program was an ill-disguised scheme
to evade the nuclear testing moratorium.[51]   Richfield soon lost interest and the project was abandoned.[52]   The whole venture, however,
was apparently never much more than an idea. There is no evidence
that anyone at the laboratory really worked through the engineering
details and the depth of Richfield's interest is unclear.[53]   As a
practical matter the most important effect of the Athabaska scheme
upon Plowshare was the negative one of reinforcing the laboratory's
commitment to excavation.

---

[51] New York Herald Tribune, May 15, 1960.

[52] The AEC's files on the Athabaska project are extensive.
Of particular interest are: Memorandum for the Record from John
Kelly dated December 10, 1959; and Memorandum from Commissioner
Floberg to Chairman McCone dated March 16, 1960.

[53] Subsequent technical analyses evidently cast serious
doubt on the feasibility of the project. See: Hearings on Peaceful
Applications, op. cit., p. 9.

The first stirrings of serious industrial interest in Plowshare did not begin in Washington, but grew out of a relationship at the working level among engineers at the Bartlesville Research Station of the United States Bureau of Mines, the AEC's San Francisco operations office, and the El Paso Natural Gas Company. The Bureau of Mines' engineers managed to interest El Paso in examining the possibilities of fully contained underground nuclear explosions to stimulate natural gas production. A network of working relations based upon mutual trust and confidence had apparently long existed between Bartlesville and El Paso.[54] The government research station began to use its technical resources to review El Paso holdings for areas potentially amenable to nuclear stimulation. They were funded in this effort directly by the Commission's San Francisco operations office. SAN also assumed overall responsibility for bringing the technical competence existing at Bartlesville to bear upon non-excavation applications of nuclear explosives.

The basis of their actions is highly interesting from our perspective.[55] First, the administrators at the operations office believed that the critical factor in developing industrial support for a

---

[54] Interview with Fred Clark, Division of Peaceful Nuclear Explosives.

[55] The following draws upon interviews with Fred Clark and Fred Van Santen, DPNE, and John Philip, SAN.

program like Plowshare was to be in close and continuous touch with
industry on a technical level. All of the informal, confidential, and
personal relationships necessary to this process were thought to be
impossible from Washington where the tendency was to deal with industrial top management on the basis of economics. SAN was convinced such approaches were worthless unless senior technical
personnel in a company were "sold" on a project on technical grounds.
Neither the Lawrence Radiation Laboratory scientists nor the Washington administrators were able to do this for Plowshare. The operations
office was sensitive to the fact that in general research and development funds are more limited in industry than in government and that
in order to secure the commitment of hard dollars from such a pool
it is necessary to begin at the technical level. Chief company technical officers can then usually be relied upon to persuade top management. Hence, SAN concentrated on working at the technical level
"exploring possibilities, exchanging information, watching for opportunities."[56]

The efforts of SAN and Bartlesville bore fruit in December of 1967 with the execution of Project Gasbuggy, the first joint
government-industry nuclear detonation for industrial purposes.

---

[56] Interview with Fred Clark, Division of Peaceful
Nuclear Explosives.

A 26 kt nuclear explosive was used to stimulate production of natural gas from a gas-bearing sand in New Mexico.[57] In one way the experiment was a gratifying success. In a two-week interval the "Gasbuggy" well produced more gas than had been recovered from five of the eight wells within one and one-quarter miles of it during their entire production history of eight to eleven years.[58] But a number of vexing problems connected with radioactivity concentrations in the gas are still unresolved. Though the AEC believes such concentrations can eventually be reduced to wholly "safe" levels through further research and development on nuclear explosives, it seems clear that public acceptance of gas containing any measurable radioactivity is at best highly problematic.

The stimulation of natural gas production has not been the only "underground engineering" application of nuclear explosives to receive serious attention in the past few years. The AEC has also received industry proposals for cooperative experiments to recover oil from oil shales, to recover copper, and to create underground storage cavities for natural gas.[59]

---

[57] For technical details see: Hearings on Commercial Plowshare Services, 1968, pp. 2250285; and Hearings on Nuclear Explosion Services for Industrial Applications, 1969, pp. 285-262.

[58] Ibid., p. 259.

[59] All of these applications are described at length in Hearings on Commercial Plowshare Services, 1968, pp. 50-225.

The industrial promise of Plowshare, however, remains highly uncertain. Gerald Johnson, now a vice-president of Gulf-General Atomic, believes that with the possible exception of the underground gas storage idea, there are real technical problems with all of the proposed industrial applications. Though it is entirely possible that these diffi-culties would yield to concentrated research and development efforts, experience to date suggests to him that in general developing technical data have not systematically supported most of the initial suppositions about the easy applicability of nuclear explosives to peaceful purposes. Radiation is not, in his view, a trivial problem in natural gas stimu-lation, nor is it likely to be in the oil shale area. It is clear that nuclear explosives will fracture large volumes of shale at relatively low cost, but in situ retorting is "a complex and sensitive process representing a considerable feat of controlled chemical engineering." As of May, 1970 the oil companies simply were not interested.[60]

Indeed, by the spring of 1970 Plowshare remained to all intents what it had been from the beginning, an AEC program, an in-stance of public policy operating independent of the sorts of external demands which many have seen as the source of governmental prior-ities. As such it neatly brackets the Commission's civilian power

---

[60] The following draws heavily upon an enormously candid and helpful interview with Gerald Johnson.

program by illuminating the other side of the argument that public

bureaucracies should be created to undertake inherently public ends.

In 1967 and 1968 a proposal by the Commission and the

Columbia Gas Company to use nuclear explosives to create gas storage

cavities in Central Pennsylvania touched off a local public debate. A

group calling itself "People Against Ketch" (the project's name) made

the essential point:

> The AEC regulates atomic energy only in the
> sense that it determines how, when, and where
> atomic energy is to be utilized. On the question
> of whether atomic energy should be used for a
> given purpose, the AEC does not regulate. As
> far as the AEC is concerned, if atomic energy
> can be used for a specific purpose it should be
> used, . . . the AEC has indicated it is more in-
> terested in applying nuclear technology . . .
> than in either evaluating actual needs or in
> judging the merits of alternative means. . . .
> the primary interest of the AEC (is) in promot-
> ing the utilization of atomic energy, not in de-
> termining . . . true needs . . . and then deciding
> on the best means to fulfill them. [61]

These points are well taken. In conjunction with the history of Plow-

share, they underline the limitations of public bureaucracies as the

principal agents for the execution of public ends. Plowshare shows

that such institutions can become both insensitive and narrowly tech-

nical. In their own fashion they seem to be quite as capable of pursuing

---

[61] Hearings on Nuclear Explosive Services for Industrial
Applications, 1969, p. 244.

a restricted view of what constitutes the public interest as a profit-

seeking company. Moreover, since such institutions are part of

government, the situation is much worse for the normal political

process can easily become short-circuited: the way priorities are

set within government inhibits the meaningful comparison of social

utilities.

Let us now return to AEC's budgetary records for more

systematic evidence on these matters.

CHAPTER V

THE CONSEQUENCES OF ADMINISTRATION

1. Introduction

The histories of the AEC's civilian power and Plowshare programs highlight an important issue about American government: how big is it to be and what is its role in the realization of public ends? On the one hand there is the position represented by Milton Shaw's reactor development policy. Vital public ends cannot be left to private means. The government itself must assume primary responsibility for operationalizing and bringing about such goals. The arguments upon which this position is based have been seen in the fast breeder case to be highly persuasive with the technical history of reactor development underlining the limitations of private firms. As the Commission has tacitly recognized in adopting its breeder policy, constraints upon the financial, technical and administrative resources of even the largest industrial concerns limit their ability to develop complicated new technologies, even when such development is intimately related to their most narrowly defined institutional self-interest. Public programs drawing upon public resources and administered by financially disinterested public servants are essential.

The Plowshare program seems to point up the flaw in this argument. Under certain circumstances public programs can

apparently become oriented around narrowly technical conceptions
of their purpose and hence become quite as insensitive to externalities as the most viscously profit maximizing business enterprise.
Administration by a public agency in the name of public purposes is
no guarantee of social responsibility. Those administering both the
Plowshare and the fast breeder programs have defined their objectives
in terms of a narrow range of technical problems which represent the
most "obvious" and most "desirable" research and development frontier
only from a particular institutional perspective.

The data generated by the executive's annual budgetary
cycles is hardly the place to look for evidence about the causes of
this behavior for a given program. Such data may however provide
important clues about an equally interesting matter. To what degree
is the process of competitive priority setting within the executive
branch responsive to the political consequences of public policies?
What evidence is available from budgetary data regarding the linkages
between public policy and public administration? The answer is by no
means obvious.

In the first place, it is not at all self-evident that the
budgetary process has anything to do with "politics" except in a very
narrow sense of the term. That is, if we take "politics" to mean the
process of accommodation among a set of more or less mutually ex-

clusive interests, then the "politics" of the budgetary process are merely the "games" or "tactics" that the participants employ to maximize their respective objectives. Thus, if I am obliged to secure for my budget request the approval of someone who to further his own ends can normally be expected to reduce such a proposal, I may well, as a matter of tactics, take to "padding" my requests in the hope that after the "inevitable" cuts have been made I will retain what I really wanted to begin with. Or, in anticipation of a major proposal of some sort, perhaps a new facility, I may try to slip a relatively minor item into one year's budget and argue in a subsequent year that approval of these funds constituted some sort of de facto commitment to the whole project. Naturally the "budget cutter" will develop counter strategies of his own. He may require the person making the request to rank all proposed budget modifications by "priority" categories; or he may try to impose absolute ceilings on new spending.

It comes therefore as no surprise that scholarly investigations of budget making within the federal government (including our own narrative in Chapter I) confirm that these sorts of practices are common. Moreover, they are evidently capable of being compactly and precisely described: "There are striking regularities in the budgetary process. . . . the behavior of the budgetary process of the United States Government results in aggregate decisions similar to those produced by a set of simple decision rules that are linear and temporally stable. "[1]

  The behavior which has been modeled by Wildavsky and others is surely a very real part of the budgetary process. But it is not the most important part. For as we have argued in Chapter II, analyses which concentrate upon the decision-making regularities of the process are necessarily unable to account for the differential success of alternative public policies; are in fact unable to describe what public policy means at all. The reduction of budget-making behavior to "a set of simple decision rules" by-passes the problem of priority setting in government; by-passes the question of whose policies have been preferred over others and why. Now it may be that the "budgetary process" is not the place to look for evidence about these matters; that the budgetary process does not, except in the limited "gamesmanship" sense, have anything to do with politics; that it is only administration. Administrators do not, it might be argued, do anything of general political interest, or rather they either do simply what they are told or what "external conditions require of them. " Aside from the "gamesmanship" to which administrators resort in order to further their own career interests, the

---

[1] Davis, Dempster and Wildavsky, op. cit., p. 529.

budgetary process is administration, not politics, and is hardly the place to look for explanations of the allocation of resources among competing priorities. Even our own data do not allow us lightly to dismiss this position. Consider, for instance, the history of another AEC program, the "raw materials"--uranium ore purchasing--program. As Table 17 suggests, the fortunes of this operation have been in monotonic decline over most of the years for which we have data.

TABLE 17

Presidential Budget (in $ millions) and Corresponding Prosperity
Scores (in parens.) for the Raw Materials Program*

Fiscal Year	Presidential Budget	Prosperity Score	Fiscal Year	Presidential Budget	Prosperity Score
1958	$599	(196)	1966	$213	(67)
1959	670	(202)	1967	163	(55)
1960	740	(205)	1968	130	(43)
1961	630	(186)	1969	112	(35)
1962	579	(167)	1970	57	(19)
1963	512	(135)	1971	18	(6)
1964	345	(98)	1972	2	(1)
1965	267	(81)			

*See Appendix A for data on other budgetary stages.

It is clear that the causes of this decline will be illuminated neither by correlating someone's requests with someone else's allocations, nor by detailing the bureaucratic infighting among line program officers and budget staff.

The federal acquisition of uranium ore began with the

Manhattan Engineer District in 1942. Between 1942 and 1946 approxi-

mately 10,000 tons of ore were purchased by the army, about three-

quarters of it from the Belgian Congo. When the Atomic Energy Com-

mission was created in 1947, American supplies were essentially de-

pendent upon ore from two foreign mines, one in the Belgian Congo,

the other in Northern Canada. Thus, one of the highest priorities of

the new agency was to assure a reliable source of raw uranium, and

special emphasis was placed upon the exploration of North American

reserves in order to reduce dependence on overseas mines.

In the late forties and early fifties the raw materials

acquisition program was guided by a single objective: "to get as

much ore as possible from every available source and as soon as

possible."[2] The most important potential domestic source was be-

lieved to be the Colorado Plateau, an area which had been mined

intermittently for several decades and which was thought to be geo-

logically well understood. Geologists, however, were pessimistic

about the existence of large quantities of uranium in the region.

Commission policy therefore came to be based on the conviction

that a successful acquisition program would have to develop supplies

from the Union of South Africa, the Belgian Congo, and Canada, as

---

[2] FY 1965 Authorization Hearings, p. 186. The following summary draws heavily upon the official account presented during
these hearings. These essential facts are not controversial.

well as Colorado.

The purchase program which evolved in the early 1950's had several components, one of which was to increase production from the Colorado Plateau and to undertake an intensive search for uranium in all parts of the United States. Simultaneously, the Commission decided to continue investigation of South African sources and to search for new bodies of ore in any country where geology looked favorable.

To secure the active assistance of prospectors in the domestic mining industry the Commission established a program of guaranteed prices for delivered ore, a system which continued with revisions until March 31, 1962. At the outset, about $1.00 per pound was paid for uranium oxide in ore which contained 0.2% U_3O_8. In 1951 this price was increased to $3.50 per pound.[3] The result of these early governmental actions was perhaps an unprecedented prospecting boom in the American West.

As a supplement to the purchase program, the AEC established ore buying stations at various locations in order to provide a convenient market for ore produced in areas where supplies were not large enough to support a processing plant (i.e., to

---

[3] Ibid.

separate the uranium oxide from the ore). The Commission also supported a variety of geological and metallurgical research programs, underwrote the dissemination of quantities of technical information, provided assaying and technical services to ore processors and milling companies, supported an access road program to provide access to the remote and often inaccessible areas where uranium had been found. In numerous public statements the AEC advertised its desire greatly to expand uranium procurement programs, and its eagerness to negotiate purchase contracts at prices which would cover all costs of production plus a reasonable profit.

In the middle of 1952 the AEC was receiving 200 - 300 tons of uranium per year from the Colorado Plateau. It was hoped that the new programs would increase this to 1,000 tons per year.

Toward the end of 1955 domestic uranium exploration apparently began to decline. Taking note of this situation, the Commission, in 1956, announced an extension of the purchase program to cover the period from March 31, 1962 to December 31, 1966. Because of the lead times involved, this extension was believed necessary to keep exploration for new sources from halting completely. The extended program offered to purchase high grade uranium for $8.00 per pound, subject to a limit of 500 tons per year from any one mining company.

Following this announcement dramatic developments occurred in the domestic uranium supply situation. Known reserves increased from 70,000 tons U_3O_8 at the end of 1955 to over 190,000 tons U_3O_8 by the beginning of 1958.[4] There had turned out to be a great deal more uranium in the Colorado hills than anyone had suspected.

In the fall of 1957 the AEC announced that the government was no longer interested in expanding the production of uranium concentrates. In spite of this change in policy, substantial exploration continued at a high level during 1958 and resulted in the discovery of yet further new reserves in New Mexico and Wyoming. By the summer of 1958 the Commission had decided on the need to limit its commitments for the purchase of uranium in the 1962-1966 period. This did not prove to be a trivial problem. The preceding several years of bountiful incentives had produced a set of vested interests within the mining industry who naturally were anxious to keep a good thing going as long as possible.[5]

---

[4] Ibid., p. 187.

[5] In discussing these matters with me, an AEC official who has been involved in this area since the days of the Manhattan District offered the opinion that the uranium mining industry of the 1950's is the only area in all of the nuclear industry where "real money" has been made.

Though I have not researched these events beyond a few discussions with AEC staff, it seems apparent that the subsequent revisions to Commission purchase policy did to some degree reflect the efforts of the mining interests to secure a compromise to their advantage.[6] Although the supply of cheap uranium now far exceeded demand, the official price of uranium ore remained pegged at $8.00 per pound. The Commission, however, was successful in substituting for its guaranteed purchase program one which limited government purchases during 1962 - 1966 to uranium produced from sources already developed.[7] In subsequent negotiations with ore suppliers the AEC was successful in obtaining the agreement of mill operators to defer delivery to the government until post-1962 of $90 million worth of U_3O_8 then scheduled for delivery prior to March 31, 1962.

During the same period discussions were also undertaken with Canadian producers where, as in the United States, production rates were building to very high levels. These negotiations produced agreement to defer until after 1962 approximately $200 million worth of U_3O_8. The AEC also exercised its contractual options not to pur-

---

[6] Mr. Paul Fine, Director of the Division of Operations Analysis and Forecasting, was particularly helpful in these matters.

[7] Announcement of the new policy was made on November 24, 1958. See ibid., p. 188.

chase additional uranium by extending contracts most of which expired
March 31, 1962.

As a further part of the new program established in
November of 1958, the Commission established annual allocations,
on the basis of "developed" reserves, for each mining property eligible
for a market. In some cases, historic production rates were used instead as a basis for allocations. Many small companies, however,
were granted allocations which were insufficient to support continued
operation. Again, pressure was apparently brought to bear and in
June of 1962 the AEC adopted a modified program under which "small
producers," irrespective of the size of their assigned allocations,
were permitted to sell ore to mills at a rate of 1,000 tons U_3O_8 per
year so long as production of all such producers did not exceed one
million pounds per year. In 1963 total production of the 150 producers
in this category was 600,000 pounds of U_3O_8.

The initial uranium purchase program and the post-1958
"stretch-put" arrangements have probably had an important though indirect effect upon AEC policy in several related areas. First, it has
long been apparent that the only long-run solution to the problems of
the vast government-generated uranium mining and milling interests
is a commercial market of sufficient size to replace the original but
since the early sixties largely fulfilled demands of the thermonuclear

weapons program. The only conceivable source of such demand is large central station reactors. At the same time, given present technology (i.e., light water reactors), the reactor industry is enormously vulnerable to upward movement in the price of uranium. A rise in ore prices to say $20 - $30 per pound would destroy the economic competitiveness of the current generation of reactors. The degree to which and the time when such a price rise is likely are matters of sharp controversy since the price of uranium is dependent upon a complex set of technical and administrative circumstances all of which are in dispute: the existence of unknown reserves of high grade ore (a substance which has had a habit of turning out to be more plentiful than experts believed at any time); modification of the federal policy which presently prohibits the importation of foreign uranium (Canada has a lot); the continued need for the huge government "stockpile"; and the extent to which technical improvements in the enriching process can overcome supply limitations (an especially sensitive and complicated matter).

Sorting out these issues would require a volume by itself, but the essential point should now be apparent. The history of the AEC raw materials program, whatever its causes and its consequences, has very little to do with the budgetary process or budgetary "politics" in the sense in which Wildavsky and others have used the term.

Much the same seems to be true for an AEC program with a markedly different history. I have noted in Chapter I that between the late 1950's and the early 1970's the "Rover" program first mushroomed from a modest research and development operation into a full-scale attempt to build and "fly" a nuclear space rocket, and then at about the point of its maximum technical success and promise it was sharply curtailed. Again this is not "budgetary politics" in the usual sense. Rover's rapid growth in the early 1960's was the result of a major new Presidentially-sponsored policy toward space exploration, and its later difficulties were due to a reassessment of that policy by politicians with different sets of priorities.

We seem, then, to be elaborating a crude model of priority setting or resource allocation within the government which at first glance does not look particularly congenial to further concern with budgetary politics. Admittedly bureaucrats play "games," as the budgetary process literature describes and even models. Government programs, meanwhile, grow, decline, or otherwise experience changes in their fortunes. But, the two sets of behavior have no relationship; bureaucratic politics does not explain changes in the prosperity of programs. The "politics" which are pertinent here are the public politics of Presidential or Congressional policy and the clash of competing clientele interests with material stakes in the fortunes of various governmental activities (the uranium mining industry) or as Plowshare and reactor development illustrate, the interests of governmental institutions themselves. When we search for the causal agents in this process, we naturally look for relationships among tangible interests. This may be the President or Congress, but more likely are the interests of the ongoing public and private institutions who have a stake in what government does. This can be a complex matter. As I have tried to indicate in discussing the Atomic Energy Commission reactor development policy, there is room for honest disagreement over the matter of whose interests are paramount in the breeder effort. The budgetary process per se is unlikely to contain all of the evidence about whose axes are being ground or whose oxen gored by a particular policy. It is unlikely that we will be able to tell "who has wanted what" by examining budgetary histories alone.

But what about the fluctuations which programs undergo across the "stages" of budgetary process? Are these fluctuations merely evidence of "politics" in the gamesmanship sense or do they have some more general significance? Again the answer is not obvious. Certainly one might argue that what really matters is the actual allocations at the end of each yearly cycle and that the intermediate variations represent no more than "confederate currency.".

The rest of this chapter will explore just this question. I will show first that programs are treated differently at successive stages of each cycle and will then argue that these differences, or rather the actions which produced them, have political meaning in the broader sense. The behavior of program directors, budgetary officers, agency heads and the Bureau of the Budget officials represents more than "gamesmanship"; in fact this behavior has a very great deal to tell us about the way priorities are set at the operating levels of government. Dismissing this process as adequately described by a combination of Presidential choices, external circumstances, and clientele group activity is almost as misleading as writing off bureaucratic behavior as simple gamesmanship.

For example, in the mid-1960's the Bureau of the Budget would have liked the AEC's merchant ship reactor program killed and its weapons material (plutonium) production program drastically cut back. In the first, they were wholly successful, in the second, less so. The important causal question is, of course, why this happened. What are the general causal patterns which explain why some programs survive while others are killed. In principle this question can be answered but to do so requires information about the behavior of all relevant participants. We would somehow, that is, have to measure the strengths of all competing interests; --in the merchant ship case, the relative strength of the shipowners, the shipbuilders, the unions, and other government agencies, among others. Intuitively these are just some of the exogenous variables which a model of this program's prosperity would have to include. While information on many of these matters is certainly available, that information is at best going to be very difficult satisfactorily to quantify. Here data collection and measurement problems, though perhaps not insoluble in principle, mean that in practice it is not at all a straight-forward matter to apply the econometric analysis of variance paradigm to questions of comparative program prosperity. They mean that it will not be at all easy to model the causal process by which priorities are established within government.

We could, of course, throw up our hands and retreat to narrative history using budgetary data only for descriptive and summary purposes. In Chapter II, I have indeed suggested several somewhat novel ways in which financial records can be used for just this limited purpose.

But, an alternative is to ask a different question. Suppose we temporarily accept the likelihood that we will have to rely largely upon narrative history to answer questions about who wants what and why, and instead ask how sensitive a particular part of the institutionalized structure of American government is to expressions of preferences among programs by other parts of the same structure. Not only does the available budgetary data contain an answer to this question, but it also contains additional information from which we can derive

numerical measures of the expressed preferences whose impact we
want to assess.

Thus, recognizing that competition over public priorities
occurs within the budgetary cycle (i. e. , that it is not all organizational
process), and admitting that for any particular case the most important
causal questions about their establishment are beyond budgetary analysis as such, we can still ask: To what extent is the politics of budgetary process an instrument of political control? This is not so much
a question about why things happen in government as it is a question of
where and how they happen.

2. The Question of Policy Preferences

The data generated by the budgetary process can tell us
more than the fact that federal administrators employ a repertoire of
tactics; it can tell us where government is putting its disputed dollars;
how different stages are influenced in the process of resource allocation.
This is because at each of the stages of the budgetary cycle a different
set of interests quantifies the value of a program in terms of its claim
upon a resource pool which may be constant, diminishing or growing.
Hence the actual dollar allocations at a given stage mirror the policy
preferences of the participants at that stage. It is true that for programs as well as agencies there is a very high statistical association
between budget requests in a given year and allocations the previous

year. Substantively, however, the apparent evidence of a strong linear relationship is of trivial significance; it merely means that between pairs of years (i. e., regarding years as replications) large programs tend to remain large and small programs, small. We might also wonder, in view of the budgetary politics literature, whether AEC program directors typically ask for a constant proportion of last year's allocation. They do not. Both within programs (across FY 1958 - FY 1972) and within years (across programs) there is great variation in division requests as proportions of the previous year's allocation. [8] The yearly variation is less for larger programs than for smaller ones, but this only means that the former fluctuate by smaller relative amounts of dollars. One might ask at this point whether there are causal variables, common across programs, which would account for this manifest behavioral variance. This is an important question but again is one on which no systematic data is available. [9]

---

[8] The curious reader can easily check this statement by selecting a number of requests and corresponding allocations from the data in Appendix A and calculating the resulting fraction.

[9] My personal impression is that the principal independent variable is the degree to which the program director is constrained by externally imposed requirements, obligations, or commitments. At one end of this dimension, budget making by the division director consists simply of "costing out" a set of requirements--a "want list." At the other, it entails substantial discretion in light of current technical or political circumstances. Within AEC the raw materials program to which we have already referred and parts of the weapons pro-

Whatever the underlying causal structures, the point to stress here is that the division director in making his program requests is not simply trying to outwit a budget-cutting adversary. The director of the AEC Rover program, for instance, wants to build and fly his rocket. In pursuit of this goal he will try to develop a case strong enough to withstand the skepticism of others both within his own agency and elsewhere in government to whom the prosperity of this enterprise is perhaps a less compelling matter. A given request may or may not be based on a set of objective external constraints (e.g., contracts with power suppliers in the case of the special nuclear materials production program); it may or may not have external support (the Canal Study Commission's requirements); and it may or may not be challenged by other parts of the permanent government (ACDA's opposition to Plowshare). The important point is that the AEC division director is fundamentally interested in the prosperity of his program. The institutionalized review structures oblige him to work for this prosperity by successive confrontations with a hostile universe.

---

gram approximate the former extreme, while an enterprise such as "advanced systems" reactor research perhaps approaches the latter. As a matter of tactics it will normally be to the division director's advantage to make as much of a given request as possible _seem_ to be constrained by some type of requirement or commitment. This tactical principle, however, should not be taken to imply that all "requirements" are imaginary. At the division level programs objectively differ on this variable.

The first skeptics that the program director must confront are the General Manager and his budget review committee. It
is their business to cut budgets. As noted in Chapter I they usually
do so to bring the aggregated division requests into conformity with
an administration (Bureau of the Budget) "ceiling" or "guideline, "
the rigidity of which varies markedly from year to year. [10] Within
the AEC the General Manager's budget staff is always exceptionally
well informed about how flexible the Budget Bureau ceilings or guidelines are likely to prove in a particular year. In light of this knowledge, the General Manager may follow a number of strategies in
dealing with the division requests. He might merely propose for
consideration by the Commission a number of recommended cuts to
meet the BoB ceiling. Alternatively, he may recommend a total
budget in excess of the Budget Bureau guidelines, perhaps supplemented by a list of cuts from which the Commission might choose
if it desires to modify his proposal. A variation of this is to recommend that the Commission supplement his own reductions with others
which the General Manager considers to be important enough to be
simply identified as matters of Commission policy determination.
Finally, the General Manager may present a recommended "low
case" budget which conforms to a BoB ceiling, while suggesting

---

[10] Arthur Smithies, op. cit.

that the Commission supplement this in its official budget with special

pleas for selected additional items, arguing that such matters ought

to be considered by the administration "on their merits," independent

of other ceilings.

Once more, most of this, if not all, is "politics" only

in the narrow tactical sense and not therefore a matter we want to

explore in great detail. The basic job of the General Manager in this

context is to cut budgets to meet ceilings, and what interests us is

how he does this. In principle, of course, he could use a number of

devices or decision rules. He might, for one thing, begin by merely

taking fixed absolute amounts from each program. Thus, as a matter

of habit or tradition, weapons might lose, say, $20 million, high en-

ergy physics might lose $17 million, and so forth. Plainly, this is

absurd on its face. Slightly (but only slightly) less so, the General

Manager's review committee might reduce each program by constant

proportions. Again, we know that this is not really plausible. What

does, however, represent a real possibility is the notion of proportional

reduction. That is, the General Manager might reduce each program

by a fraction exactly equal to the percentage by which the aggregated

division requests exceed the pertinent ceiling.

The latter is an interesting possibility for a number of

reasons. First, the literature on the budgetary process suggests that decision rules of this sort are an important part of administrative behavior. It has been argued that the most significant administrative feature of the budgetary process is its potential complexity.[11] Because of this complexity, it is impossible, as a practical matter, for each program to be reconsidered in its entirety at each review stage. Adoption by the General Manager of some sort of "proportional reduction" rule would provide him with a device which corresponds closely to conventional notions of fairness.

Professor Wildavsky has commented upon the expectation in government that programs are somehow entitled to "fair shares" of new money and that each should pay an approximately "fair share" of overall fiscal cuts.

> Having a project included in the agency's base
> this year means more than just getting it in the
> budget for a particular year. It means establish-
> ing the expectation that the expenditure will con-
> tinue, that it is accepted as part of what will be
> done, and, therefore, that it will not normally
> be subjected to intensive scrutiny. (The word
> "base," incidentally, is part of the common
> parlance of officials engaged in budgeting and it
> would make no sense if their experience led them
> to expect wide fluctuations from year to year
> rather than addition to or subtraction from some
> relatively steady point.) "Fair share" means

---

[11] Crecine, (1969), op. cit., Chapter II. The definitive statement of this perspective on administrative behavior in general is, of course: Herbert A. Simon, Administrative Behavior, (New York: The Free Press, 1965). See especially the introduction to the second edition.

not only the base an agency has established
but also the expectation that it will receive
some proportion of funds, if any, which are
to be increased over or decreased below the
base of the various governmental agencies.
"Fair share," then reflects a conveyance of
expectations on roughly how much the agency
is to receive in comparison with others. [12]

Given these expectations, application of a proportional

reduction rule would appear to be an admirable expedient if the General

Manager's objective is to attain a predetermined budget ceiling in a

manner which will minimize internal conflict. Within the AEC more-

over, proportional reductions are a commonly proclaimed norm for

action by the General Manager and his staff. A standard complaint

by program directors at this and later stages of the review process

is that their activities have been treated "unfairly" in just this sense:

the General Manager, or later the Commission or the Bureau of the

Budget, has reduced their particular program disproportionately in

view of the total budget reduction. Finally, there are pervasive myths

among AEC program staff about the behavior of various budget review-

ers. Staff in the division of peaceful nuclear explosives can often be

heard to complain that "the Commissioners always reduce Plowshare

unfairly. "

I will shortly report the results of the simple calculations

---

[12] Wildavsky, (1964), op. cit., p. 17.

needed to substantiate these beliefs. As a preliminary, though, consider some of the reasons why we might anticipate that the proportional reduction model will not adequately account for the General Manager's behavior. Those reasons relate to some very fundamental issues of the political control of public administration.

The General Manager is the Commission's chief executive officer, charged with the execution not the formulation of policy, and he has no reason whatever to consider that "proportional reduction" represents Commission policy toward its various programs. Whatever its merits as a conflict avoidance technique, the "fair share" treatment of each program as being equal in all respects to every other program hardly represents the Commission's view about the relative priority of its numerous activities. The General Manager's reductions should reflect these preferences; his behavior should to some degree be caused by Commission policy.

But the General Manager also plays an important role vis-a-vis the Bureau of the Budget and the administration. His information about their policies (and once again, these are most decidedly not to treat all AEC programs "fairly") is more complete than that of any other AEC participant in the budgetary process. His actions should therefore represent some attempt to adjust Commission priorities to BoB and administration preferences. Evidence that this is the case are the common exchanges between the Commissioners and the General Manager during budget review sessions in

which the latter defends particular reductions as having been made

in anticipation of Budget Bureau actions.

What about the General Manager's own policy preferences?

Is he in the end only an executive officer or does he use his position to

impress his own set of priorities upon Commission activities? Does

the General Manager, for instance, "protect" certain programs even

in light of known Commission and Bureau of the Budget antipathy? We

would like to know, that is, how much of the General Manager's differ-

ential treatment of particular programs can be explained by Commis-

sion, Budget Bureau, or Presidential support or opposition to the same

programs. If it develops that some programs are indeed, as myth has

it, repeatedly treated "unfairly" by the General Manager, it would be

interesting to know if this represents an attempt by this official to

execute Commission policy (perhaps adjusted by that of the Bureau of

the Budget), or whether the AEC General Manager uses the budget re-

view procedure as a device for expressing his own programmatic

preferences about AEC activities. These preferences of course are

not necessarily arbitrary or capricious. Among all AEC personnel,

the General Manager has the most detailed knowledge of the overall

status of the agency's activities.

Let us now check to see if the General Manager's review

really does consist simply in reducing each division request by an amount exactly proportional to his reduction in the total operating budget--which we assume was made to bring the total into line with a Bureau of the Budget ceiling or guideline. We simply calculate for each year the total General Manager budget as a proportion (expressed as a per cent) of the aggregated division requests. That is, we divide each element of the second column of Table 11 in Chapter II, page 102, by the correspondent element of the first and multiply by 100. We repeat the operation for each program, again for each year, and subtract the proportional change in the total budget from the corresponding proportional change for each program. The entries in Table 18 are the results of these subtractions. There can be a zero entry for a program if and only if it happens to have been cut by a percentage just equal to the percentage reduction in the overall budget. An asterisk next to an entry means that the program request in question was left unchanged by the General Manager.

As expected, it is clear from Table 18 that the General Manager's review is not well described as the application of a proportional reduction decision rule. For example consider fiscal year 1967. The "fair share" was a 5.2 per cent reduction. Two programs, raw materials and naval reactors, were not changed; they show a deviation from fair share of +5. 2 per cent. Others fared less well.

TABLE 16

Deviations from "Fair Shares" (Expressed in Per Cent)
at the General Manager Review Stage*

PROGRAM	FY1958	FY1959	FY1960	FY1961	FY1962	FY1963	FY1964	FY1965	FY1966	FY1967	FY1968	FY1969	FY1970	FY1971
1. Raw Materials	4.4	1.2	2.2	1.7	-0.4	6.1*	11.2*	3.1*	3.1*	5.2*	16.7*	8.7	4.1	4.5
2. Special Nuclear Materials	-2.1	0.7	-1.1	3.0	0.9	2.6	10.2	2.2	2.6	3.6	11.1	1.8	1.3	2.1
3. Weapons	4.5	3.4	2.0*	3.2	0.5	-6.3	-4.5	-0.5	1.1	3.1	-9.0	2.2	-0.1	1.5
4. Civilian Power Reactors	-5.0	-2.3	-1.4	-3.2	1.6*	-7.0	-9.8	3.1*	5.4	3.2	8.8	-1.7	-0.4	-1.4
. Cooperative Power Reactor Program	---	7.4*	-8.7	3.4*	1.6*	-22.4	-8.8	3.1*	3.1*	0.0	9.6	6.8*	-4.7	-11.0
6. Euratom	---	7.4*	2.9*	3.4*	1.6*	6.1*	11.2*	3.1*	3.1*	-17.0	16.7*	-43.2	-94.2	---
7. Merchant Ship Reactors	-70.2	-35.6	-63.1	-28.0	1.6*	-12.3	-27.6	3.1*	3.1*	-44.8	-63.3	-91.2	---	7.3*
8. Army Reactors	5.1*	-2.2	-15.3	-37.2	1.6*	2.4	-9.5	-45.9	3.1*	-61.5	---	---	---	---
9. Naval Propulsion Reactors	-9.5	-3.4	-0.4	-3.4*	1.6*	6.1*	5.6	3.1*	5.1*	5.2*	16.7*	6.8*	3.8*	7.2
10. Aircraft Nuclear Propulsion	-7.8	7.4*	-0.8	-3.8	-5.9	---	---	---	---	---	---	---	---	---
11. Pluto	5.1*	-16.3	2.0*	3.4*	1.6*	8.0	-88.8	3.1*	3.1*	4.4	7.8	3.3	0.5	6.1
12. Rover	5.1*	7.4*	2.9*	3.4*	1.6*	8.1	-3.5	3.1*	3.1*	-16.2	-22.2	-23.6	-11.6	-13.3
13. SNAP	---	-7.4	2.0*	-23.9	1.6*	3.4	-6.4	3.1*	-10.4	0.2	7.8	-3.4	0.0	-0.2
14. General Reactor Technology	5.1*	-18.1	-22.6	-6.4	1.6*	-14.5	-1.1	3.1*	-2.9	-5.6	-5.8	-7.1	-6.6	-3.3
15. Nuclear Safety	5.1*	-18.5	2.9*	-13.6	1.6*	-4.0	3.5	3.1*	-8.6	-14.6	-7.9	-11.8	-8.1	-2.3
16. Advanced Reactor Systems	5.1*	7.4*	-3.1	-6.6	-6.8	-5.9	-19.6	3.1*	-5.7	-11.3	-2.2	0.1	-8.7	-9.1
17. High Energy Physics	5.1*	-23.1	2.0*	-5.5	1.6*	1.1	-2.7	-13.2	-12.4	-6.3	-6.3	-2.6	0.7	-9.1
18. Sherwood	-6.2	3.0	-9.8	-6.0	1.6*	6.1*	11.2*	-3.9	-9.9	-6.3	5.7	0.5	1.2	0.8
19. Biology and Medicine			1.9		-2.2	4.7	7.1	-3.6	-0.8	-2.1			0.0	1.1
20. Training, Education and Information	-34.9	-40.6	-18.2	-37.9	-9.6	-6.3	-3.2	-4.6	-4.2	-3.2	-0.1	-2.9	2.3	-6.1
21. Isotopes	5.1*	-68.6	2.0*	-49.0	-10.5	6.1*	-13.5	-7.6	-5.1	-21.1	-25.1	-6.0	-7.8	-4.0
22. Plowshare	---	---	2.9*	-15.0	1.6*	6.1*	11.2*	-4.3	-3.4	-18.3	-34.0	-17.4	-13.9	-29.1
23. Program Direction and Administration	-0.4	2.8	-2.8	-3.8	1.6*	0.0	4.8	2.6	3.1*	4.7	14.6	0.1	1.4	1.9

* These data calculated before FY 1972 figures became available.

Army reactors emerged from the review with only about half of what its director might have anticipated had the General Manager applied a proportional reduction rule. Euratom, SNAP, advanced systems, high energy physics, isotopes and Plowshare all were cut by at least ten per cent more than a proportional reduction.

Reading across the rows of Table 18 does in fact seem to confirm the belief that certain programs are continually treated "unfairly" by the General Manager. Plowshare, isotopes, advanced systems, SNAP and merchant ship reactors have all repeatedly been reduced by amounts substantially in excess of a "fair share" of the total cut. Though we cannot yet be more precise about whose policies are being expressed here, we now know that the General Manager's budget review reflects someone's programmatic preferences, someone's notions of relative priorities--unless, of course, we just dismiss the numbers in Table 18 as random departure from a substantively meaningless mode. But it is not clear what "policy preference" means in this context aside from departure from "fairness" as we have defined it.

Recall that the program directors are given the opportunity to appear before the Commission to appeal the General Manager's actions. If possible, he will base his case upon the existence of some set of "requirements" which he will endeavor to claim are inflexible.

His position will be most sound when he can successfully present a particular client or set of unambiguous commitments. The Commission's actions, both here and to a greater degree later in the budget review sequence, are probably much more strongly influenced by political than by technical considerations. Partly, of course, these political considerations are the questions of "tactics" or "budgetary gamesmanship" about which we have commented previously. But only partly. Or to be more precise, "politics" in this narrow sense affects Commission behavior as an intervening variable. Essentially, programs prosper or decline from Commission action because of their political effects. What will be the consequences upon Los Alamos of a failure to support the Rover program? How much of a fight is Plowshare really worth in light of administration cynicism and strident, though localized, public opposition?

Does our historical data contain any evidence to support these assertions? Once again we can examine the actual pattern of Commission restoration compared with some frankly non-political "null" model. The data in Table 19 have been calculated by the same procedure used to produce Table 18. (In this case the AEC September budget has become the numerator and the General Manager's budget the denominator for calculating "fair shares.")

We first notice that on the whole the magnitude of the

TABLE 19

Deviations from "Fair Shares" (Expressed in Per Cents) at the Commission Review Stage*

PROGRAM	FY1958	FY1959	FY1960	FY1961	FY1962	FY1963	FY1964	FY1965	FY1966	FY1967	FY1968	FY1969	FY1970	FY1971
1. Raw Materials	-6.6	-1.5*	-6.1	-2.7	0.3*	-0.8*	-4.8*	-0.8*	-0.3*	-1.0*	-5.6*	-0.7	-1.6*	2.3
2. Special Nuclear Materials	-0.7	1.0	3.1	0.3	0.3*	-0.8*	-5.3	-1.8	-0.0	0.4	-5.0	1.3	-0.3	-0.9
3. Weapons	1.0	0.3	-3.7	0.7	0.3*	3.5	-3.9	-3.0	-0.3*	-1.0*	3.5	0.8	1.9	0.3
4. Civilian Power Reactors	32.7	-1.5*	1.0	1.7*	-4.0	2.1	21.6	-0.2	11.0	-1.0*	-4.4	4.4	-1.6*	0.4
5. Cooperative Power Reactor Program	--	-1.5*	-0.4*	1.7*	0.3*	-0.8*	20.2	-0.8*	-40.0	3.5	24.2	0.1*	-1.6*	-0.3*
6. Euratom		-1.5*	-0.4*	1.7*	-0.7	-20.8	-4.8*	-0.8*	-0.3*	-1.0*	-5.6*	0.1*	-1.6*	
7. Merchant Ship Reactors	533.2	-1.5*	93.7	1.7*	42.9	-0.8*	0.7	-0.8*	-0.3*	65.7	-5.6*	0.1*		-0.8*
8. Army Reactors	-6.8*	-1.5*	21.8	44.4	-10.9	-10.8	1.4	-0.8*	-0.3*	-1.0*	-5.6*		-1.6*	-0.8*
9. Naval Propulsion Reactors	10.3	-1.5*	3.0	1.7*	-1.1	-0.8*	-2.9	-0.8*	-0.3*	-1.0*	-5.6*	0.1*		-0.8*
10. Aircraft Nuclear Propulsion	8.1	-1.5*	3.2	1.7*	3.0	--	--	153.2	--	--	--	--	--	--
11. Pluto	-6.8*	-1.5*	-0.4*	1.7*	0.3*	-19.6	--	0.3	--	--	--	--	--	--
12. Rover	-6.8*	-1.5*	-0.4*	1.7*	10.0	-0.8*	12.3	0.3	-0.3*	-1.0*	1.6	-25.8	-0.8	-0.8*
13. SNAP	--	-1.5*	-0.4*	1.7*	0.3*	4.8	10.4	15.7	9.8	3.0	5.4	4.6	-0.3	7.0
14. General Reactor Technology	-6.8*	--	100.8	-1.0	-5.3	6.3	-0.2	-0.8*	-0.3*	-1.0*	-3.6*	0.1*	-1.0*	6.4
15. Nuclear Safety	-6.8*	-1.1*	-0.4*	1.7*	0.3*	-3.6	-0.3	-0.8*	-0.3*	-1.0*	-5.5*	0.1*	-1.0*	-0.8*
16. Advanced Reactor Systems	-6.8*	-1.5*	-0.4*	1.7*	-16.8	-3.6	-8.6	14.7	-0.3*	6.8	-17.9	0.1*	-1.6*	-100.6
17. High Energy Physics	-6.8*	-1.5*	-0.4*	-1.1	2.8	-1.4	25.9	4.8	-0.3*	0.1	1.8	0.8	-1.6*	0.7
18. Sherwood	-6.8*	11.8	13.6	1.7*	-1.7	-3.5	-4.8*	0.0	3.9	-0.5	12.0	10.5	-1.6*	-0.8*
19. Biology and Medicine	0.3	-1.5*	1.7	1.7*	-6.8	-1.0	-3.0	-0.6*	-0.3*	0.2	1.5	1.2	-1.6*	-0.8*
20. Training, Education and Information														
21. Isotopes	26.5	52.7	6.5	2.4	-0.2	4.2	-8.3	-0.8*	2.7	12.4	-0.3	-0.4	-1.6*	-0.5*
22. Plowshare	-6.8*	-1.5*	-0.4*	1.7*	10.3	-10.2	17.2	-0.3*	-0.3*	0.7	-0.7	0.1*	-1.6*	-0.8*
23. Program Direction and Administration	--	--	149.6	1.7*	0.3*	-0.8*	-4.8*	-14.0	-0.3*	5.4	62.9	0.1*	-1.6*	-0.8*
Administration	-3.1	-1.5*	-0.4*	2.6	0.3*	-0.8*	2.6	-0.8*	-0.34	-1.0*	-5.5	1.0	-1.6*	0.6

*These data calculated before FY 1972 figures became available.

entries in Table 19 are smaller than in Table 18. This reflects the fact that the total budget is usually changed less at the Commission review state and means that many conflicts have already been settled and will not be reopened. We saw in Chapter I that as the review process progresses through successive stages the number of items in dispute is reduced.

Now we have more systematic evidence that the Commissioners use the budget review operation to further preferred programs. Note additionally that the Commission does not always favor the same ones as the General Manager. Again using FY 1967 for illustration, ten programs, though unchanged in absolute dollars by Commission consideration, still were budgeted one per cent lower than purely proportional treatment would have implied. The reason is that three other programs were treated particularly well. Merchant ship reactors, which the General Manager had cut drastically, received notably more sympathetic treatment from the Commission. Advanced systems and training, education and information programs also fared well in the context of a "proportional restoration" model.

So, just as the General Manager does not invariably reduce division requests "fairly" to meet the Bureau of the Budget ceiling or guideline, neither does the Commission typically restore a "fair share" to each program. But is this evidence of any more substantial significance? Perhaps not. For one thing, we may choose to regard the data in Tables 18 and 19 as merely reflecting capricious additions or subtractions of incremental dollars to various activities. We reject this possibility as silly on its face. Second, we may be seeing here no more than traces of "budgetary gamesmanship." The General Manager sharply reduces the merchant ship reactor program and the Commission gives some (or all) of the money back. So what? Well, the point is that policies are being purchased with these dollars; policies to support pure rather than applied research, to favor civilian over military reactors, or to explore space instead of expand commercial maritime transport.

The world consists of deviations from central tendencies, and the deviations evident in Tables 18 and 19 represent differential policy preferences within government. The problem we have set for ourselves is to use budgetary process data to better understand how public administration is linked to public politics. These discrepancies from a "fair share" model partly capture the politics of public administration and therefore are the first step to that end.

We might be tempted simply to read the entries in Tables 18 and 19 as respective numeric measures of General Manager and Commission "support" for alternative programs. We might, that is, argue from Table 19 that in FY 1967 the Commissioners "supported"

the merchant ship program about five times more strongly than they
"supported" training, education and information. The next step presumably would be somehow to combine such separate indicators of
support in each year into an overall measure across all fiscal cycles
by adding each column of the two tables. The problem is that the
budgetary process is, in part, a matter of tactics. Any single stage
is to some degree both a response to previous stages and an anticipation of later stages. Unless we take account of this tactical complexity,
the "politics" of the process in the narrower sense, we will be misled
in our effort to use this data as evidence of a different sort of politics--
the magnitude of conflict among alternative programmatic preferences,
among real differences about the priorities of what the government is
doing.

In discussing the factors which affect the General Manager's
review actions we have already set forth the reasons why we cannot read
Table 18 as a straightforward proxy for his personal opposition to or
support for particular programs. The informal ties between the AEC
budget staff (the "working level" of the General Manager's budget review apparatus) and the Bureau of the Budget have historically been
very strong. But this is not the only possible interpretation of these
figures. Take Plowshare for example. John Abbadessa, the AEC
controller, maintains that the pattern of "unfair" reductions which

we see in Table 18 does not reflect any personal evaluation of Plowshare's worth. He claims to personally believe Plowshare to be an
important and exciting program. The Bureau of the Budget, however,
has been consistently hostile to the growth of this program, and by
anticipating BoB cuts the Commission "gains credibility" when it
strongly supports its highest priority activities: civilian power reactor development and the production of special nuclear materials.[13]

Even if one chooses to be cynical about such protestations
of "real" versus "apparent" preferences, the fact remains that the behavior reflected in Table 18 is caused by a more complex set of factors
than an ordering of preferences by the AEC senior budget staff regarding program priorities. Part of our ultimate problem is to try to sort
out these causal threads.

Similar considerations apply to the Commission review.
The Commissioners, as they respond to the General Manager's recommended reduction from division requests, are aware that there will
normally be modifications of specific program budgets at later stages
of the process. There is, therefore, little need for them to adopt an
intransigent position on a program director's plea for restoration of
a cut. Moreover, the format of the review process at this stage favors

---

[13] Interview with John P. Abbadessa.

the program director. He can appear before the assembled Commission in a formal, on-the-record meeting fully buttressed by his own
technical experts. He is therefore usually able to develop the strongest
possible case in support of his original request. As a rule, the Commissioners have little to gain by taking a hard line in the face of a
forceful appeal. They may have something to lose in terms of working
harmony with their staff. Successful restoration of a General Manager
reduction, thus, says more about the program director's initial case
than about Commission policy. It may be more nearly a measure of
the former's strength than of the latter's priorities. The process
can be conceived as one where the special "requirement" and technical-
based pleadings of the program director are evaluated by the Commission in light of pertinent political consideration. But since the Commission is aware that it will be able to modify its decisions at later
stages, a large restoration is a measure of how strong a particular
program division is in competition with the other divisions, how
successful, that is to say, a particular program director has been
in making his requirements case.

But what is a "large restoration"? The obvious problem
is that this is a highly relative notion. We require an estimate of how
much has been restored to a program relative to some expected value
in light of both the initial reduction by the General Manager and the

total restoration by the Commission. That is, we need to combine the data of Tables 18 and 19 into a composite.

3. The Effects of Administration: Evidence from Budgetary Data

Consider the actions taken each year by the General Manager and the Commissioners. Our problem is to define a measure of the way each program request is treated during these two successive review processes. This measure will have to take account simultaneously of several factors. It should on the one hand take account of what the General Manager has done, both to specific program requests and to the aggregated total of all requests. At the same time the measure should be sensitive to how the Commission treats a particular program in light of what the Commission does to the overall budget recommended by the General Manager.

The same logic applies to the events during the next two "stages" of the budget cycle. An index, that is, which successfully captures the way programs are treated by the General Manager and Commissioners during the internal review can also be used to gauge Commission support for programs in the face of Bureau of the Budget reductions. The logic of this latter review and restoration sequence is identical to the former. In both cases, a list of requests is acted upon by someone "in the budget-cutting business" (the AEC General Manager in the first instance, the AEC's Budget Bureau examiners in the second). In both cases, we want to measure the Commission's responses to the treatment each program has received in light of action on the aggregated total. The Commissioners response to the Bureau of the Budget actions can plausibly be considered a measure of their support for particular programs.

We have, in fact, been able to take account of all these considerations in a new mathematical formalism. The properties of this algorithm are described in some detail in Appendix B. We have transformed the "treatment scores" generated by the algorithm into two ordinal scales, each with four degrees of positive and negative treatment around a zero point defined in terms of the "fair share" or proportional reduction concept. Thus a given program in a given year will be assigned a "division strength" score of zero if and only if it was treated "fairly" (i.e., proportionally) by the Commissioners in light of the General Manager's action. (Similarly, "fair" treatment by the Commissioners vis-a-vis the Bureau of the Budget produces a "Commission support" score of zero. Deviations from fair treatment are assigned scores ranging from -4 (most unfair) to +4 (most preference). Hence we have two entirely new and completely independent ordinal scales which measure the treatment accorded each AEC program at two points in the budget review process against the concept

of fair share.[14]

The final scores for all AEC programs for the years

FY 1958 to FY 1972 are also reproduced in Appendix B. Inspection

of these values reconfirms the arguments elaborated in Chapter II,

namely, programs do appear to be in competition with each other for

new money--for most years the treatment scores for both "division

strength" and "Commission support" sum to approximately zero.

And, more important for our purposes, in a given year the benefits

to particular programs are anything but equal.

But the object of this elaborate measurement exercise

was not merely to confirm some intuitively obvious characteristics

of the budgetary process. The real test of the validity of these two

new indices is whether they help us to move beyond descriptive state-

ments of the sort we made in Chapter II, and to begin to address the

causal significance of all the budgetary actions we have discussed.

Does the jockeying among the program divisions, the General Manager,

---

[14]Though the point is made in the Appendix, I want to
stress that the algorithm itself is completely compatible with sub-
stitution of any substantively or mathematically interesting zero point.
An example might be "splitting the difference"--assignment of a zero
treatment score for, say, division strength, if only the Commission
restores precisely half of a General Manager reduction. For the
reasons set forth in the text, the fair share notion seemed to me to
be the most interesting anchor point for the index.

and the Commissioners make any difference to the prosperity of the AEC's various activities?

The General Manager's annual recommendations (stage two in our data) are the most likely place to look for an answer. As a working hypothesis one might argue that the General Manager and his budget review committee attempt to adjust the individual program requests in light of both anticipated Commission preferences and likely BoB action. Of all the budget stages on which we have data, the General Manager stage is probably most sensitive to events which we can also measure from the same data. Moreover, we know from both the budgetary process literature and our own descriptive analysis that the stages themselves are highly intercorrelated, i. e., that on the average any given stage in a given year is a very good predictor of any other stage for that year. Because of this, any progress we are able to make in accounting causally for what happens to programs at the hands of the General Manager and his review committee is also progress in accounting for actual changes in the prosperity of Commission programs.

But even so, any success in accounting for the General Manager's behavior is in itself not devoid of theoretical interest. As the AEC's chief executive officer and senior civil servant, he is strategically located between programs and politicians. Our concern throughout has been with the nature of the relationship between public administration and public policy.

By taking the behavior of the Commission's General Manager as the dependent variable, we focus our analysis on what a traditional metaphor proposes as the bridge between politics and policy. It is now possible to test the hypothesis that the administrative mechanism is sensitive to the expressed policy preferences of other governmental agents (e. g. , the Commission and the Bureau of the Budget) who may be presumed to be more sensitive to the pressures arising from public politics. Using the transformed data now in hand a simple test of this hypothesis can be devised. The test consists of asking whether changes in the prosperity scores of AEC programs at the General Manager stage of the budget in a given year can be explained as linear, additive effects of the program's "division strength" the previous year plus its "Commission support" in a previous year plus a simple "dummy" variable.[15] More precisely, I propose to regress the prosperity change scores of a program upon the corresponding division strength scores, Commission support scores, and

---

[15]The Presidential dummy was allowed to take the value "1" if the President restored a tentative Bureau of the Budget cut on the basis of a Commission appeal, and "0" otherwise. I resorted to this very crude measure because restoration was by far the most common Presidential action across all years and programs.

Presidential treatment scores, each lagged one year.

Since this procedure explicitly treats the strength and support scales as given or exogenous, we can assume but not demonstrate that they in turn capture the political consequences of public policy. However, if that assumption is granted, then the test I propose will provide important new evidence about the "where" and "how" questions regarding the linkage between public administration and public policy.

A comment on two further preliminary matters before taking up the results of this test. First should the regression model not be fit across all AEC programs taken together? No, for to do so would contradict a fundamental point made in Chapter II. Programs are the behaviorally meaningful unit of analysis for governmental activities. Agencies and bureaus merely reflect how government is organized; programs reflect what it is doing. Different programs, in addition, are treated differently precisely because their political consequences vary. If this variation is ignored by lumping programs together, there is no reason whatever to expect the strength and support variables to have an effect. Indeed, to the degree that the critical analytic assumption is correct--that variations (across programs and time) in the latter are caused by the political consequences of public policy--then it follows that the impact of these variables should vary in form sharply among different programs.

The second preliminary matter is the absence of a
Congressional variable from the proposed explanatory equation.
It is true that the Joint Committee on Atomic Energy is directly
represented neither in the equation nor in the basic data set. But
this is a limitation of fact, not principle. Certainly the "stage"
dimension of the AEC budgetary array could be expanded to include
the JCAE's authorization actions. But so for that matter could it
be expanded to include several other potentially interesting and
comparable "stages, " e. g. , "spring flash estimates, " Bureau of
the Budget "guidelines, " and others. Not only that, but the basic
formalism that has been suggested to measure "treatments" across
the division-General Manager-Commission stages and the Commission-
Budget Bureau appeal stages is applicable to any comparable triad.
(Commission-Presidential-JCAE is perhaps a possibility to measure
"Joint Committee support. ") The purpose of the present exercise,
though, is not fully to account for the General Manager's behavior,
nor to gauge the causal impact of the Joint Committee upon the prosperity of AEC programs (surely large). It was to determine if a set
of data dealing with activities within the executive branch--data not
normally available to scholars--could be used as a source of evidence
about the relationship between public administration and public policy.

We are, at last, in a position to answer that question.

To test whether the preferences expressed during the budget process help to account for turning points in the prosperity of an AEC program, I have attempted to fit a simple linear model. The fourteen available prosperity change scores for the civilian power program were regressed against "division strength," "Commission support," and "Presidential action"--all three lagged one year. The initial results were not encouraging; none of the coefficients was statistically significant. Hence I could not confidently reject the null hypothesis that the factors measured from the budgetary stage data have no influence upon changes in the prosperity of the civilian power program.[16]

Consider, though, the column of residuals (i. e. , arithmetic differences between actual and predicted values of the dependent variable) as arrayed in Table 20.

In fiscal year 1967 (December 1965) the Commission's Presidential budget allowed for approximately $89 million in operating expenses for the civilian power program. The following September

---

[16] The coefficients and their associated standard errors (in parentheses) were: division strength, 1. 08 (3. 55); Commission support 1. 00 (3. 01); and Presidential action, 0. 80 (9. 13). These coefficients along with all others reported here were estimated by the ordinary least squares solution programmed as part of the "Regression Analysis Program for Economists," written by William J. Raduchel.

TABLE 20

Preliminary Regression Analysis of the Effects of Division
Strength, Commission Support, and Presidential Action on
Changes in the Prosperity of the Civilian Power Program

Prosperity Change Score For:	Actual Value of Change Score	Predicted Value	Residual
FY 1958-1959	5	6.5	-1.5
FY 1959-1960	0	3.2	-3.2
FY 1960-1961	2	4.5	-2.5
FY 1961-1962	-6	5.4	-11.3
FY 1962-1963	-7	7.2	-14.2
FY 1963-1964	2	5.5	-3.3
FY 1964-1965	6	4.6	1.4
FY 1965-1966	7	8.6	-1.6
FY 1966-1967	12	5.7	6.3
FY 1967-1968	46	5.2	40.8
FY 1968-1969	-3	4.2	-7.2
FY 1969-1970	18	7.6	10.3
FY 1970-1971	-1	3.4	-4.4
FY 1971-1972	-3	6.6	-9.6

the division submitted to the General Manager a request for more

than $147 million and eventually received over $134 million. As we

know from the material in Chapters I and III, this $45 million in-

crease represented a major policy change regarding the priority

assigned to development of the fast breeder. Now an important

assumption of the general linear model is that the error terms are

normally distributed. In the world of real data, however, and

especially in what is believed to be a system responding to a political environment, the constraint will have to be somewhat relaxed. In

such a system it seems plausible only to expect that small perturba-

tions will be reasonably close to a normal distribution. The larger

shocks to the system, such as the sharp change in the priority of the

civilian power program, are events to be explained in themselves.

In the context of the streamlined assumptions of the general linear

model their effect is an extreme skewing of the error distribution.

Hence when we can isolate an observation which we believe responsible

for the violation of the normality of the residuals, and when we have

independent evidence (as we do in the reactor case) that this obser-

vation represents an "unusual" historical event, in effect a shock to

the underlying causal system, then it is reasonable simply to remove

this observation from the data set. [17]

The data in Table 21 result from removal of the FY 1967-

1968 change score from the civilian power program. These results

are more than gratifying. Turning points in the prosperity of the

---

[17] Edward J. Kane, Economic Statistics and Econometrics, (New York: Harper & Rowe, 1968), Chap. 14. Kane states: "The reader should notice that the unbiasedness, consistency, and BLUE (i. e., Best, Linear, Unbiased, Estimate) properties of least-squares estimators depend in no way on the assumption that u follows a particular probability distribution. The assumption that u is normally distributed serves (1) to establish an identity between least-squares and maximum-likelihood estimators, and (2) to justify strictly the use of t, F, and z test procedures. The fact that least-squares estimators possess nice properties even in the absence of normality suggests that the precision of the conventional test procedures is not very sensitive to departures from normality. " pp. 356-357 (emphasis added).

civilian power program at the General Manager budget stage can now

be seen to be strongly affected by the strength of the operating division

in the previous year.

TABLE 21

Regression Analysis of Changes in the Prosperity
of the Civilian Power Program
at General Manager Budget

Fiscal Year	Actual	Estimated	Residual
1958-1959	5	5.8	-0.8
1959-1960	0	-5.4	5.4
1960-1961	2	2.6	-0.6
1961-1962	-6	0.3	-6.3
1962-1963	-7	-4.8	-2.2
1963-1964	2	0.3	1.7
1964-1965	6	8.0	-2.0
1965-1966	7	5.9	1.1
1966-1967	12	10.8	1.2
1968-1969	-3	-5.2	2.2
1969-1970	18	8.4	9.6
1970-1971	-1	-0.2	-0.8
1971-1972	-3	5.6	-8.6

Independent Variable	Coefficient	Standard Error	$T(d.f.=9)$	Sig.
Lagged Div. Strength	2.8	1.2	2.3	.05
Lagged Comm. Supp.	0.1	1.1	0.1	ns*
Lagged Pres. Action	-5.0	3.2	-1.5	ns

Intercept = 12.4 $R^2 = .58$

*not significant

A substantial part of the General Manager's yearly budgetary actions--his choices in allocating scarce dollars among competing claims--can be accounted for by an index derived from evidence of programmatic preferences as they are expressed during the annual intra-agency review process. This process is not merely budgetary gamesmanship; it is causally important in the eventual establishment of the agencies' operating priorities.[18]

The data in Table 21 are at the very least unambiguous evidence in support of the basic hypothesis first proposed in Chapter I and advanced with more force in the immediately preceding pages. The internal budgetary records of the AEC contain information on how priorities are determined at the operating levels of government. The chief executive officer of the AEC is sensitive to the comparative strengths of the program divisions and his budgetary actions in part reflect this sensitivity.

---

[18] Dropping the non-significant "Commission support" variable from the model naturally decreases the standard errors of the two remaining independent variables. They become 1.0 and 2.9 for "division strength" and "Presidential action," respectively. The effect is to render the coefficient of the latter significant at the .10 level. One might, therefore, conceivably reject the null hypothesis, i.e., believe the coefficient. This is tempting especially since it is a negative coefficient, implying that the General Manager and his review committee are "fighting" or "attempting to correct" for last year's Presidential action. Though this is both intriguing and wholly plausible in the case of civilian power, it is rather a lot of interpretive weight for a crudely measured and dubiously significant result to bear.

Budgetary process data is also data about budgetary politics, but politics of a different sort from that described by Wildavsky and others. The annual sequence of intra-AEC requests - reductions - restorations described in Chapter I has systemic implications; it provides clues about the strengths of the operating divisions which are constant neither over time nor among the different divisions. For a particular program--civilian power reactors-- variations over time (which we cannot systematically explain) has causal significance for how governmental priorities are eventually determined. Perhaps even more interesting, the regression test suggests that the impact of this variation is indirect. Variation in the strength of the division of reactor development help account for turning points in the prosperity of the civilian power program because this variation partly explains the behavior of the agency's chief executive officer in adjusting division requests to fiscal and policy constraints.

The same pattern holds for Plowshare. Once more the only coefficient which can be accepted (at the .04 level in this case) is that associated with the division strength variable. The events of the intra-AEC review process, as distinct from the actions of the Bureau of the Budget and the Commission's response to them, are causally important in explaining changes in Plowshare's prosperity at the hands of the General Manager. The overall relationship is, however, less impressive than was the case for civilian power where division strength and Presidential action accounted for more than half the variance in the prosperity change scores. For Plowshare, division strength is the only significant predictor variable and accounts for about 40 per cent of the variance in the dependent variable. The details are in Table 22.[19]

The Rover program to develop a nuclear propelled space rocket has been cited as an example of an AEC activity which briefly benefitted from the Kennedy inspired national space exploration commitment but then suffered from the subsequent administrations' downgrading of this priority. As a consequence of these shifting priorities the prosperity change scores of the Rover program fluctuated quite widely during the period FY 1958 - FY 1972. Moreover since Rover, unlike many of the other AEC operations we have considered, does truly represent a homogeneous output category, i.e., is a "real"

---

[19] Plowshare, as we know, has been a sharply controversial program subject to a number of large political shocks. It is reasonable to suppose that the assumptions of the general linear model are unable to defend themselves from such shocks, hence the fairly substantial residuals. This is simply to say that the simple model which is used here as a test is misspecified and that removal of one observation will not help matters a great deal. This is indeed the case. Dropping the "Commission support" variable and removing FY 1965-1966 observation does not markedly affect the results. The coefficient for "division strength" remains large, positive (14.1) and significant at about the .05 level. The overall R^2 increases microscopically to .42.

TABLE 22

Regression of Plowshare Prosperity Change Scores
on Division Strength, Commission Support
and Presidential Action

Fiscal Year	Actual	Predicted	Estimated
1960-1961	21	43	-22
1961-1962	21	-2	-23
1962-1963	-1	-16	15
1963-1964	37	16	21
1964-1965	30	14	16
1965-1966	32	-16	48
1966-1967	-23	-2	-23
1967-1968	-32	-3	-29
1968-1969	41	43	-2
1969-1970	16	-13	29
1970-1971	-37	-3	-34
1971-1972	-83	-40	-43

Independent Variable	Coefficient	Standard Error	T(d.f. =8)	Sig.
Lagged Div. Strength	14.2	6.1	2.3	.04
Lagged Comm. Supp.	-0.6	3.7	-0.2	ns*
Lagged Pres. Action	-27.9	23.6	-1.2	ns

$$\text{Intercept} = -54.4 \qquad R^2 = .41$$

*not significant

program, it represents something of a critical test for the hypothesis that budgetary data contains important causal information. Moreover, Rover has been regarded, even by its critics, as an exceptionally well managed and technically successful operation. [20] Thus it is an instance where one would predict the division strength variable to be causally important.

It is. Again following the practice of removing the observation which produces the largest residual in fitting the model across all available observations (FY 1965-1966 in this case) we find that the strength of the program division has an unambiguous causal impact upon changes in the program's prosperity at the General Manager budget stage. The results are reproduced in Table 23.

Our ability successfully to "track" the wide variations in Rover's prosperity change scores must be regarded as a true theoretical and methodological triumph. <u>Division strength counts</u>, as in this case does Commission support (if we are willing to reject the null hypothesis with a ten per cent chance that we may be wrong). At the risk of flogging an already dead horse, I want to stress that the striking success of this test was by no means a foregone conclusion. The two significant independent variables were measured

---

[20] Interview with Fred Schuldt of the Bureau of the Budget.

TABLE 23

Regression of Rover Prosperity Change Scores
on Division Strength, Commission Support
and Presidential Action

Fiscal Year	Actual	Predicted	Estimated
1958-1959	-1	7.6	-8.6
1959-1960	3	8.9	-5.9
1960-1961	12	7.6	4.3
1961-1962	6	-2.7	8.7
1962-1963	73	44.0	29.0
1963-1964	56	45.3	10.7
1964-1965	-3	40.1	-43.1
1966-1967	-5	19.3	-4.3
1967-1968	0	-17.0	17.0
1968-1969	1	18.0	-17.0
1969-1970	-71	-54.7	-16.3
1970-1971	22	3.7	18.2
1971-1972	-20	-27.4	7.4

Independent Variable	Coefficient	Standard Error	T (d.f. =9	Sig.
Lagged Div. Strength	15.6	3.6	4.3	.00
Lagged Comm. Supp.	10.4	5.8	1.8	.10
Lagged Pres. Action	-1.3	13.0	-0.1	ns

Intercept = 120.8 $R^2 = .70$

*not significant

by means of an algorithm wholly derived from the set of unproven theoretical propositions elaborated in Chapter II and at the beginning of this chapter. The scale derived from that algorithm necessarily reflects some fairly arbitrary decisions, in many cases based upon little more than judicious guesses.

The dependent variable itself is not free from measurement problems. In our desire to correct for loss of information because of the tininess of strictly proportional changes, we developed an index number with the opposite problem. Relatively small absolute differences are magnified into very large prosperity change scores for programs of modest size like Rover.

In a very real sense, the surprising thing about the outcome of the experiment is that, as Table 23 suggests, it has all worked. The net effect is to provide a new way of thinking about how to look at budgetary records where the object is not to simulate the process but to gather evidence about what makes a difference in government. Within the Atomic Energy Commission, administration is indeed policy-making.

That the method I have developed for testing this theory is not trouble-free is, however, clear when the analysis is extended to all of the AEC programs for which data across stages was collected. The salient points are summarized in Table 24.

A number of observations are in order about these results.

TABLE 24

Summary of Regression Results for All Available AEC Programs

Program	R^2	Observation Removed	Statistically significant (.05 level or better unless otherwise indicated) independent variables (with sig. in parenthesis)
Raw Materials	.60		Div. str. (-); Comm. supp. (+); Pres. act. (+)
Special Nuclear Materials	.38	FY 1971-1972	Div. str. (+); (.07 level)
Weapons*	.85		Comm. supp. (+)
Civilian Power Reactor	.58	FY 1967-1968	Div. str. (+)
Cooperative Power Reactor	-		--
Merchant Ship Reactor	-		
Army Reactor	.65		Pres. act. (+)
Naval Reactor	-		--
ANP-Pluto**	.79		Div. str. (+); Pres. act. (-)
Rover	.70	FY 1965-1966	Div. str. (+); Comm. supp. (+); (.10 level)
SNAP	-		--
General Reactor Technology	.60	FY 1964-1965	Div. str. (-)
Nuclear Safety	-		--
Advanced Reactor Systems	.53		Comm. supp. (+)
High Energy Physics	-		--
Sherwood	-		
Biology and Medicine	.33		Comm. supp. (+) (.07 level)
Training, Education & Inf.	.85		Div. str. (+); Comm. supp. (+); Pres. act. (+)
Isotopes	.60		Comm. supp. (+)
Plowshare	.41	FY 1965-1966	Div. str. (+)
Program Dir. & Adm.	-		--
Euratom	-		--

*Seaborg years only: FY 1964 - FY 1972. See Chapter VI for discussion.

**Combined into one program because of limited number of observations for each.

First, the model being fitted makes a good deal less sense for some of the programs than for others. Operating expenses for raw materials, for instance, represent in most cases simply a costing out of contractual obligations for fulfillment of which the General Manager and his committee probably regard as a nearly absolute constraint. A glance at the raw data for this program (Appendix A) reveals that there is in fact very little variation across stages in allocation for raw materials regarding this program as almost a limiting case of the sufficiency of a budgetary process model of the sort fitted by Wildavsky and his colleagues.[21]

Much the same argument can be made about the co-operative power program, though here the problem is not the short-term inflexibility of contractual commitments so much as the long lead times involved in cooperative arrangements between industry and government to build large facilities. In these circumstances there is little reason to expect that the one-year lag used in the basic model will measure forces to which the General Manager is sensitive.

Another problem is the behavior of the dependent variable. The fact is that for several programs there is precious little variance to be explained. This is the case for special nuclear materials, naval

---

[21] The same point could be made somewhat differently by merely noting that for raw materials prosperity changes at the General Manager level correlate almost perfectly (.85) across years with changes at the division level.

reactors, weapons, biology and medicine, and program direction and administration, the standard deviations of the change scores for all of which are less than ten compared with an average of twenty-eight for all of the programs. In two instances we have the opposite problem. Euratom and merchant ship reactors were both very small programs (several million dollars at most), the comparative fluctuations in whose fortunes have been enormously magnified by the prosperity index device.

Finally, the artificiality of the "program" category has almost certainly caused problems in at least one instance. I have already noted that "SNAP" represents a collection of quite distinct projects, each of which has been subject to widely varying political and technical considerations. Here different projects have tended to be the object of controversy over priorities in different years. By aggregating them into a single artificial output category we ignore this variation. To a lesser degree the same thing applies to "advanced systems" and "general reactor technology," both of which are frankly treated by the program division (the division of reactor development and technology) as residual categories.

Nevertheless having said all of this, several entries (or non-entries) in Table 24 probably have to be frankly accepted as failures. Most notably, the model should have worked for high energy physics. This is a homogeneous and meaningful output category representing an AEC activity over whose priority there has been controversy both within the Commission and between the AEC and various administrations. As we saw in Chapter II, it has been a strong and prosperous program and numerical behavior of our indicator of its prosperity does not behave outrageously.

Sherwood and nuclear safety, too, should fit the model, and army reactors might be expected to show significant coefficients for division strength and Commission support.[22]

Still, as an exercise in methodological innovation, especially in the area of measurement, it seems reasonable to regard the results of those tests as encouraging. At the very least, it is true that the fundamental theoretical argument developed here and in Chapter II have survived an empirical test, and while outcomes of this test are not uniformly heartening, neither are they wholly discouraging. Given the measurement problems that have had to be confronted, with both the

---

[22]Army reactors really was a "turkey." At the time of its cancellation it was an effort to develop a compact reactor as an energy source to convert water and nitrogen (from the atmosphere) into ammonia. The ammonia was then to be used to fuel military vehicles, freeing the army from reliance upon petroleum. Commissioner Robert C. Wilson, at one time chairman of the Board of Standard Oil (Indiana) was instrumental in cancelling the program largely by insisting that the development of ammonia driven engines represented a major research and development undertaking in itself. Finally the program had a general reputation within the AEC for having been rather poorly managed. For all of these reasons significant coefficients for the strength and support variables would have been pleasant confirmation of our propositions.

dependent and the independent variables, this is perhaps as much as
can be expected.

A final comment on methodological matters. An obvious
criticism of the model which I have attempted to fit in order to account
for the priorities established by the General Manager is that it completely ignores the Joint Committee on Atomic Energy. This is perfectly true; as is the observation that the beginning of wisdom in accounting for anything which the Atomic Energy Commission has done
is to recognize the pervasive and massive causal impact of this extraordinary legislative body. This is a matter to which I shall return in
the final chapter. In terms of the foregoing quantitative analyses,
though, the purpose of the exercise was to see if a set of internal
executive branch data of a type that has not been generally available
for scholarly analysis could be made to yield information of any
political significance. The tentative answer is that it can. The algorithm used to scale the outcomes of the division-General Manager-
Commission and the Commission-Budget Bureau-Commission sequence of request, reduction, and restoration is applicable to any
formally similar triad of actions. One possibility, perhaps to measure
"Joint Committee support" would be Commission Budget-Presidential
Budget-Joint Committee Authorization. Indeed, given time and information one could in principle expand the basic data set used in this study
by the addition of several further budgetary stages (JCAE authorization,

spring flash estimates, etc.), or even by including as "stages" alternative budgets (i. e. , "high" case and "low" case estimates) submitted
by particular participants. As a practical matter the only limitations
in doing this are time and knowledge. Compilation of the present six-
stage data set was not a trivial matter in either regard.[23]

I have already noted that as a scholar one can develop
theories which are convincing to oneself and which may even be valid
but which those who participated in the events being explained would
neither recognize nor accept. Bearing this in mind, I now want to
return to the AEC and try to place these methodological matters in
a broader historical and theoretical perspective. My intent throughout, recall, has been not to become obsessed with budgetary data
for what it can tell us about budgeting, but to use it as a tool to understand part of the government--in this case the Atomic Energy Commission.

---

[23] With hindsight it is also clear that I should have worried
less about spanning the whole AEC budget with a mutually exclusive set
of "programs" for the maximum number of years. Instead, I should
have selected a few "real" output categories (Rover, plutonium production, Plowshare) and concentrated on assembling the maximum number of stages for the years during which the program existed.

CHAPTER VI

ORGANIZATIONAL ADAPTABILITY
AND
PROGRAM PROSPERITY

1. Special Nuclear Material Production: The Heartland of AEC
    Policy Space

At first the Kennedy Administration did little to modify

the nuclear weapons policies inherited from the Eisenhower years.

Weapons production, research and development continued at the

very high levels achieved under the Republicans. It took more than

two years, essentially Kennedy's full tenure as President, for new

policies to be developed; then in the late summer of 1963 after months

of analysis the Office of the Secretary of Defense decided that the

United States had built enough atomic and thermonuclear weapons.

The stockpile would, of course, continue to be modified over time

as new weapons systems were introduced to replace those becoming

obsolete. But the net quantity of nuclear weapons of all types, from

tactical missiles to ICBM warheads, would henceforth remain roughly

constant. Robert McNamara, in one of his most important single

acts as Secretary of Defense had determined that (after seventeen

years) the nation's stockpile of nuclear weapons had finally approached a height beyond which further sheer accumulation was useless. [1]

Since much of the special nuclear material needed to fabricate new devices could be recovered from obsolete weapons, this decision had immediate and profound implications for the AEC's uranium and plutonium (special nuclear materials) production programs.

I have described how the AEC had already recognized that its uranium purchase program had produced a substantial surplus of raw ore and had moved to "stretch out" deliveries and curtail ore refinement. These actions were not accompanied by equivalent cut-backs in the rate of weapons fabrication which had accelerated rapidly throughout the second Eisenhower Administration. During the first two Kennedy years, the Joint Committee and the military continued to press for maximum weapons production. In principle, Department of Defense "requirements" determined the number and types of weapons to be built by the Commission and, in turn, the amounts of special nuclear material to be manufactured. We have seen how this theory was belied by the laboratories activities with regard to need for new types of weapons. In the matter of determin-

---

[1] Jonathan Spivak, "Nuclear Cutback," Wall Street Journal, December 30, 1963. See also, John W. Finney, "Defense Study Favors Cut in Atomic Weapon Output," New York Times, December 21, 1963.

ing quantities of weapons and weapons material, practice was equally remote from principle. It is only a mild exaggeration to say that during the Eisenhower years military "requirements" for nuclear weapons were generally totaled up to provide an outlet for all the weapons material the AEC plants could produce. When McNamara made his decision the AEC's capacity to produce such material was considerable; special nuclear material production was the AEC's most successful program.

At the end of FY 1963 the government had spent $4.6 billion on equipment and facilities to produce fissionable materials, excluding plant and equipment costs for actual weapons fabrication and storage. This compared with a total cumulative AEC expenditure of $7.7 billion on plant and equipment.[2] This investment was the result of a series of decisions made between January, 1947 and July, 1952 in what appears to have been considered by the participants, particularly the JCAE, a straight-forward response to a major national security crisis.[3]

When the civilian Atomic Energy Commission assumed control of the Manhattan District's nuclear materials production com-

---

[2] "AEC Production History," p. 2; an unclassified summary prepared in 1965 for public information purposes by the Historian's Office of the AEC. It is on file in the Secretariat, USAEC. The following draws heavily upon this document.

[3] Hewlett and Duncan, op. cit.

plex in 1947, it took over two gaseous diffusion process buildings at
Oak Ridge and three "production reactors" at the Hanford Works
near Richland, Washington. The gaseous diffusion plants were built
to produce uranium enriched in the isotope U-235 and the production
reactors were used to transform U-235 into plutonium-239, another
fissionable isotope.[4]

When the Manhattan District's production facilities
were turned over to the Atomic Energy Commission, the Oak Ridge
diffusion complex was trouble-free but the Hanford reactors were
showing signs of wear.[5]

The special nuclear materials production program
was therefore a high Commission priority from the very beginning;
construction of a fourth production reactor at Hanford was begun

---

[4] Uranium, fashioned into metallic fuel elements, is
the heart of "production" reactors as well as power reactors. In
the former, the thermal energy released as one of the consequences
of the natural fissioning of the U-235 atoms is treated as a waste
product. The idea in the production reactor is to use the neutrons
which are also released in the fission process to transform U-235
into fissionable Pu-239 which like U-235 can be used in weapons.
Gaseous diffusion plants separate U-235 from U-238 by forcing a
gaseous uranium compound (uranium hexafloride) through ingene-
ously designed porous barriers. The gas which passes through
these barriers is slightly richer in U-235 and the process is repeated as many as several thousand times until the desired enrichment is achieved.

[5] Hewlett and Duncan. op. cit., p. 141

in December, 1947 and design of a fifth was authorized with a view toward completion by June, 1949. [6]

During 1948 the Commission pressed for maximum weapons material output from the existing facilities and began design studies for a third gaseous diffusion process building.

I have noted in Chapter II that the initial AEC response to the first Soviet nuclear test was to propose expansion of its production facilities. These plans were approved in late 1949 and included a fourth process facility at Oak Ridge. (Along with new feed materials--uranium hexafloride--facilities and additions to Hanford chemical processing facilities for separating Pu-239.) Presidential approval of the thermonuclear weapon meant there would be a need for yet more production capacity, and in March, 1950 the Commission announced plans to build an entirely new production reactor complex on the Savannah River near Aiken, South Carolina. The new site would include two large reactors of a novel type. Six months later the President approved construction of an additional gaseous facility at another new site (Paducah, Kentucky), three more heavy water moderated reactors at Savannah River, and another expansion of ore refining and feed materials plants.

The AEC response to the entry of Chinese troops into

---

[6] Ibid., pp. 145-147.

the Korean battle was a proposal made in January of 1951 to build

a sixth reactor at Hanford. Though it was evident by this time

that significant advances were being made in the operating efficiencies

of existing production facilities, both gaseous diffusion and plutonium

production, the Commission and the JCAE continued to be concerned

with capacity. As a result, the President was asked in 1952 to ap-

prove a further major expansion. The new proposal involved, among

other things, the addition of a fifth gaseous diffusion process build-

ing at Oak Ridge, two more (for a total of four) at the Paducah site,

and three at another new site in the Ohio River Valley at Portsmouth,

Ohio. For plutonium, the Commission decided to build two large re-

actors (numbers 7 and 8) at Hanford.

By February, 1956 all of these facilities were operating,

many at rates well above initial design estimates.

To summarize, between January, 1947 and July, 1952

a series of decisions were made to construct: a) three additional

gaseous diffusion process buildings at Oak Ridge for a total of five;

b) two new sites (Paducah and Portsmouth) with a total of seven

process facilities between them; c) five additional plutonium reactors

at Hanford plus two new chemical processing facilities to separate

the plutonium; and d) five heavy water moderated reactors at Savannah

River.

All of these plants were completed and placed in operation well in advance of schedule, and in most cases technical advances resulted in operating levels significantly above design capacities.

I have argued in another chapter that programs reflect what government does, rather than how it happens to be organized; that they are the behaviorally as distinct from the administratively significant unit of analysis. To illustrate a theory about priority establishment within government, I have reviewed two AEC programs--civilian power and Plowshare--in some detail and have more selectively tried to capture the salient aspects of a few others-- Rover, merchant ship reactors, raw materials, and now special nuclear materials. From all of this material it is clear that at least one early prophecy about the AEC has been more than fulfilled. Because of the breadth of its mandate for development of all aspects of nuclear energy it has had to enter into an extraordinarily complicated set of relations with other government agencies and non-governmental agents. The "domain" of AEC power is unusually large. [7] At the center of the domain is the production of special nuclear materials; here, as in none of its other activities, the Com-

---

[7] James D. Thompson, Organizations in Action: Social Bases of Administrative Theory, (New York: McGraw-Hill Book Co., Inc., 1967).

mission had been "the sole determinant of social policy. "[8]

Predictably, then, the administration's attempt during the fall and early winter of 1963 to translate the weapons production decision into a reduction in special nuclear material production resulted in a major confrontation. The Commission was able to deploy some powerful arguments in defense of its production complex. In 1963 about 5200 persons were employed at the three gaseous diffusion plants, about 8400 at Hanford, and 7600 at Savannah River.[9] Additionally, because of their prodigious appetite for electrical power, the former provided indirect employment for thousands. At the time, about six per cent of the country's total electrical generating capacity was being consumed by the diffusion plants and the energy to generate this electricity came largely from Appalachia coal mines.[10]

The situation at Hanford was somewhat different.

---

[8] Anthony Downs, op. cit., p. 213. In defining the notion of a "policy space" (i.e., domain) Downs draws a direct analogy with the zoological concept of "territoriality. " "The interior of the bureau's territory is where it exercises the dominant role over social policy. It consists of two sub-zones: the heartland, in which the bureau is the sole determinant of social policy; and the interior fringe, where it is dominant, but other social agents exercise some influence. "

[9] FY 1965 Authorization Hearings, pp. 237-238.

[10] Ibid., p. 232. See also, Finney, op. cit.

While in the short-run any production cut would probably have had a smaller impact on plutonium reactor operations, the longer term implications for Hanford were more serious, for eventually the diffusion plants could look toward an alternative source of demand, power reactor fuel. No such alternative was on the horizon for plutonium. The Commission's "isotopes" program was (and still is) an effort to develop the potential of other radioactive isotopes such as cobalt-60, cesium-137, curium-244, plutonium-238, and uranium-233 for a variety of applications ranging from power sources for cardiac assistance devices to food preservation. None of these projects showed promise of imminent technical success in 1963. The problem at Hanford was exacerbated by the utter economic dependence of this remote and otherwise barren area upon the plants which had been built during the fifties. At this time, the economic prosperity of Richland, Washington, and the neighboring cities was heavily dependent on high and growing operating levels at the Hanford production facilities.[11]

---

[11] "Diversification" of the Hanford facilities had been an important AEC objective for some time. The most widely discussed possibility was establishment of a private plant to fabricate certain radioactive by-products of the plutonium production process into a form suitable for use as power sources in space satellites and remote weather stations. In 1963, however, the commercial value of such an enterprise remained highly problematic. The more general point is that all the production facilities had to rely on progress in other Commission activities--nuclear power, isotopes development, peaceful nuclear explosives--as a potential source of demand. In turn, most of these were based on the "requirements" of other government programs. For further detail on these matters see, FY 1965 Authorization Hearings, pp. 254-259.

In discussions with the administration on these issues, the AEC took the general position that it was necessary to maintain a capability to respond to non-military "requirements" for special nuclear material while still fulfilling the military "mission." To buttress this argument, stress was laid on the fact that the production facilities represented a unique industrial enterprise. Indeed, by all accounts, the AEC did have every right to be proud of its production accomplishments. The diffusion plants and production reactors are clearly a massive technological and engineering achievement. The efficiency of the former was a principal factor in the competitive position of power reactors, and if "requirements" for exotic isotopes did materialize as a result of the development activities in other parts of the AEC, it was undeniable that the production reactors at Hanford and Savannah River were the only source of supply.

The Commission was also concerned about the government's contractual commitments to the utilities supplying electrical power to the diffusion plants. In order to meet the demand for power implied by the expansion decisions of the early fifties, these utilities had built generating facilities specifically to service the diffusion plants. To protect such investments their contracts with AEC had stipulated notice periods as long as four years required before the government could drop power without paying monetary penalties.

The idea was to allow the utilities time to integrate any output dropped
by AEC into normal commercial load growth.[12]

Actually the Commission had been slowly dropping power
in accordance with these provisions since 1958 when the operating
levels of the diffusion plants had reached a peak. The Commission
position in the fall of 1963 was that any modification of its current
plans in this regard would eventually cost the government a great
deal of money. While admitting that present demand for enriched
uranium did not wholly justify current and planned future operating
levels of the diffusion plants, this picture could change sharply with
growth of the nuclear power industry. The Commission argued that
its projections of such growth plainly indicated that demand for
uranium would outstrip supply within the next twenty years. The
government's original contracts with the utilities had provided
electricity for the diffusion plants at extremely low prices. If the
government now cancelled these contracts and then had to go back
into the open market for electricity to meet projected demand for
power reactor fuel, it was highly improbable that such attractive
rates would be available. Hence, the Commission contended, in
the long-run the government would minimize costs by being "conservative" in dropping power, even though that meant continuing

---

[12] FY 1965 Authorization Hearings, pp. 234-236;
FY 1966 Authorization Hearings, p. 80.

to accumulate an "inventory" of enriched uranium. [13]

The Commission did not prevail. In his January, 1964 State of the Union message President Johnson announced that three of the nine plutonium reactors at Hanford and one of the five reactors at Savannah River would be shut down over the twelve-month period beginning July 1, 1964. Additionally, combined electrical power consumption at the three diffusion sites would be curtailed by about twenty-five per cent below the current level. [14]

Later in the spring the AEC announced yet further reductions in the rate of production of enriched uranium beyond the twenty-five per cent curtailment announced in January. [15] The supplementary reduction meant a net decrease in enriched uranium production by about forty per cent compared with levels planned prior to the McNamara decision.

These were not trivial matters. While Seaborg's

---

[13] FY 1966 Authorization Hearings, pp. 80-96; see FY 1967 Authorization Hearings, pp. 48 ff.

[14] The details are drawn from Chairman Seaborg's public statement the same day. The power reduction to the diffusion plants meant a $50 million reduction in the special nuclear materials operating costs, while affecting some 2900 contractor positions. The reactor shutdown would result in further cost reductions of about $13 million. When shutdowns were complete, employment levels at Hanford and Savannah River would be cut by about 2500 positions.

[15] Statement by Glenn T. Seaborg released April 20, 1964.

April 20 statement referred to the reductions as having been "recommended by the Commission," the fact is they represented several
months of intense negotiation between the AEC and the administration.
Anthony Downs' zoological metaphor is quite to the point. The administration's desire to bring nuclear material production rates into line
with revised short-run weapons requirements represented an invasion
of the heartland of the AEC policy space. In the end, the Commission's
defense was only partially successful.[16] To understand the nature of
the problems the Commission faced and to assess the adequacy of its
response to them, it is necessary to review from a different perspective
some of the structural characteristics of the agency and its programs.

2. Administrative Responsibility and the Active Government

In 1947 the AEC was not thought by those who fashioned
it to be merely another quasi-independent executive agency.

> For, make no mistake, the Atomic Energy Act
> is a radical piece of legislation--in some re-
> spects as radical and unprecedented as the
> scientific discovery that occasioned it. It is,
> in sober fact, an act without precedent in the
> legislative history of this or any other country.
> Never before have men in any state, standing
> on the threshold of a new technological era,
> attempted to provide in advance for rational
> control of the forces to be unleashed. And
> never before in the peacetime history of the

---

[16] Cf. Downs, op. cit., pp. 213-216. The AEC's assessment of the costs of modifying its program does, as Downs' theory pre-
dicts, seem to have exceeded "true social value" of such costs.

> United States has Congress established an
> administrative agency vested with such
> sweeping authority and entrusted with such
> portentious responsibilities . . . [17]

Nor was there any illusion about the possibility of separating administration from policy-making.

> It appears certain that within our generation
> further, further discoveries in the science of
> nuclear physics and a steadily growing number
> of inventions applying atomic energy to indus-
> trial and commercial ends will confront the
> Commission with decisions calling for the
> highest order of political judgment. [18]

Some twenty years later a former senior staff aid to Presidents Kennedy and Johnson was able plausibly to refer to the Atomic Energy Commission as "a minor barony."[19] The observation, moreover, would have been apt even in 1963. As a matter of fact the Commission had very few cards to play in its confrontation with the Johnson Administration over special nuclear materials production rates. What had happened? Why was the AEC in 1970 no more (to change metaphors) than a third or fourth magnitude star in the Washington power firmament?

The first course was sheer intellectual error about the short-run practical implications of the nuclear fission process. The fact is that in 1947 mankind was not exactly "on the threshold of a new technological era." Or if we were, it had more to do with

---

[17] Newman and Miller, op. cit., pp. 3-4.

[18] Ibid., p. 122.

[19] Professor Francis Bator in Richard E. Neustadt's seminar on the Presidency (spring, 1969).

transportation and communication technology than with energy production.[20] The now defunct merchant ship reactors program makes
the point as well as anything.

The merchant ship program faltered in part because it
became clear after several years of research and development that
nuclear power could not by itself revolutionize oceanic transport.
In fact, upon analysis it developed that in this area nuclear energy
held decidedly marginal technological promise. Nuclear powered
merchant ships could merely transport certain cargoes over certain
routes for a somewhat lower unit cost than conventional vessels.
Which cargoes, which routes, and precisely how much lower were
all at the time of the program's demise a matter of inconclusive
study by both the Atomic Energy Commission and the Maritime
Administration.[21]

Meanwhile no one had proposed a plan to supplement
nuclear merchant ships with nuclear longshoremen. All of the

---

[20] As this is written, we learn that the coal industry
is on the verge of laying waste to a substantial fraction of the American West to strip mine coal, the energy source of the Nineteenth Century industrial revolution. See Ben A. Franklin, "Coal Rush is on in
West as Strip Mining Spreads," New York Times, August 22, 1971.
See also Jurgen Schmandt, "The Dismal State of Energy R & D," a
paper delivered before the Southwest Social Science Conference,
Dallas, Texas, March 1971.

[21] FY 1967 Authorization Hearings, pp. 110 ff.

problems of the American maritime industry, that is, would be un-affected by successful development of an economically attractive nuclear power plant. In fact, as the director of the Commission's division of reactor development and technology pointed out to the Joint Committee, nuclear power might actually make solution of the industry's labor and cargo handling problems more difficult.[22]

While nuclear power might provide a speed advantage over certain very long routes (e. g. , Tokyo to New York), it would give none at all on a run of the New York to London type. Sufficient fuel oil could handily be carried by conventional ships to permit them to make such trips at thirty knots. Since thirty knots is the effective limiting speed for large surface vessels regardless of propulsion mechanism, nuclear power would provide no marginal advantages. In his 1965 testimony, Milton Shaw observed that in the early days of the naval nuclear ship program a number of people thought the application of nuclear power "would automatically make better sonar systems, better missile systems, and better torpedoes. Nuclear power was advertised by many as a cure-all."[23] It was not. Nuclear propulsion gives combat vessels one significant advantage over conventional systems; it permits a warship to go anywhere, any-

[22] Ibid. , p. 112.

[23] Ibid. , p. 112.

time. This is a much less important consideration for civilian mari-

time ships which, after all, normally adhere to fixed schedules.

The point is that the practical advantages of nuclear

energy in this and many other ares have turned out to be marginal

not revolutionary. The spectacularly obvious comparative and abso-

lute advantages of nuclear explosives as a weapon of large scale de-

struction apparently represent something of a deviant case. Far the

more typical circumstance has been that realization of the "benefits

of the atom" has depended upon applied research and development

and complicated engineering and that even then, the advantages of

nuclear energy are comparative rather than absolute and are highly

sensitive to the ends being sought and the costs deemed acceptable.[24]

Technological determinism, however, can at best only

partially explain the problems that have beset the AEC. Such a per-

spective cannot for example account for the fact that the fast breeder

-----

[24] One could conceivably make a case that the military
advantages of nuclear explosives are less absolute than commonly
thought. However, since the administrative structures invented to
provide such explosives to the armed forces were perfectly designed
to minimize the incentives for anyone to consider the question, the
issue remains in doubt. It is incidentally my own guess, which I
cannot substantiate in any formal way, that the Russians have always
been more concerned with the comparative costs of nuclear weapons,
especially tactical devices, than our own officials. It is at least
arguable that the Russians really wanted to avoid development of
tactical nuclear weapons in the late fifties. As noted, the Eisenhower
Administration never took the possibility seriously, perhaps in part
because none of its members ever thought to balance the benefits of
such devices against their costs.

program is (at least temporarily) thriving in the face of enormous technical uncertainities, while the completely straight-forward idea of using nuclear explosives to create storage facilities for natural gas is moribund. Whatever the nature of the causal relationships among technology, society, and public policy, it is self-evident that one cannot get very far by supposing that technical opportunities and the economic pressures they produce determine the direction of policy. [25]

It has been noted that Chester Barnard stood classical management theory on its head by switching emphasis from the business firm as a command organization to the firm as an adaptive organization. [26] This theory has been suggested as a basis for explaining patterns of innovation in public organizations as well as profit-seeking firms and hence provides the proper framework within which to carry a discussion of the Atomic Energy Commis-

---

[25] Theodore Lowi has also made the point about the inadequacies of technological determinism in accounting for the relationship between technology and policy. Noting that the "interesting question is always the social inventions through which a technical invention becomes revolutionary instead of a museum curiosity, " he argues that "by far the most important mechanism of administered social relations is modern government. " Theodore J. Lowi, The End of Liberalism, (New York: W. W. Norton & Co. , 1969), pp. 30-31.

[26] The point is made by W. J. M. MacKenzie, Politics and Social Science, (Baltimore: Penguin Books, 1967), p. 252. Barnard's seminal argument is of course contained in his The Functions of the Executive, (Cambridge, Mass.: Harvard University Press, 1938).

sion beyond technological considerations.[27]

The postulate that organizations are adaptive entities naturally suggests that there may be causally significant variations in the mechanisms they employ in order to maintain themselves in some sort of equilibrium with their environment. It suggests that one should ask how different organizations "adjust themselves to the world about them; their relations with each other and competing organizations, with the general public."[28] I would argue that the institutional arrangements invented to administer development of nuclear energy plus some highly unusual political aspects of the early stages of that development combined to inhibit the ability of the AEC to adapt to its political environment. The history of the Commission strikes me as the history of a notably maladaptive organization.

> For most goals in society there are antithetical
> or conflicting interests. Hence programs that

---

[27] The development of Barnard's theory is closely linked with the work of Herbert A. Simon. The definitive statement of its relevance to public administration is Herbert A. Simon, Donald W. Smithburg and Victor A. Thompson, Public Administration, (New York: Alfred A. Knopf, 1950).

For a thorough summary of the pertinent literature see: Joseph L. Bower, "Descriptive Decision Theory from the 'Administrative' Viewpoint," in Raymond A. Bauer and Kenneth J. Gergen, eds., The Study of Policy Formation, (New York: The Free Press, 1968), pp. 103-149.

[28] Simon, Smithburg and Thompson, op. cit., p. 381. The authors go on to note that "these adjustments and relations are essentially of a political character, and indeed, . . . are sometimes referred to as 'the politics of public administration'."

> satisfy one group of people often reduce satis-
> factions of other groups. . . . Few indeed are
> the administrative agencies that have all friends
> and no enemies. There is almost certain to be
> some hostility towards any administrative organ-
> ization and its program. To survive with any
> given program of activities, an agency must find
> friendly groups whose political support is strong
> enough to overcome the opposition to hostile
> groups. To preserve its friends, it must to
> some degree adapt its program to their interests.
> To neutralize its enemies, it must sometimes
> sacrifice elements in its program that attract
> the most effective political opposition. Hence,
> organizations are in a continual process of ad-
> justment to the political environment that sur-
> rounds them--an adjustment that seeks to keep
> a favorable balance of political support over
> political opposition. [29]

The Atomic Energy Commission's repeated failures on

all of these counts are the principal causes of the episodic success

of its development programs. While it is true that the facts of nuclear

technology have not generally been able to sustain some early wide-

eyed optimism about the practical implications of the discovery and

control of the fission process, this is less important to an under-

standing of the AEC than the Commission's repeated inability to sus-

tain "a favorable balance of political support over political opposition. "

It is clear from previous studies of organizational be-

havior that successful adaptation may require the development of a

---

[29] Ibid. , pp. 388-389.

broad array of strategies to protect a program.[30] In view of the
range of adaptive mechanisms used by other public agencies to obtain
the resources and authority to control their programs, the AEC performance has been unimaginative to say the least. Time and again
the Commission, its staff, and its contractors have relied upon one
basic pattern; its programs have been presented as responses to
"requirements." Why should fast breeders be developed? Because
projected shortages of uranium may "require" them. Why should
the production reactor be kept operating? As a "contingency"
against future "requirements." Why develop nuclear excavation
technology? Because of the "requirement" for a sea-level trans-
isthmus canal.

The Commission's resort to this gambit apparently
illustrates Graham Allison's observation that "what government

---

[30]Highly suggestive case studies of successful adaptation
include: Grant McConnell, The Decline of Agrarian Democracy, (Berk-
eley: Univ. of California Press, 1953); Arthur Maass, Muddy Waters,
(Cambridge: Harvard Univ. Press, 1951); and Philip Selznick, TVA
and the Grass Roots, (Berkeley: Univ. of California Press, 1953).
See also by the same author (Philip Selznick), "Cooptation: A Mechanism for Organizational Stability" in Robert Merton, et al., eds.,
Reader in Bureaucracy, (Glencoe, Ill.: The Free Press, 1952).
An extremely interesting recent study is Harvey M.
Sapolsky, Creating the Invulnerable Deterrent, (Cambridge: MIT
Press, 1971). Sapolsky's most intriguing point is that the highly regarded PERT computerized management system was a conscious
adaptive contrivance by the managers of the Polaris program and
that it had only incidental impact upon the technical and administrative success of the program.

does. . . can. . . be understood as outputs of large organizations

functioning according to standard patterns of behavior. . . each

with a fixed set of operating procedures and repertoires. . . The

behavior of these organizations . . . relevant to an issue in any

particular instance therefore, is determined primarily by routines

established in these organizations prior to that instance. "[31]

The idea of explaining an organization's behavior in

terms of standard operating procedures invoked to produce specific

actions provides the critical clue to explaining the Commission's

difficulties in sustaining support for its non-military development

programs.

I have commented in Chapter I on the quite remarkable

degree of amity which characterizes the relations both among the

AEC's senior staff and between the staff and the Commissioners.

This is actually a common observation about the Commission and

reflects the extent to which the agency is even now being managed

---

[31] Graham T. Allison, "Conceptual Models and the
Cuban Missile Crisis," American Political Science Review, LXIII,
no. 3, Sept. 1969. Allison also notes: "Where situations cannot be
construed as standard, organizations engage in search. The style
of search and the solution in any particular case are largely determined by existing routines. Organizational search for alternative
courses of action is problem oriented; it focuses on the atypical dis-
comfort which must be avoided. It is simple-minded: the neighborhood of the symptom is searched first, then the neighborhood of the
current alternative. Patterns of search reveal biases which reflect
the special training and experience of various parts of the organization, its expectations and communication distortions. "

by a group of officials who have been working with each other since the days of the Manhattan District.[32]   Until August of 1964, when Alvin R. Leudecke retired, all AEC general managers had been former general officers with extensive experience in nuclear weapons matters.   Leudecke's replacement, Robert C. Hollingsworth (who still holds the position) was the first civilian official to assume the post of the Commission's chief executive.   Hollingsworth, however, had been an "Oak Ridge colonel," having served in the army from 1942 to 1946.   During most of this period he was stationed at Oak Ridge.   During his subsequent career as a civilian administrator, he held numerous positions of responsibility in the Commission's division of production, including assistant director and chief of administration.   Richard Hewlett notes that Hollingsworth's rise to power within the Commission parallels that of most of the agency's senior staff.   During the fifties the production division (i. e. , the special nuclear materials program) was "the place where all the action was."[33]

The programs which resulted from the series of de-

---

[32] The following biographical data is all drawn from copies of official biographies kept on file in the Historian's Office, USAEC.   I am indebted to Richard G. Hewlett for providing me this material.

[33] Private communication.

cisions to expand the facilities to produce plutonium and uranium-235
in a very real sense were the AEC throughout most of the Eisenhower years. These programs entailed a massive mobilization of industrial and technical expertise, representing an administrative
achievement at least comparable to that of the more highly publicized
Manhattan District.[34]

As a public program, however, this effort had a very
unusual characteristic. It was completely non-controversial. As
a political enterprise the job of the division of production could not
have been simpler; its administrators merely had to get something
built as quickly and efficiently as possible. They were under a
minimum of pressure to justify a program which could be billed as
no more than the execution of a mandate. As with weapons production, there were few incentives any place in government to question
the need to maximize production of special nuclear materials, and
none at all to question the AEC's expertise regarding the most effective

---

[34] Appointed as Hollingsworth's deputy in 1962 (he, too,
still holds the post) was E. J. Bloch. Bloch had been an engineer in
the Army Corps of Engineers from 1931 through 1946, following which
he held among other things a series of positions in the production division. Milton Shaw's predecessor as director of reactor development,
Frank K. Pittman, had been in charge of plutonium production at Los
Alamos from 1944 until 1948, after which he held several positions in
the production division. As Hewlett suggests, the pattern is remark-
edly constant. Virtually all of the top fifteen or so senior officials in
the AEC during the period 1956-1971 at one time had major responsibility for matters relating to the production of special nuclear materials.

means of doing so.

The AEC production division was, hence, an almost paradigm illustration of a "policy space" in which the responsible administrative officials were for all practical purposes "the sole determinants of social policy." As such it is plausible to suppose that the behavioral routines, --the standard, rehearsed operating procedures--, which were so successful in coping with problems in this domain would be transferred to different programs in subsequent years.

But the problem with reactor development, Plowshare, Rover, merchant ship reactors, and assorted SNAP devices (among others) was precisely that all soon became politically controversial. Like most public programs they generated "antithetical or conflicting interests." While perhaps satisfying one group of people, they manifestly reduced the satisfaction of others. This was a political situation for which the AEC response routines, most of which were learned under the highly unusual circumstances of the weapons, raw materials, and special nuclear materials programs, were wholly inappropriate. Using the term "politics" in the same sense as Simon and his colleagues, the author of a recent study of a successful public program observes: "Politics is a systemic requirement. What distinguishes programs from one another in government is not that some play politics while others do not, but rather that some are better at it than others. "[35]

The Atomic Energy Commission was obliged to learn the rules of the game and to develop coping mechanisms in highly unusual circumstances. It was given a mandate to execute programs which for a time had no meaningful political opposition. When opposition to one aspect of these programs--atmospheric testing--did develop it could be handled, as we saw in Chapter IV, by drawing upon a fully articulated consensus about national priorities. The effect was to postpone further the reassessment of apparently still serviceable response routines. But as circumstances changed the shortcomings of these routines became clear.

Consider, for example, the Pluto program. The Lawrence Radiation Laboratory was funded for approximately seven years at about $10 - $20 million per year a program to develop a nuclear missile. By the end of FY 1964 total AEC expenditures on Pluto were about $130 million. The result was a device which met all technical requirements. It was a completely successful technical operation which had developed a novel and sophisticated reactor technology. However, it had been undertaken by AEC ostensibly as a response to a Department of Defense "requirement," a "requirement"

---

[35] Sapolsky, op. cit. , pp. 255-256.

which turned out to be quite different from that for special nuclear
materials production during the fifties. Like the latter in the sixties,
it suddenly evaporated. The Department of Defense concluded that
Pluto would have to be sacrificed to its own priorities and the Commission had little choice but to abide by the decision.[36]

But both Pluto and special nuclear materials also suggest the need to look to more than the career pattern of senior Commission officials and the special characteristics of the program they
administer to account for the AEC difficulties in responding to changing circumstances.

Institutional factors were also important, and there is no
question that in this regard the place to begin is with the Green and
Rosenthal analysis of the consequences of the attempt to insure administrative responsibility through the creation of an extraordinarily
privileged Congressional committee.[37] Some ten years after their
study was undertaken, little doubt can remain that in one sense the
Joint Committee on Atomic Energy has been an almost total failure;
it has destroyed, not promoted, administrative responsibility. The
effect of the JCAE - Commission axis has been to make the develop-

---

[36] Minutes of Commission Meeting 2022, June 22, 1964.

[37] Green and Rosenthal, op. cit.

ment of nuclear technology what Theodore Lowi terms a "partici-

patory program"--one "split off with a special imperium to govern

itself." He notes:

> Beside making conflict-of-interest a principle
> of government rather than a criminal act, par-
> ticipatory programs shut out the public. To be
> more precise, programs of this sort tend to
> cut out all that part of the mass public that is
> not specially organized around values strongly
> salient to the goals of the program. They shut
> out the public, first, at the most creative phase
> of policy-making, the phase where the problem
> is first defined. Once problems are defined,
> alliances form accordingly and the outcome is
> both a policy and a reflection of superior power. [38]

Green and Rosenthal have noted that from the first the

members of the Joint Committee have experienced comparatively

little pressure from back home.[39] In the early years, because of

its preoccupation with military needs, Atomic Energy Commission's pol-

icies conferred few direct benefits and inflicted few direct depri-

vations. For these reasons, the nature of the transactional rela-

tionships between the Joint Committee and the various atomic energy

issue publics has never been one of simple one-way causality. In-

stead it has resembled the more complex and subtle causal pattern

discovered in a recent analysis of the 1962 Trade Expansion Act.[40]

---

[38] Lowi, op. cit., p. 86.

[39] Green and Rosenthal, op. cit., Ch. I.

[40] Raymond A. Bauer, Ithiel de Sola Pool, and Lewis
Anthony Dexter, American Business and Public Policy, (New York:
Atherton Press, 1963).

As the Commission's programs became more controversial, the JCAE served to insulate rather than transmit the resulting political pressures. My own evidence fully bears out the
judgment that:

> The Joint Committee has over the years de-
> veloped a distinctive approach. It favors a
> vigorous, imaginative, and aggressive atomic
> energy program, demanding boldness and risk-
> taking rather than caution and economy. ...the
> JCAE has consistently initiated, supported, and
> encouraged certain broad policies: the H-bomb
> program; expansion and diversification of nuclear
> weaponry; expanded production of fissionable
> material, especially plutonium; development of
> nuclear-propelled submarines and aircraft; and
> an accelerated program for developing nuclear
> power. The Committee has supported the AEC
> and the executive branch when they have taken
> the initiative, but it has usually prodded and
> pulled the Executive in its direction. ...Gener-
> ally, the JCAE has desired more and bigger pro-
> grams than the Executive deemed prudent or eco-
> nomical. [41]

The effect of this was that the Commission could rely
upon the Committee's own institutional interest in the success of
nuclear development programs to fend off doubts and criticisms
originating elsewhere in the Executive Branch or arising out of the
political system at large. The Joint Committee became at once the
AEC's sovereign and its most powerful constituency.[42]   This ex-

---

[41] Green and Rosenthal, op. cit., p. 105.

[42] Downs, op. cit., developes the notion of bureau
sovereigns (pp. 44 ff). Green and Rosenthal also make the point

tremely unusual set of institutional "dependency relationships" did

not prepare the Commission to deal with the problems which de-

veloped as its programs became more public. [43]

As we have seen, two fundamental things have happened

to atomic energy programs during this transition. First, they have

become more controversial. They have generated the opposition of

interests which either are or in some way believe they are diminished

by AEC activities. The Commission has, of course, been sensitive

to the growth of this opposition, but has been extremely slow to grant

its "objectivity. " It has tended to assume that such opposition is

based upon misperception or lack of information. It has also been

---

that the Commission's dependence upon the JCAE plus the multi-
headed commission form of administration combined to reduce the
President's effective control over the atomic energy program and
probably his interest as well. This institutionally reinforced separ-
ation of the Commission from Presidential policy was particularly
unfortunate for the AEC in a period when the central value around
which other administrative agencies were being organized was
executive leadership. See, Herbert Kaufman, "Emerging Conflicts
in the Doctrines of Public Administration, " reprinted in Alan A.
Altshuler, ed. , The Politics of the Federal Bureaucracy, (New
York: Dodd, Mead and Co. , 1968).

On the normative question of administrative responsibility, an older generation of scholars has produced more
insight than I can possibly do justice to here. For a thoughtful
analysis of the matter see, Glendon Schubert, The Public Interest,
(Glencoe, Ill.: The Free Press, 1960).

[43] On the notion of "dependency relationships" see,
James D. Thompson, op. cit. One might even argue that the dis-
tinctive feature of those which characterized the AEC's institutional environment was the presence of dual sovereigns and the absence
of any meaningful constituency.

inclined to underestimate the potential size of the antithetical interests aroused by various programs. The old Cold War tradition of
locating it among a few random cranks and screwballs has generally
prevailed among AEC staff, if not within the Commission itself. This,
of course, misses the whole point. While it may be arguable that Don
Charles Foote and his Episcopal missionaries were cranks, they represented a set of very real interests which were not, to say the least, well
served by the Chariot project: the Eskimos whose fishing grounds happened to be located on the site the AEC chose to demonstrate the technical feasibility of an extremely discretionary program. The same
considerations are pertinent to present opposition to power reactors.
It may well be that the costs of reactors (including the potential and
hugely controversial health hazards) are in the end out-weighed by the
benefits. The AEC's technical case is at least presumptively a strong
one.

What once however may have been the case in atomic
energy matters is, however, no longer true. The resolution of
technical issues cannot be counted upon automatically to guarantee
the prosperity of a research and development program. The reason
is that differences over "technical matters" have come to represent
real differences over public priorities; over what government ought
to be doing and what it ought to be doing first. Because of the AEC's
Joint Committee abetted insulation from the political process; because

the atomic energy program has been effectively "split off with a
special imperium to govern itself, " a sensitivity to the political
nature of such ostensibly technical questions has not developed.

In a less complicated time a great scholar could write
of administrative responsibility:

> Whether we call it "objective" or "functional" or
> "technical" the fact remains that throughout the
> length and breadth of our technical civilization
> there is arising a type of responsibility on the part
> of the permanent government, the man who is
> called upon to seek and find the creative solution
> for our crying technical needs which cannot be ef-
> fectively enforced except by fellow technicians
> who are capable of judging his policy in terms
> of the scientifid knowledge bearing upon it.
> "Nature's laws are always enforced, " and a
> public policy which neglects them is bound to
> come to grief, no matter how eloquently it may
> be advocated by popular orators, eager partisans,
> or smart careerists. [44]

However, as the history of Plowshare suggests, reliance
upon technical competence can be inadequate when the fundamental
goals of a program become a matter of controversy. There is an old
quip to the effect that "there is no Republican or Democratic way to
build a road; only a right way and a wrong way. " True enough, but
presumably the function of the Republicans and the Democrats is to
guarantee that somewhere along the line someone has asked whether
the road is needed at all. The value of the technical competence,

---

[44] C. J. Friedrich, op. cit. , p. 14.

Friedrich's "functional responsibility, " which the AEC has continually
displayed comes only after that question has been asked and answered.
If it has not been resolved, it will be impossible to wish the resulting
political problem away, as the AEC has been inclined to do, by refer-
ring to technical criteria. Analysis, if I may be permitted an aphorism,
is no substitute for politics. A decision to build fast breeders because
of their comparative efficiencies as energy producers is nonetheless
a decision to build reactors.

The technical considerations are pertinent only after
conflict over the need for the road has been resolved.

Another important change has also occurred in AEC
programs. They have less and less been determined by externally
established priorities. Again the point is illustrated by my reviews
of civilian power and Plowshare on the one hand and special nuclear
materials and raw materials on the other. The former have been seen
to reflect a great deal more discretion on the part of the Commission
than have the latter. I have in fact argued that both civilian power
and Plowshare can be seen as instances of public policy being determined by the skills and perspectives of public administrators. Without pressing the point too far, it is certainly true that neither represented a response to an external demand as did the special nuclear
material production effort.

Just as a different type administrative responsibility is

called for as the goals of programs become controversial, a different type is also needed as the source of those goals varies. The
original atomic energy programs were both non-controversial and
concerned with externally determined goals. The appropriate administrative officer to carry out such programs probably resembles
a limiting case of Friedrich's technically competent and "functionally
responsible" official. He is a manager and is closely approximated
by the superbly competent public servants who administered the early
special nuclear materials production program. As programs come
to be controlled by priorities largely established within an agency,
the responsible administrator must become less a manager and more
an executive. The AEC experience suggests that many of the quali-
ties that make for efficient management are also pertinent to executive
leadership. But something else is clearly needed, for the executive is
required to provide direction to policy, to define goals and to establish
objectives. A standard complaint within AEC has been that this sort
of leadership has been notable for its absence over much of the agency's
history. It is, for example, this lack which Milton Shaw had in mind
in arguing that prior to 1964, "reactor development (had) never been
an AEC program."[45]

But it is not the distinction between managers and execu-

----

[45] Interview with the author. See also: Herbert A. Simon,
"On the Concept of Organizational Goal," 9, Administrative Science
Quarterly, 1964, pp. 1-22.

tives which primarily interests me. For it does not relate to what strikes many as the central issue in public administration: how can an active government, wielding immense economic power and often in possession of effective monopolies of both information and technical skills, be brought under effective political control?[46] The central problem in this regard is the means of insuring the appropriate adaptive behavior (administrative responsibility) as programs vary along the first dimension; as they become the subject of public controversy. Here the lessons of the AEC's experience are clear; both executives and managers are inadequate to insure responsibility.

Again, consider the instance of externally determined goals, perhaps an agency established with a specific mandate to, say, "provide better health care," or "solve the housing problem," or "straighten out the ecological mess." In these instances goals have arisen directly from the public political arena, and because of this are likely to remain controversial even as they are pursued.

---

[46] For a thoughtful and suggestive essay on this point (though one which I believe overly optimistic), see: Andrew Shonfield, Modern Capitalism: The Changing Balance of Public and Private Power, (New York: Oxford Univ. Press, 1965), esp. Pt. 4, pp. 385-428. Frederick C. Mosher has addressed the same problem: "The accretion of specialization and of technological and social complexity seems to be an irreversible trend, one that leads to increasing dependence upon the protected, appointive public service, thrice removed from direct democracy. Herein lies the central and underlying problem--how can a public service so constituted be made to operate in a manner compatible with democracy?" Frederick C. Mosher, Democracy and the Public Service, (New York: Oxford Univ. Press, 1968), p. 4.

Here, administrative responsibility almost completely merges with political responsibility; administrators must be politicians, not merely managers or executives.

There is a fourth possibility. In an active, wealthy, and technically proficient administrative system there will inevitably be many programs--Plowshare, fast breeders--which are not direct responses to external demands; which did not initially arise from public politics. Because they are public programs, however, they continually threaten to become political issues. Such issues may arise from entirely exogenous causes. They may, for example, actually come about because of the activities of a very few random screwballs of the sort which AEC is inclined to blame for many of its problems. But the point which the Commission misses is that this does not matter. The real problem is that in such circumstances a fourth type of administrative responsibility or adaptive behavior is required. The _function_ of public administration is different under these conditions from what it is when public programs are not political issues.

Whom do we call upon to perform this function? Increasingly, the government has been relying upon _professionals_ and once more the AEC is a case in point. Though not members of a uniformed career service, AEC staff obviously are professionals with regard to atomic energy matters.[47]   Professionalism however is clearly

incompatible with the adaptive patterns required to administer public

programs which have become political issues.

> Professionalism rests upon specialized know-
> ledge, science, and rationality. There are
> correct ways of solving problems and doing
> things. Politics is seen as constituting ne-
> gotiations, elections, votes, compromises--
> all carried on by subject matter amateurs.
> Politics is to the professions as ambiguity
> to truth, expediency to rightness, heresy to
> true belief.[48]

One could hardly find a more apt description of the AEC's

conception of the nature of its administrative responsibility. My point,

of course, is that such a conception is inappropriate.[49] No single term

comes readily to mind to describe this fourth type of administrative re-

sponsibility. Perhaps the idea of "political administrator" conveys the

central point that the function has far more in common with politics

than with management. In terms of attributes, it should be stressed

---

[47] Note that I have used the terms "manager," "executive,"
and "politician" to denote functions. "Professionalism" as I am using
it is an attribute. I suspect that some of the traditional confusion over
how to draw the line between politics and administration stems from
failure to make the distinction. Both are functions and have no necessary
connections with any particular set of attributes.

[48] Mosher, op. cit., p. 109 (emphasis added).

[49] Mosher's basic argument is that the growing dependence
of the public service upon professionals is inconsistent with many of our
democratic ideals. I fully agree.

that technical competence (either with or without profession certi-
fication) is not the key. The function of such an administrator is
not analysis. The job requires sensitivity to questions about the comparative political strengths and weaknesses of programs as well as
their technical promise. It also requires a willingness to adjudicate
competing claims about their value.

Figure 1 summarizes many of these thoughts.

Figure 1
A Typology of Administrative Functions

	Controversial Programs	Non-controversial Programs
Internally Determined Goals	Political Administrator	Executive
Externally Determined Goals	Politician	Manager

The central proposition is that the types of adaptive
behavior necessary to insure the prosperity of a government program can be classified according to the nature of that program.
I have suggested four broadly different categories (representing
the extremes of two dimensions) and have argued that for each

a particular type of administrative responsibility (i. e. , adaptive behavior) is required to guarantee prosperity.

With specific regard to the AEC, I have proposed that many of its recent problems can be traced to an unusual set of dependency relations, the net effect of which has been to insulate the agency, especially at the senior staff level, from a changing political environment. The Commission has become frozen into a particular conception of administrative responsibility, closely resembling Friedrich's "functional responsibility," that is highly inappropriate to these changes.

Above all, the AEC has never learned that "government is different because government is politics. "

APPENDIX A

Operating Expenses in $ millions for 23 AEC
Programs by Stage, FY 1958 - FY 1972
(Associated "prosperity scores"
in parentheses)

OPERATING EXPENSES IN MILLIONS. (ASSOCIATED PROSPERITY SCORE.)

RAW MATERIALS

	DIVISION	GENL MNGR	COMMISSION	BOB	APPEAL	PRESIDENT
FY1958	614.3(196)	610.0(197)	611.0(190)	599.0(191)	599.0(195)	599.0(196)
FY1959	714.2(204)	670.0(199)	670.0(202)	570.0(198)	670.0(202)	670.0(202)
FY1960	786.0(211)	781.0(208)	736.5(201)	736.5(200)	736.5(222)	739.5(205)
FY1961	724.3(201)	712.0(196)	680.5(197)	630.0(190)	642.0(139)	630.5(185)
FY1962	590.1(161)	578.5(154)	578.5(159)	578.5(168)	578.5(170)	578.5(167)
FY1963	512.1(137)	512.1(140)	512.1(143)	512.1(142)	512.1(134)	512.1(135)
FY1964	384.6(95)	384.6(103)	384.6(102)	344.6(97)	344.6(92)	344.6(98)
FY1965	267.4(73)	267.4(73)	267.4(74)	267.4(77)	267.4(79)	267.4(81)
FY1966	212.7(63)	212.7(63)	212.7(64)	212.7(67)	212.7(55)	212.7(67)
FY1967	163.0(51)	163.0(51)	153.0(52)	163.0(54)	163.0(54)	163.0(55)
FY1968	130.0(37)	130.0(43)	130.0(42)	129.5(43)	129.5(42)	129.5(43)
FY1969	113.7(32)	113.6(33)	112.6(34)	112.4(34)	112.4(34)	112.4(35)
FY1970	89.5(26)	88.0(26)	88.0(26)	86.0(27)	86.0(27)	57.0(19)
FY1971	25.0(7)	24.3(7)	25.0(7)	14.0(4)	24.0(7)	18.0(6)
FY1972	2.3(0)	1.5(0)	1.5(0)	1.5(0)	1.5(0)	1.5(0)

SPECIAL NUC MATERIALS

	DIVISION	GENL MNGR	COMMISSION	BOB	APPEAL	PRESIDENT
FY1958	649.6(152)	602.5(144)	639.1(144)	600.7(143)	600.7(142)	594.1(140)
FY1959	620.0(130)	578.0(127)	592.0(129)	592.0(127)	592.0(130)	592.0(128)
FY1960	596.2(117)	572.3(113)	592.0(117)	581.0(115)	592.0(118)	581.0(116)
FY1961	580.3(118)	578.0(118)	570.0(119)	547.5(120)	570.0(122)	567.6(121)
FY1962	581.8(116)	577.7(114)	577.7(115)	559.7(119)	560.5(120)	560.5(117)
FY1963	570.2(112)	550.4(112)	550.4(111)	547.3(111)	541.4(103)	541.1(103)
FY1964	493.3(90)	488.0(97)	485.6(93)	483.6(99)	483.6(94)	483.6(99)
FY1965	448.4(91)	444.3(90)	440.0(89)	440.0(93)	410.0(88)	401.5(87)
FY1966	385.1(84)	383.1(84)	384.1(84)	374.1(86)	376.5(84)	378.5(87)
FY1967	363.0(83)	357.0(84)	362.0(84)	337.7(82)	355.7(86)	355.7(87)
FY1968	373.4(79)	352.4(87)	354.3(83)	339.4(82)	355.4(86)	346.3(83)
FY1969	363.9(75)	346.6(75)	349.9(76)	339.3(76)	339.3(75)	334.3(75)
FY1970	361.7(77)	345.4(76)	349.2(75)	319.7(73)	338.5(77)	324.8(78)
FY1971	398.4(82)	377.1(81)	376.7(81)	339.4(81)	344.7(80)	348.5(84)
FY1972	420.9(88)	401.0(91)	401.6(92)	355.1(88)	355.1(89)	355.1(87)

WEAPONS

	DIVISION	GENL MNGR	COMMISSION	BOB	APPEAL	PRESIDENT
FY1958	429.8(65)	426.8(68)	460.0(69)	452.2(69)	452.2(69)	452.2(69)
FY1959	545.0(74)	523.0(77)	532.0(77)	532.0(75)	532.0(69)	532.5(75)
FY1960	542.0(69)	542.0(71)	524.0(69)	517.0(67)	524.0(69)	517.0(67)
FY1961	501.0(66)	500.0(68)	495.0(69)	495.0(72)	495.0(68)	495.0(68)
FY1962	650.0(84)	643.0(85)	643.0(85)	546.1(76)	556.1(77)	590.1(80)
FY1963	572.0(85)	589.0(80)	614.0(83)	603.2(81)	764.0(94)	761.2(94)
FY1964	877.6(104)	739.6(99)	746.2(95)	681.6(92)	760.3(96)	688.3(92)
FY1965	833.3(110)	803.3(109)	785.7(106)	780.7(109)	771.7(109)	771.7(109)
FY1966	750.0(106)	735.0(108)	735.0(107)	712.3(108)	721.5(105)	705.3(105)
FY1967	701.0(104)	636.0(108)	686.0(107)	653.0(105)	662.0(104)	659.0(104)
FY1968	874.5(120)	650.1(107)	709.0(111)	595.5(111)	705.5(110)	700.5(110)
FY1969	873.8(118)	833.5(121)	837.5(122)	835.6(124)	851.6(123)	840.7(122)
FY1970	915.5(127)	862.0(127)	892.0(129)	844.0(128)	850.0(126)	828.2(129)
FY1971	966.0(129)	909.0(131)	918.5(131)	859.5(136)	876.1(132)	841.7(133)
FY1972	963.8(131)	886.6(134)	878.7(135)	848.0(138)	876.0(137)	848.0(136)

CIVILIAN POWER REACTORS

	DIVISION	GENL MNGR	COMMISSION	BOB	APPEAL	PRESIDENT
FY1958	78.8(75)	70.8(71)	98.8(90)	95.0(102)	95.0(94)	95.0(97)
FY1959	92.0(78)	83.0(77)	83.0(74)	83.0(83)	83.0(76)	83.0(78)
FY1960	97.1(77)	93.0(77)	94.2(75)	89.0(82)	91.6(76)	89.0(77)
FY1961	98.5(81)	92.0(79)	92.0(78)	78.5(80)	87.0(77)	87.0(80)
FY1962	87.5(71)	87.5(72)	83.6(67)	75.2(74)	81.0(72)	81.0(73)
FY1963	87.3(69)	76.0(64)	78.1(64)	78.1(73)	78.1(62)	78.1(64)
FY1964	101.7(75)	80.2(67)	101.4(79)	85.0(80)	92.8(75)	85.0(76)
FY1965	86.6(71)	86.6(74)	87.1(71)	72.3(71)	85.8(77)	79.3(75)
FY1966	86.7(77)	88.7(81)	98.7(88)	82.0(87)	85.8(82)	85.5(85)
FY1967	103.7(96)	94.9(93)	94.9(90)	76.2(86)	89.0(90)	89.0(94)
FY1968	147.2(126)	135.6(140)	137.1(131)	122.1(137)	134.0(135)	134.0(140)
FY1969	164.4(139)	150.5(137)	157.0(139)	121.0(126)	154.4(143)	132.0(129)
FY1970	179.5(156)	168.0(156)	168.5(149)	135.0(144)	153.2(146)	125.8(131)
FY1971	186.6(156)	170.0(154)	172.2(151)	102.6(114)	140.5(137)	130.0(137)
FY1972	170.5(145)	158.7(151)	155.7(146)	134.7(154)	144.7(150)	144.7(155)

OPERATING EXPENSES IN MILLIONS. (ASSOCIATED PROSPERITY SCORE.)

COOP POWER REACTORS

	DIVISION	GENL MNGR	COMMISSION	BOB	APPEAL	PRESIDENT
FY1958	0.0(0)	0.0(0)	0.0(0)	0.0(0)	0.0(0)	0.0(0)
FY1959	14.5(60)	14.5(67)	14.5(68)	14.5(70)	14.5(70)	14.5(71)
FY1960	23.2(90)	20.5(85)	20.5(86)	16.5(73)	20.5(90)	16.5(74)
FY1961	25.3(101)	25.3(109)	25.3(113)	25.3(125)	25.3(122)	25.3(122)
FY1962	24.5(96)	24.5(102)	24.5(104)	24.5(117)	24.5(116)	24.5(116)
FY1953	18.5(71)	13.2(56)	13.2(57)	10.4(47)	13.2(51)	10.4(44)
FY1954	15.0(53)	12.0(50)	15.0(61)	15.0(69)	15.0(64)	15.0(69)
FY1955	18.0(71)	18.0(77)	18.0(77)	14.6(70)	16.0(76)	16.0(79)
FY1966	37.7(162)	37.7(174)	22.7(106)	22.7(118)	22.7(113)	22.7(118)
FY1967	46.7(210)	44.7(221)	46.7(233)	35.2(193)	35.2(189)	35.2(194)
FY1958	23.8(99)	22.1(115)	28.7(144)	28.7(156)	28.7(153)	28.7(157)
FY1969	25.6(104)	25.6(117)	25.6(119)	25.6(130)	27.6(135)	27.6(140)
FY1970	19.1(80)	17.1(79)	17.1(80)	16.1(84)	16.1(81)	13.1(71)
FY1971	21.6(87)	17.6(80)	17.6(80)	12.6(68)	12.6(64)	11.6(63)
FY1972	26.8(110)	13.0(62)	13.0(64)	13.0(72)	13.0(71)	13.0(73)

EURATOM

	DIVISION	GENL MNGR	COMMISSION	BOB	APPEAL	PRESIDENT
FY1958	0.0(0)	0.0(0)	0.0(0)	0.0(0)	0.0(0)	0.0(0)
FY1959	5.0(106)	5.0(107)	5.0(118)	5.0(116)	5.0(116)	5.0(105)
FY1960	9.0(180)	9.0(172)	9.0(192)	9.0(193)	9.0(191)	9.0(175)
FY1961	5.0(103)	5.0(99)	5.0(113)	5.0(119)	5.0(113)	5.0(103)
FY1962	3.0(61)	3.0(57)	2.6(59)	2.6(62)	2.6(61)	2.6(54)
FY1963	5.0(99)	5.0(98)	4.0(87)	4.0(88)	4.0(81)	4.0(74)
FY1954	7.0(130)	7.0(136)	7.0(145)	7.0(155)	7.0(144)	7.0(140)
FY1965	5.5(113)	5.5(108)	5.5(120)	5.5(126)	5.5(126)	5.5(117)
FY1966	5.8(131)	5.8(125)	5.8(140)	5.8(147)	5.8(141)	5.8(132)
FY1967	4.5(105)	3.5(80)	3.5(88)	2.0(53)	3.5(90)	3.5(83)
FY1958	2.5(53)	2.5(60)	3.5(63)	2.5(65)	2.5(63)	2.5(58)
FY1959	5.0(105)	2.5(52)	2.5(59)	2.5(61)	2.5(59)	2.5(54)
FY1970	0.4(8)	0.0(0)	0.4(9)	0.4(10)	0.4(9)	0.0(0)
FY1971	0.0(0)	0.0(0)	0.0(0)	0.0(0)	0.0(0)	0.0(0)
FY1972	0.0(0)	0.0(0)	0.0(0)	0.0(0)	0.0(0)	0.0(0)

OPERATING EXPENSES IN MILLIONS. (ASSOCIATED PROSPERITY SCORE.)

MERCHANT SHIP REACTORS

	DIVISION	GENL MNGR	COMMISSION	BOB	APPEAL	PRESIDENT
FY1958	6.3(115)	1.0(30)	6.3(139)	3.6(103)	3.6(93)	3.6(107)
FY1959	6.5(105)	3.6(102)	3.6(78)	3.6(95)	3.6(86)	3.6(94)
FY1960	10.0(152)	3.3(84)	6.5(125)	6.0(142)	6.0(127)	6.0(140)
FY1961	12.0(190)	8.2(212)	8.2(167)	6.7(179)	8.2(189)	8.2(208)
FY1962	8.6(134)	3.6(215)	12.3(234)	8.0(203)	11.3(260)	11.3(280)
FY1963	8.6(131)	7.0(180)	7.0(138)	6.1(150)	6.1(126)	6.1(138)
FY1954	9.0(126)	5.5(137)	5.7(107)	5.7(142)	6.7(140)	5.7(140)
FY1955	5.0(78)	5.0(127)	5.0(97)	2.5(63)	4.5(103)	2.5(64)
FY1966	3.8(65)	3.8(107)	3.8(82)	0.0(0)	2.2(53)	0.3(10)
FY1957	6.0(106)	3.0(80)	5.0(113)	0.5(14)	0.5(12)	0.5(12)
FY1968	0.5(8)	0.0(3)	0.0(2)	0.0(2)	0.0(2)	0.0(2)
FY1969	5.0(80)	0.0(2)	0.0(2)	0.0(2)	0.0(2)	0.0(2)
FY1970	0.0(0)	0.0(0)	0.0(0)	0.0(0)	0.0(0)	0.0(0)
FY1971	0.2(4)	0.2(8)	0.2(6)	0.0(0)	0.0(0)	0.0(0)
FY1972	0.0(0)	0.0(0)	0.0(0)	0.0(0)	0.0(0)	0.0(0)

ARMY REACTORS

	DIVISION	GENL MNGR	COMMISSION	BOB	APPEAL	PRESIDENT
FY1958	5.5(55)	5.5(69)	5.5(64)	5.5(76)	5.5(74)	5.5(78)
FY1959	6.1(54)	5.5(64)	5.5(62)	5.5(70)	5.5(69)	5.5(72)
FY1960	11.0(91)	9.0(92)	11.0(110)	11.0(128)	11.0(123)	11.0(130)
FY1961	19.6(169)	11.6(124)	16.6(177)	11.0(142)	14.0(168)	14.0(177)
FY1962	18.1(153)	18.1(186)	14.6(148)	14.6(183)	11.5(138)	11.5(142)
FY1963	13.5(111)	13.0(137)	11.6(120)	11.6(139)	11.6(125)	11.6(132)
FY1964	19.5(150)	15.5(161)	16.4(160)	12.9(156)	12.9(141)	12.9(158)
FY1955	20.3(174)	10.3(109)	10.3(107)	9.0(111)	9.0(109)	9.0(116)
FY1966	11.5(105)	11.5(131)	11.5(128)	4.7(65)	9.7(124)	4.7(65)
FY1957	2.6(26)	0.8(11)	0.8(10)	0.8(12)	0.8(12)	0.8(12)
FY1968	0.8(8)	0.8(11)	0.8(10)	0.8(12)	0.8(12)	0.8(13)
FY1969	0.0(0)	0.0(0)	0.0(0)	0.0(0)	0.0(0)	0.0(0)
FY1970	0.0(0)	0.0(0)	0.0(0)	0.0(0)	0.0(0)	0.0(0)
FY1971	0.0(0)	0.0(0)	0.0(0)	0.0(0)	0.0(0)	0.0(0)
FY1972	0.0(0)	0.0(0)	0.0(0)	0.0(0)	0.0(0)	0.0(0)

NAVAL REACTORS

	DIVISION	GENL MNGR	COMMISSION	BOB	APPEAL	PRESIDENT
FY1958	90.1(95)	77.0(82)	90.1(90)	84.0(84)	84.0(85)	84.0(85)
FY1959	97.5(93)	87.0(85)	87.0(84)	87.0(81)	87.0(83)	87.0(82)
FY1960	93.0(83)	90.0(79)	93.0(81)	93.0(79)	93.0(80)	93.0(80)
FY1961	87.5(80)	87.5(79)	87.5(81)	85.0(80)	85.0(79)	85.0(78)
FY1962	100.0(90)	100.0(88)	98.6(87)	94.6(86)	94.5(88)	94.5(85)
FY1963	96.2(85)	96.2(87)	96.2(86)	96.2(84)	96.2(79)	96.2(79)
FY1964	102.7(85)	96.9(86)	98.7(84)	98.7(87)	98.7(83)	98.7(88)
FY1965	98.8(90)	98.8(89)	98.8(88)	94.6(86)	94.6(89)	94.6(89)
FY1966	96.2(95)	96.2(93)	96.2(93)	96.2(96)	96.2(94)	96.2(96)
FY1967	102.3(106)	102.3(107)	102.3(106)	102.3(108)	102.3(108)	97.3(103)
FY1968	96.6(92)	96.6(106)	96.6(100)	94.6(99)	96.6(101)	96.6(101)
FY1969	115.2(108)	115.2(111)	115.2(111)	115.2(112)	115.2(111)	115.2(112)
FY1970	129.3(125)	129.3(126)	129.3(125)	125.8(125)	129.3(128)	121.8(127)
FY1971	138.5(129)	138.1(132)	138.1(131)	132.0(136)	132.0(133)	132.0(139)
FY1972	142.5(135)	142.5(143)	142.5(141)	140.0(149)	140.0(151)	140.0(150)

AIRCRAFT NUC PROPULSION

	DIVISION	GENL MNGR	COMMISSION	BOB	APPEAL	PRESIDENT
FY1958	104.0(139)	90.5(131)	104.0(137)	75.0(140)	75.0(129)	75.0(129)
FY1959	66.5(80)	66.5(89)	66.5(85)	66.5(115)	66.5(106)	66.5(105)
FY1960	86.1(97)	83.1(99)	86.1(99)	68.6(109)	68.6(99)	68.6(100)
FY1961	78.6(91)	73.0(90)	73.0(89)	43.0(75)	73.0(113)	73.0(113)
FY1962	80.5(92)	74.5(89)	76.5(89)	35.0(59)	33.0(51)	33.0(50)
FY1963	0.0(0)	0.0(0)	0.0(0)	0.0(0)	0.0(0)	0.0(0)
FY1964	0.0(0)	0.0(0)	0.0(0)	0.0(0)	0.0(0)	0.0(0)
FY1965	0.0(0)	0.0(0)	0.0(0)	0.0(0)	0.0(0)	0.0(0)
FY1966	0.0(0)	0.0(0)	0.0(0)	0.0(0)	0.0(0)	0.0(0)
FY1967	0.0(0)	0.0(0)	0.0(0)	0.0(0)	0.0(0)	0.0(0)
FY1968	0.0(0)	0.0(0)	0.0(0)	0.0(0)	0.0(0)	0.0(0)
FY1969	0.0(0)	0.0(0)	0.0(0)	0.0(0)	0.0(0)	0.0(0)
FY1970	0.0(0)	0.0(0)	0.0(0)	0.0(0)	0.0(0)	0.0(0)
FY1971	0.0(0)	0.0(0)	0.0(0)	0.0(0)	0.0(0)	0.0(0)
FY1972	0.0(0)	0.0(0)	0.0(0)	0.0(0)	0.0(0)	0.0(0)

OPERATING EXPENSES IN MILLIONS. (ASSOCIATED PROSPERITY SCORE.)

PLUTO

	DIVISION	GENL MNGR	COMMISSION	BOB	APPEAL	PRESIDENT
FY1958	10.0(61)	10.0(74)	10.0(74)	3.0(30)	3.0(24)	3.0(29)
FY1959	19.3(108)	14.7(102)	14.7(106)	5.0(46)	5.0(38)	5.0(45)
FY1960	12.3(64)	12.3(76)	12.3(80)	12.3(106)	12.3(86)	12.3(104)
FY1961	19.2(104)	19.2(123)	19.2(132)	0.0(0)	19.2(143)	19.2(173)
FY1962	20.0(105)	20.0(123)	20.0(130)	20.0(184)	20.0(148)	20.5(180)
FY1963	26.0(135)	26.5(168)	21.5(143)	21.5(189)	26.5(175)	26.5(212)
FY1964	39.8(193)	0.0(0)	7.6(48)	7.6(69)	18.3(123)	2.0(17)
FY1965	5.0(26)	5.0(31)	12.6(84)	8.0(73)	9.0(60)	4.0(36)
FY1966	0.0(0)	0.0(0)	0.0(0)	0.0(0)	0.0(0)	0.0(0)
FY1967	0.0(0)	0.0(0)	0.0(0)	0.0(0)	0.0(0)	0.0(0)
FY1968	0.0(0)	0.0(0)	0.0(0)	0.0(0)	0.0(0)	0.0(0)
FY1969	0.0(0)	0.0(0)	0.0(0)	0.0(0)	0.0(0)	0.0(0)
FY1970	0.0(0)	0.0(0)	0.0(0)	0.0(0)	0.0(0)	0.0(0)
FY1971	0.0(0)	0.0(0)	0.0(0)	0.0(0)	0.0(0)	0.0(0)
FY1972	0.0(0)	0.0(0)	0.0(0)	0.0(0)	0.0(0)	0.0(0)

BOVER

	DIVISION	GENL MNGR	COMMISSION	BOB	APPEAL	PRESIDENT
FY1958	12.0(20)	12.0(21)	12.0(20)	12.0(23)	12.0(24)	12.0(25)
FY1959	12.0(18)	12.0(20)	12.0(22)	12.0(22)	12.0(22)	9.7(19)
FY1960	15.5(22)	15.5(23)	15.5(23)	15.5(25)	15.5(26)	15.5(28)
FY1961	22.7(34)	22.7(35)	22.7(35)	18.0(32)	18.0(32)	18.0(34)
FY1962	27.7(41)	27.7(41)	33.0(49)	28.2(49)	28.2(51)	30.3(56)
FY1963	73.2(106)	74.7(115)	74.7(114)	74.7(125)	76.7(123)	74.7(128)
FY1964	132.5(179)	113.0(171)	132.2(191)	91.2(155)	124.2(203)	101.2(187)
FY1965	109.0(163)	109.0(167)	120.0(183)	106.0(185)	106.0(193)	84.0(165)
FY1966	85.5(138)	85.5(141)	85.5(156)	84.0(160)	85.5(162)	84.0(174)
FY1967	89.1(151)	88.5(157)	88.5(156)	86.5(175)	86.5(177)	79.0(173)
FY1968	92.6(145)	84.3(157)	90.3(160)	60.3(121)	60.3(122)	60.3(131)
FY1969	98.5(152)	97.0(159)	72.0(118)	72.0(134)	72.0(134)	72.0(145)
FY1970	55.3(87)	52.5(87)	53.0(87)	46.5(88)	50.0(96)	47.9(103)
FY1971	68.2(104)	67.3(110)	67.3(109)	50.0(99)	50.0(98)	43.0(94)
FY1972	84.6(131)	52.0(89)	52.0(90)	0.0(0)	15.0(31)	15.0(33)

OPERATING EXPENSES IN MILLIONS. (ASSOCIATED PROSPERITY SCORE.)

SNAP

	DIVISION	GENL MNGR	COMMISSION	BOB	APPFAL	PRESIDENT
FY1958	0.0(0)	0.0(0)	0.0(0)	0.0(0)	0.0(0)	0.0(0)
FY1959	5.3(9)	4.5(9)	4.5(9)	4.5(10)	4.5(9)	4.5(10)
FY1960	13.0(20)	13.0(24)	13.0(23)	12.3(26)	12.3(24)	12.3(25)
FY1961	22.0(35)	16.0(31)	16.0(30)	14.0(33)	14.0(29)	14.0(31)
FY1962	19.0(30)	19.0(35)	19.0(33)	19.0(44)	19.0(39)	19.0(41)
FY1963	51.3(80)	50.0(97)	48.0(87)	48.0(106)	56.3(104)	56.3(112)
FY1964	110.5(161)	90.9(173)	113.0(194)	87.5(195)	113.0(213)	92.0(197)
FY1965	86.2(140)	86.2(167)	100.5(182)	73.0(169)	73.5(155)	73.0(166)
FY1966	96.2(168)	83.2(174)	91.7(181)	48.5(122)	84.6(135)	70.5(168)
FY1967	64.5(118)	50.7(114)	52.7(110)	46.6(124)	47.9(113)	45.9(115)
FY1968	89.5(151)	54.6(129)	60.6(128)	57.7(153)	57.7(135)	57.7(145)
FY1969	102.3(170)	71.2(147)	74.4(146)	59.4(146)	64.4(139)	59.4(139)
FY1970	62.9(107)	52.0(109)	52.6(103)	41.4(104)	43.6(96)	38.4(96)
FY1971	66.1(109)	52.4(108)	56.5(109)	39.5(104)	42.5(96)	35.5(90)
FY1972	56.5(95)	35.1(76)	29.0(60)	20.2(55)	22.5(54)	22.5(58)

GENL REACTOR TECH

	DIVISION	GENL MNGR	COMMISSION	BOB	APPEAL	PRESIDENT
FY1958	0.0(0)	0.0(0)	0.0(0)	0.0(0)	0.0(0)	0.0(0)
FY1959	0.0(0)	0.0(0)	0.0(0)	0.0(0)	0.0(0)	0.0(0)
FY1960	35.2(59)	26.2(46)	52.8(89)	50.8(89)	50.8(88)	50.8(89)
FY1961	40.7(70)	36.7(67)	35.7(64)	35.7(69)	35.7(66)	35.7(67)
FY1962	50.0(84)	50.0(88)	47.1(80)	47.1(88)	47.1(89)	47.1(87)
FY1963	80.0(133)	63.4(115)	68.0(118)	57.0(102)	63.0(104)	60.0(101)
FY1964	74.5(115)	65.3(116)	68.3(112)	60.0(109)	64.0(108)	60.0(109)
FY1965	65.0(111)	65.0(118)	65.0(113)	58.0(108)	60.0(113)	60.0(115)
FY1966	66.0(122)	62.0(121)	62.0(117)	58.8(120)	62.0(121)	58.8(119)
FY1967	65.3(127)	51.0(130)	62.0(125)	59.0(127)	59.0(125)	59.0(127)
FY1968	56.0(100)	51.0(109)	51.0(103)	51.0(109)	51.0(106)	51.0(108)
FY1969	59.0(104)	53.0(103)	53.0(99)	50.0(99)	53.0(102)	50.0(99)
FY1970	52.0(94)	49.0(96)	49.0(91)	46.0(93)	46.0(91)	47.0(99)
FY1971	52.0(90)	48.0(92)	51.4(95)	45.0(95)	49.0(99)	42.0(90)
FY1972	48.0(85)	44.0(89)	44.0(87)	39.5(84)	38.5(83)	38.5(84)

NUCLEAR SAFETY

	DIVISION	GENL MNGR	COMMISSION	BOB	APPEAL	PRESIDENT
FY1958	8.0(27)	8.0(30)	8.0(28)	8.0(30)	8.0(31)	8.0(31)
FY1959	10.1(31)	7.5(26)	7.5(26)	7.5(26)	7.5(27)	7.5(27)
FY1960	12.7(37)	12.7(39)	12.7(40)	12.7(41)	12.7(42)	12.7(42)
FY1951	11.1(33)	9.2(30)	9.2(30)	9.2(33)	9.2(33)	9.2(32)
FY1952	11.0(32)	11.0(34)	11.0(34)	11.0(38)	11.0(39)	11.0(38)
FY1953	27.7(80)	25.0(80)	25.0(80)	22.2(74)	22.2(70)	22.2(70)
FY1954	41.5(111)	38.3(121)	40.0(122)	35.0(117)	36.1(116)	35.0(119)
FY1965	39.5(117)	39.5(127)	39.5(127)	32.0(111)	32.0(115)	32.0(115)
FY1956	42.5(136)	37.5(130)	41.3(131)	36.5(138)	36.5(136)	35.5(135)
FY1957	46.3(156)	41.3(154)	38.3(154)	38.3(154)	38.3(154)	38.3(154)
FY1968	44.0(137)	35.0(136)	35.0(130)	35.0(139)	35.0(139)	35.0(139)
FY1959	50.3(154)	43.3(149)	42.3(150)	40.3(149)	40.3(149)	40.3(150)
FY1970	47.9(150)	42.0(146)	42.0(145)	39.0(147)	39.0(147)	38.0(151)
FY1971	46.5(141)	41.5(142)	41.5(142)	38.0(149)	38.0(147)	35.9(144)
FY1972	49.0(151)	42.0(150)	42.0(154)	35.9(146)	35.9(148)	35.9(147)

ADVANCED SYSTEMS

	DIVISION	GENL MNGR	COMMISSION	BOB	APPEAL	PRESIDENT
FY1950	7.5(37)	7.5(43)	7.5(38)	6.0(37)	6.0(36)	6.0(38)
FY1959	13.5(60)	10.0(52)	10.0(49)	6.1(35)	6.1(34)	6.1(36)
FY1960	16.6(69)	15.6(73)	15.6(70)	15.6(83)	15.6(80)	15.6(85)
FY1961	17.0(73)	15.2(74)	15.2(72)	15.2(90)	15.2(83)	15.2(89)
FY1952	22.1(94)	22.1(104)	18.3(82)	10.2(58)	14.2(78)	11.5(65)
FY1963	44.0(182)	38.2(184)	37.1(170)	36.6(200)	36.6(178)	36.6(191)
FY1964	40.2(155)	27.8(132)	26.7(116)	24.9(137)	25.7(129)	24.9(140)
FY1965	34.1(146)	34.1(165)	39.5(181)	27.0(153)	27.0(149)	29.0(173)
FY1966	45.2(209)	41.2(215)	41.2(205)	29.5(182)	39.5(228)	29.5(185)
FY1957	38.5(187)	30.8(172)	33.8(179)	25.8(170)	25.8(160)	21.0(142)
FY1968	16.6(74)	12.5(73)	11.0(58)	9.8(63)	9.8(60)	9.8(64)
FY1959	11.0(48)	8.9(46)	8.9(44)	7.9(48)	7.9(45)	7.9(48)
FY1970	7.1(32)	6.1(32)	6.1(30)	6.0(37)	6.0(34)	6.0(39)
FY1971	6.1(26)	5.5(28)	0.0(0)	0.0(0)	0.0(0)	0.0(0)
FY1972	0.0(0)	0.0(0)	0.0(0)	0.0(0)	0.0(0)	0.0(0)

OPERATING EXPENSES IN MILLIONS. (ASSOCIATED PROSPERITY SCORE.)

HIGH-ENERGY PHYSICS

	DIVISION	GENL MNGR	COMMISSION	BOB	APPEAL	PRESIDENT
FY1958	16.0(19)	16.0(21)	16.0(19)	16.0(19)	16.0(20)	16.0(20)
FY1959	21.6(23)	21.6(26)	21.6(25)	21.6(24)	21.6(24)	21.6(25)
FY1960	32.2(32)	32.2(34)	32.2(33)	32.2(33)	32.2(33)	32.2(34)
FY1961	39.2(40)	35.7(40)	34.7(39)	32.2(37)	32.2(36)	32.2(36)
FY1962	53.6(54)	49.1(53)	50.3(53)	46.8(52)	46.8(52)	46.8(51)
FY1963	88.9(88)	84.5(93)	84.0(90)	78.6(84)	82.4(82)	81.1(82)
FY1964	99.3(91)	85.5(93)	111.8(114)	109.0(118)	115.8(110)	109.0(119)
FY1955	117.6(120)	98.5(109)	104.0(112)	92.5(103)	92.5(105)	97.5(107)
FY1956	123.5(136)	104.2(124)	104.2(122)	100.5(122)	101.5(119)	102.5(122)
FY1967	133.3(154)	111.2(142)	112.5(140)	111.5(143)	111.5(142)	111.5(144)
FY1968	135.0(144)	109.0(147)	117.5(148)	116.5(148)	116.5(147)	116.5(149)
FY1969	137.0(144)	127.7(151)	128.3(149)	123.3(146)	128.3(149)	123.3(147)
FY1970	135.1(146)	128.3(154)	128.3(149)	128.3(156)	128.3(153)	122.5(156)
FY1971	153.9(159)	128.4(151)	130.4(149)	121.0(153)	130.1(159)	119.4(154)
FY1972	137.0(145)	125.5(155)	125.5(154)	118.6(154)	118.6(154)	114.3(150)

SHERWOOD

	DIVISION	GENL MNGR	COMMISSION	BOB	APPEAL	PRESIDENT
FY1958	21.6(82)	21.6(90)	21.6(82)	21.6(85)	21.6(87)	21.6(87)
FY1959	32.3(110)	27.5(86)	25.5(94)	25.5(92)	25.5(95)	25.5(95)
FY1960	39.2(126)	34.2(118)	39.0(130)	38.0(127)	38.0(129)	38.0(130)
FY1961	28.6(95)	26.0(92)	26.0(92)	26.0(96)	26.0(94)	26.0(95)
FY1962	25.0(81)	25.0(86)	24.5(82)	24.5(97)	24.5(89)	24.5(88)
FY1963	27.2(87)	27.2(96)	26.5(90)	26.5(90)	26.5(85)	26.5(86)
FY1964	23.7(70)	23.7(82)	23.7(77)	23.7(82)	23.7(78)	23.7(83)
FY1965	28.5(94)	26.5(93)	26.6(91)	21.5(76)	21.5(79)	21.5(80)
FY1956	27.5(98)	24.0(91)	25.0(92)	23.5(91)	23.5(89)	23.5(92)
FY1967	27.6(103)	24.5(100)	24.5(97)	23.5(101)	24.5(101)	24.5(103)
FY1958	29.5(102)	22.7(98)	26.7(106)	26.1(106)	26.1(107)	26.1(108)
FY1969	32.0(108)	29.0(109)	32.0(118)	28.2(107)	28.2(106)	28.2(109)
FY1970	30.7(107)	29.3(113)	29.3(108)	29.3(114)	29.3(113)	27.7(114)
FY1971	34.3(115)	32.0(120)	32.0(116)	30.0(121)	30.5(121)	29.6(123)
FY1972	34.2(117)	29.8(118)	29.8(116)	28.4(118)	28.4(119)	23.0(97)

OPERATING EXPENSES IN MILLIONS. (ASSOCIATED PROSPERITY SCORE.)

BIOMED RESEARCH

	DIVISION	GENL MNGR	COMMISSION	BOB	APPEAL	PRESIDENT
FY1958	39.5(55)	35.0(51)	37.5(51)	36.0(51)	36.0(51)	36.0(51)
FY1959	45.0(56)	43.0(58)	43.0(56)	43.0(56)	43.0(57)	43.0(56)
FY1960	50.0(59)	49.5(59)	50.5(61)	49.0(59)	49.0(59)	49.0(59)
FY1961	58.0(70)	54.1(68)	54.1(69)	52.0(69)	54.1(70)	54.1(70)
FY1962	67.0(80)	64.5(79)	59.8(73)	57.5(74)	57.5(74)	59.8(75)
FY1963	72.9(86)	71.9(89)	71.8(89)	70.3(86)	71.8(82)	70.3(81)
FY1964	81.4(89)	78.0(95)	79.4(93)	80.0(99)	81.5(95)	76.4(95)
FY1965	94.2(114)	88.0(109)	88.0(109)	77.0(99)	80.0(104)	80.0(105)
FY1966	93.0(122)	89.5(120)	89.5(120)	84.0(117)	89.5(122)	85.0(118)
FY1967	96.0(132)	89.0(128)	90.0(129)	89.0(132)	89.0(130)	89.0(131)
FY1968	95.5(121)	85.0(128)	91.0(131)	90.8(133)	90.8(132)	90.3(132)
FY1969	101.3(126)	95.0(126)	96.0(128)	92.0(126)	94.5(127)	92.0(125)
FY1970	100.7(129)	95.0(128)	95.0(126)	92.0(129)	92.0(126)	90.7(132)
FY1971	103.5(128)	97.0(128)	97.0(127)	89.5(130)	92.5(130)	88.2(130)
FY1972	99.7(125)	92.7(128)	92.7(130)	88.2(132)	88.2(132)	88.2(132)

TRAINING, EDUC, INFO

	DIVISION	GENL MNGR	COMMISSION	BOB	APPEAL	PRESIDENT
FY1958	25.0(126)	15.0(92)	20.0(112)	15.5(103)	17.5(111)	17.5(115)
FY1959	23.0(105)	12.0(68)	18.5(114)	18.5(114)	18.5(108)	18.5(112)
FY1960	22.2(95)	17.5(89)	18.7(93)	14.7(84)	14.7(79)	14.7(82)
FY1961	23.5(103)	13.7(72)	13.8(72)	13.8(87)	13.8(79)	13.8(83)
FY1962	19.6(85)	17.5(89)	17.3(86)	14.1(86)	14.1(81)	14.1(83)
FY1963	22.0(93)	19.2(101)	20.2(102)	13.4(79)	20.2(103)	15.1(81)
FY1964	21.4(84)	18.3(94)	17.6(84)	16.6(97)	17.0(88)	17.1(99)
FY1965	22.0(96)	20.3(106)	20.3(103)	16.6(101)	18.6(108)	17.6(108)
FY1966	20.2(95)	18.7(105)	19.3(106)	16.7(111)	18.3(112)	16.8(108)
FY1967	20.4(101)	18.7(113)	21.2(124)	17.2(121)	17.7(116)	17.2(117)
FY1968	23.0(105)	19.1(122)	20.1(118)	17.1(119)	18.1(117)	17.8(121)
FY1969	22.2(100)	20.1(112)	20.0(109)	16.5(107)	17.7(105)	17.0(106)
FY1970	20.3(94)	19.6(111)	19.6(109)	16.4(109)	16.5(101)	15.9(107)
FY1971	21.7(96)	18.8(104)	18.9(101)	13.0(89)	16.7(105)	12.7(87)
FY1972	25.2(114)	19.7(115)	12.7(73)	12.1(86)	12.1(81)	12.1(84)

OPERATING EXPENSES IN MILLIONS. (ASSOCIATED PROSPERITY SCORE.)

ISIDORES_DEVELOPMENT

	DIVISION	GENL MNGR	COMMISSION	BOB	APPEAL	PRESIDENT
FY1958	2.8(24)	2.8(32)	2.8(30)	2.8(37)	2.8(34)	2.8(41)
FY1959	15.0(113)	3.5(37)	3.5(36)	3.5(42)	3.5(39)	3.5(47)
FY1960	8.0(57)	8.0(74)	8.0(74)	6.0(64)	6.0(51)	6.0(73)
FY1961	10.5(77)	5.0(47)	5.0(48)	4.0(48)	4.5(48)	4.5(57)
FY1962	7.5(54)	6.0(55)	6.5(61)	4.5(52)	5.5(59)	5.5(69)
FY1963	11.0(78)	11.0(105)	9.0(85)	5.8(65)	9.0(86)	9.0(75)
FY1964	10.9(72)	8.2(77)	10.0(90)	11.5(129)	12.2(119)	9.2(114)
FY1965	14.0(102)	12.5(118)	12.5(117)	10.2(119)	10.2(112)	10.2(135)
FY1966	19.5(153)	17.8(182)	17.8(183)	12.2(155)	14.2(161)	12.7(177)
FY1957	22.7(188)	16.7(184)	17.0(186)	14.7(198)	14.7(180)	14.7(217)
FY1968	35.2(268)	20.4(235)	21.4(235)	19.0(252)	20.9(254)	8.3(122)
FY1969	11.0(82)	9.5(96)	9.5(96)	7.0(86)	8.5(94)	7.1(97)
FY1970	10.4(80)	9.0(92)	9.0(91)	6.8(86)	7.6(87)	6.3(92)
FY1971	10.1(75)	9.0(90)	9.0(90)	6.0(78)	7.2(85)	6.0(88)
FY1972	9.1(69)	6.6(70)	6.6(71)	5.8(80)	5.8(73)	5.8(88)

PLOWSHARE

	DIVISION	GENL MNGR	COMMISSION	BOB	APPEAL	PRESIDENT
FY1958	0.0(0)	0.0(0)	0.0(0)	0.0(0)	0.0(0)	0.0(0)
FY1959	0.0(0)	0.0(0)	0.0(0)	0.0(0)	0.0(0)	0.0(0)
FY1960	4.0(15)	4.0(20)	10.0(49)	7.5(72)	8.0(55)	8.0(59)
FY1961	9.7(40)	8.0(41)	8.0(40)	5.0(53)	8.0(59)	8.0(63)
FY1962	12.5(50)	12.5(62)	12.5(60)	5.0(51)	6.5(48)	6.5(50)
FY1963	11.7(46)	11.7(61)	11.7(58)	3.7(37)	11.7(78)	8.7(62)
FY1964	19.3(71)	19.3(98)	19.3(90)	12.0(119)	17.5(119)	15.5(119)
FY1965	27.0(109)	25.0(129)	21.5(105)	9.5(97)	12.0(90)	11.0(89)
FY1966	30.9(135)	28.9(161)	28.9(154)	16.7(187)	23.2(183)	17.8(153)
FY1967	30.0(138)	23.0(137)	24.0(136)	17.1(204)	22.4(190)	17.1(156)
FY1958	34.0(144)	16.7(105)	28.2(161)	11.5(135)	12.5(105)	19.5(175)
FY1969	35.0(146)	26.5(146)	26.5(141)	2.5(28)	6.5(50)	14.5(121)
FY1970	36.2(155)	29.1(163)	29.1(154)	14.0(157)	26.1(208)	14.5(129)
FY1971	36.1(149)	22.9(126)	22.9(120)	8.0(93)	8.0(65)	8.0(72)
FY1972	22.8(96)	7.5(43)	5.0(23)	5.0(60)	5.0(43)	5.0(46)

OPERATING EXPENSES IN MILLIONS. (ASSOCIATED PROSPERITY SCORE.)

PROGRAM DIRECTION

	DIVISION	GENL MNGR	COMMISSION	BOB	APPEAL	PRESIDENT
FY1958	49.0(65)	46.2(63)	48.0(61)	44.5(58)	44.5(59)	44.5(59)
FY1959	49.2(59)	47.0(59)	47.0(58)	46.5(56)	46.5(57)	46.5(57)
FY1960	59.7(67)	54.3(63)	56.3(63)	52.0(57)	52.0(58)	52.0(58)
FY1961	58.5(68)	54.3(63)	54.8(65)	53.5(65)	54.8(66)	54.8(65)
FY1962	58.3(66)	58.3(65)	58.3(66)	57.1(68)	57.1(69)	58.0(68)
FY1963	65.8(74)	62.4(72)	62.4(72)	61.2(69)	62.4(67)	61.9(66)
FY1964	74.7(78)	69.9(79)	75.0(82)	72.5(83)	74.5(81)	73.4(85)
FY1965	78.8(91)	78.5(91)	78.5(90)	76.0(90)	76.7(93)	76.7(94)
FY1966	83.2(104)	83.2(104)	83.2(104)	81.5(105)	81.5(103)	81.5(105)
FY1967	86.0(113)	85.5(114)	85.5(114)	84.0(115)	84.0(114)	84.0(115)
FY1968	98.8(119)	96.9(136)	97.0(130)	96.9(131)	96.9(131)	94.0(127)
FY1969	111.2(132)	103.8(128)	104.6(130)	99.9(126)	99.9(125)	102.8(130)
FY1970	121.3(148)	116.0(145)	116.0(144)	111.3(143)	111.3(142)	110.8(150)
FY1971	133.5(157)	126.1(155)	127.9(157)	124.0(166)	125.8(165)	111.1(152)
FY1972	127.0(152)	120.6(155)	117.7(155)	116.7(161)	117.0(163)	117.0(163)

APPENDIX B

Methodological Appendix to Chapter V:
Measuring "Division Strength" and "Commission Support"[*]

Our problem, it will be recalled, is to define a measure
of the treatments received by individual programs across a triad of
budgetary review stages consisting of "request" - "reduction" - "restoration." It was argued that this measure should simultaneously take
account of several factors. Using the "division request" - "General
Manager reduction" - "Commission restoration" sequence for purposes
of illustration, the measure should on the one hand take account of what
the General Manager has done, both to specific program requests and to
the aggregated total of all requests. At the same time the measure should
be sensitive to how the Commission treats a particular program in light
of what the Commission does to the overall budget recommended by the
General Manager.

To meet all these conditions it is necessary first to specify
a somewhat more elaborate model of a mechanism which might be postulated to produce some sort of "expected Commission restoration." The
purpose of this hypothetical "expected restoration" is to provide an interpretable "zero point" for our eventual scale.

Suppose that in the absence of specific response by the
Commission to the special pleadings of a particular division director, an
act of restoration is caused by the balancing of a decision rule (say, the

---

[*]I am indebted to Mr. Fred Bookstein for his collaboration on these
matters.

"fair share" notion) against some idea of the net costs to a particular program in a particular year which the Commission considers "tolerable" given the circumstances of that year. We propose a model which weights deviations from any decision rule we care to supply (the "fair share" notion is only one possibility; "splitting the difference" would be another) relative to net cost given the General Manager's action, and assumes some tolerance for total discrepancy. (The Commission knows that it cannot get all it wants.)

If D_1 and D_2 are the changes in a given program by the General Manager and Commission respectively, and a constant 'a' is determined so that $D_2 = -aD_1$ is the expected restoration, then the model is, algebraically:

$$/D_1 + D_2/ + k/D_1 + aD_2/ = \text{Tolerance}$$

The second constant 'k' is the unknown weight and the expression $/D_1 + aD_2/$ represents the deviation from some "expected restoration."

Re-stated to preserve the continuity of marginal utilities, the model is:

$$(D_1 + D_2)^2 + k^2 (D_2 + aD_1)^2 = \text{Tolerance}^2$$

When we computed the "tolerance," we could deduce the net change in a given program budget conceivable under model if the only forces operating were the psychological mechanisms we have postulated. Deviations from this minimum would then be a measure of support for the specific program in question. The minimum of $D_1 + D_2$ (net change) for a fixed tolerance occurs when $(D_2 + aD_1) = 0$, and the value of the minimum is:

$$-\text{sqrt}(\ (D_1 + D_2)^2 + k^2(D_2 + aD_1)^2).$$

We determine the "division strength" index, S, to be:

$$S = D_1 + D_2 + \text{sqrt} (\ (D_1 + D_2)^2 + k^2(D_2 + aD_1)^2\ )$$

This number, S, will have to be divided by some normalizing

term and we will have to perform some monotonic transformation to get

its metric properties into shape.*

We have noted that the postulated constant, k, expresses

the proposed balancing operation. It is simply the number which "balances"

or equates the discrepancy from the decision-rule norm ("fair share") with

actual net cost to the program $(D_1 + D_2)$. This constant can be <u>estimated</u>

as the average ratio of the two terms, $/D_2 + aD_1/$ and $/D_1 + D_2/$ over <u>all</u>

the data at hand.

It now remains to compute (or assign) the other constant,

"a," which expresses the assumed decision-rule or restoration norm.

For example, its value would be 0.5 if the Commission's rule-of-thumb

were to "split the difference" between the program division and the

General Manager. We could fix "a" at the value of 0.5 or anything else.

---

* To normalize S we merely divide by the "root mean square" (i.e., the
standard deviation around zero) of the three pertinent program allocations
(actual division request, actual General Manager budget, and actual Commission budget). This operation, however, still leaves us with a real number (of whatever precision we wish) whose interval properties we have no
reason whatever to believe. Moreover, we have no idea what a given value
for S, <u>other than zero</u>, (which we understand precisely) means except in
comparison with other values. We obviously need to collapse this interval
measure into some tractable <u>ordinal</u> scale, preserving only the sign and
the zero point. Unfortunately there are few rules available for doing this;
it is inevitably a matter of trial and error. (For a brilliant discussion of
all these issues, see: John Galtung, <u>Theory and Methods of Social Re-
search</u>, New York: Columbia University Press, 1967). We chose to follow
the standard practice of defining ordinal cut points in terms of the distribu-
tional properties of the initial array of scores, and after some experimentation, i.e., trying different cut points and looking at the results, settled upon
the nine-point scale described in the text. The important additional point
about this particular scale is that virtually <u>any</u> deviation from zero in the
initial S value is transformed into a scale score of at least ±1.

Such arbitrariness is unnecessary; for there are several interesting ways to estimate it. Suppose, for instance, that the rule is to restore to each program its fair (i.e., proportional) share of the total proposed restoration. If we use $T_j k$ to refer to the total budget for stage 'j' in year 'k', and $F_j k$ the "norm" for stage 'j' in year 'k', then this proportion is:

$$(F_3 k - F_{2,} k) / (F_{2,} k - T_{1,} k).$$

We suggest using the <u>actual</u> total, $T_3 k$, as an estimate of the "ceiling," $F_3 k$, since there is usually good information available to all participants, thanks to the informal ties between the AEC budget staff and the Bureau of the Budget about what an "acceptable" total submission might be. Then $D_2 = -aD_1$ is the expected restoration based on this norm, and $/D_1 + aD_2/$ is the discrepancy in this aspect of the Commission's tolerance.

Let us again emphasize that we do not suppose that this formalism describes what the Atomic Energy Commissioners do during their annual budget review sessions. Indeed, as we have been at some pains to point out, we do not believe that budget making is most helpfully seen as problem-solving; that decision rules offer insights into the causes of program prosperity and decline. We <u>do</u>, however, propose that changes in relative program prosperity, changes in the allocation of values, may be a consequence of what the participants in the budgetary process do; may in this instance be partly a consequence of what the Commission does with the General Manager's recommendations. We have argued this is not all "budgetary politics" in the narrow sense.

The problem is to find a measure of this treatment which takes account of several factors. The measure should take account on the one hand of what the General Manager has done, both to specific programs

and to the aggregated total of division requests. On the other hand, the
measure should be sensitive to how the Commission treats a particular
program in light of what the Commission does to the overall budget. The
index of support which we have described is presented as one way of simul·
taneously taking all these facts into account.

The test of the validity of this endeavor is whether it helps
us in addressing the issue which intrigues us, namely the causal significance of all of these budgetary actions. Does the jockeying among the
divisions, the General Manager, and the Commission make any difference
to the prosperity of the AEC's various activities?

These matters are addressed in the text. Tables A and B
report the results of the present measurement exercise. ("Commission
support" scores being computed according to exactly the same logic as
"division strength" scores.)

The numbers in parentheses are the algebraic sums down
columns and across rows. They merely reconfirm that (a) some years
are different (e.g., FY 1963); and (b) some programs are consistently
treated differently (e.g., civilian power reactors).

It remains only to comment briefly on the two constants
required by the model, "a" and "k." Recall that in the case of the former,
instead of arbitrarily fixing it at, say, 0.5, we chose to estimate it as the
average restoration across all programs.

By this definition, the actual values (for the division-General
Manager-Commission sequence) for the fifteen years on which data are
available are:

FY 1958 -- .017	FY 1963 -- 3.504	FY 1968 -- .458
FY 1959 -- 0.0	FY 1964 -- .817	FY 1969 -- .623
FY 1960 -- .397	FY 1965 -- -.075	FY 1970 -- .384
FY 1961 -- .639	FY 1966 -- .595	FY 1971 -- .346
FY 1962 -- .103	FY 1967 -- .364	FY 1972 -- .496

These numbers are, of course, readily interpretable: In FY 1966 the Commission actually did, on the average, split-the-difference between the General Manager and the division.

The second constant, "k" is a bit more complicated. The first thing to note is that unlike "a" it has no self-evident behavioral interpretation. It is simply a formal property of the model we have specified. The model postulates that the Commissioners make their restoration in part by balancing two discrepancies. The constant, k, is merely the mathematical consequence of this postulate; the only way algebraically to express the notion of "balancing" is to multiply the second discrepancy by some number which makes it equal the first. Such a number is of course the ratio of the two discrepancies. (If $k(x) = y$, then $k = y/x$) As with the first constant, "a," we actually use the ratio of the average discrepancies across all programs. Thus, for the nth year, and the ith program;

$$k_n = \sum_{i=1}^{23} \left| \text{discrepancy} -1_{(i,n)} \right| \bigg/ \sum_{i=1}^{23} \left| \text{discrepancy} -2_{(i,n)} \right|$$

where,

$$\text{discrepancy} -1_{(i,n)} = D1_{(i,n)} + D2_{(i,n)}$$

and

$$\text{discrepancy} -2_{(i,n)} = D2_{(i,n)} + A_n (D2_{(i,n)})$$

Though "k" has no behavioral interpretation, it will be useful to check its values given our data for two reasons. First, if across all fifteen years it is roughly constant, this will be a crude test of the validity of the underlying model. Second, we will be impressed if it turns out to be a small number. The only way for "k" to become large is for "discrepancy-2" to be small, which in turn will only happen when deviations from a fair share solution are minimal. Hence, small "k's" are <u>prima facie</u> evidence that the Commissioners express preference in making restorations.

Actual values for "k" for the division-General Manager-Commission sequence are:

FY 1958 -- 30.1	FY 1963 -- 0.7	FY 1968 -- 1.4
FY 1959 -- 14.0	FY 1964 -- 0.7	FY 1969 -- 1.2
FY 1960 -- 1.4	FY 1965 -- 1.1	FY 1970 -- 2.3
FY 1961 -- 1.0	FY 1966 -- 2.1	FY 1971 -- 2.9
FY 1962 -- 7.3	FY 1967 -- 1.7	FY 1972 -- 2.5

At least during the Seaborg years, our model does not, by this weak test, grossly violate reality.

TABLE A

All "Division Strength" Scores

Program		Fiscal Years														
	1958	1959	1960	1961	1962	1963	1964	1965	1966	1967	1968	1969	1970	1971	1972	
RM	-1	-1	-1	-1	1	0	0	0	0	0	0	-1	-1	2	2	(-1)
SNM	-1	1	1	-1	0	-1	-1	-1	1	1	-1	1	0	-1	1	(-1)
Weap	2	1	-1	-1	0	1	-1	-1	0	-1	-1	1	1	1	0	(1)
Civ	3	-1	0	-1	-1	-1	2	0	3	2	-1	2	-1	-1	-1	(8)
Coop	--	0	0	0	0	-1	2	0	-4	-1	4	0	-1	-1	3	(4)
Eur	--	-2	0	0	-2	-4	0	0	0	-1	0	1	4	0	--	(-2)
Mer	-2	-1	1	2	4	-4	-1	0	0	4	-4	1	--	--	--	(-1)
Army	0	-1	2	4	-2	-4	-1	-1	0	-3	0	--	--	--	--	(-6)
Navy	-1	-1	1	0	-1	0	0	0	0	0	0	0	0	0	--	(-2)
ANP	-1	0	1	1	1	--	--	--	--	--	--	1	--	--	--	(2)
Pluto	0	-1	0	0	0	-4	-2	4	--	--	--	--	--	--	--	(-3)
Rover	0	0	0	2	3	1	2	3	0	-1	2	-4	-1	-1	2	(6)
SNAP	--	-1	0	2	0	-2	2	3	2	-1	-2	1	-1	2	-3	(0)
GRT	--	--	4	1	-1	1	0	0	-1	-1	-2	0	-1	3	1	(4)
Saf	0	-1	0	1	0	-1	1	0	-1	1	-2	0	-1	-1	1	(-5)
Adv	0	-1	0	1	-2	-4	-2	3	-1	2	-4	0	-1	-4	--	(-13)
Hep	0	0	0	1	1	-1	3	0	-1	-1	1	1	-1	-1	1	(3)
Sher	0	1	2	1	-1	-1	0	-1	-1	-1	3	3	-1	-1	1	(6)
Bio	-1	-1	-1	1	-1	1	0	-1	0	0	2	1	-1	-1	1	(-1)
TEI	-2	4	1	2	1	1	-1	-1	1	3	-1	0	-1	-1	-4	(2)
Iso	0	-3	0	2	2	-4	1	-1	-1	-3	-3	0	-1	-2	2	(-10)
Plow	--	--	4	1	0	0	0	-2	-1	-1	4	0	-1	1	-1	(1)
PDA	-1	-1	0	1	0	-1	1	0	0	-1	-1	1	-1	1	-2	(-4)
	(-5)	(-8)	(16)	(19)	(2)	(-28)	(5)	(5)	(-2)	(-3)	(-6)	(8)	(-10)	(-5)	(4)	

TABLE B

All "Commission Support" Scores

Program	Fiscal Years															
	1958	1959	1960	1961	1962	1963	1964	1965	1966	1967	1968	1969	1970	1971	1972	
RM	-1	0	0	-1	0	0	-1	0	0	0	0	0	-1	4	0	(0)
SNM	-1	0	1	1	-1	-1	-1	-2	-1	1	2	-1	-1	-1	-1	(-4)
Weap	-1	0	1	0	4	-4	2	-1	-1	-1	1	-1	-1	-1	-1	(2)
Civ	-1	0	1	0	0	0	-1	4	-1	2	-1	2	-1	2	3	(17)
Coop	—	0	3	0	0	-4	0	2	0	-2	0	3	-1	-2	0	(-1)
Eur	—	0	0	0	0	-1	0	0	0	4	0	0	0	—	—	(3)
Mer	-2	0	-1	2	4	0	4	4	-1	-4	0	0	—	-4	—	(2)
Army	0	0	0	-1	-4	0	-2	-1	2	0	0	—	—	—	—	(-4)
Navy	-1	0	0	-1	-1	0	0	0	0	0	0	1	-1	-1	-1	(-3)
ANP	-1	0	-1	3	-4	—	—	—	—	—	1	—	—	—	-1	(-5)
Pluto	-2	0	0	4	0	4	1	1	-1	-1	-2	0	-1	-2	—	(11)
Rover	0	0	0	-1	-1	2	0	1	1	—	-1	0	-1	-1	4	(2)
SNAP	—	0	-1	-1	0	4	-1	1	2	—	0	-1	—	2	2	(4)
GRT	—	—	-1	0	0	-3	-1	1	1	—	0	-1	-1	-1	-1	(-3)
Saf	0	0	0	0	0	-3	—	1	—	-1	0	-1	-1	-1	—	(-8)
Adv	-1	0	0	0	4	-4	-1	1	2	-2	-1	-1	-1	-4	-1	(-7)
Hep	0	0	0	-1	-1	-2	2	1	-1	0	-1	-1	0	2	-1	(-2)
Sher	0	0	-1	0	0	0	0	1	—	—	0	0	—	-1	—	(-5)
Bio	-1	0	-1	1	-1	-1	2	1	1	-1	-1	0	-1	-1	-1	(1)
TEI	4	0	-1	0	4	-4	4	3	0	1	-1	0	-2	3	-1	(-3)
Iso	0	0	-1	-1	3	-4	-1	2	-1	3	-2	-3	0	-4	-1	(2)
Plow	—	—	-1	2	-1	-4	4	1	-1	-1	0	-1	4	1	0	(-2)
PDA	-1	0	-1	1	-1	-1	0	1	-1	-1	0	-1	-1	—	1	(-4)
	(-9)	(0)	(-4)	(7)	(4)	(-18)	(9)	(24)	(-1)	(-8)	(-3)	(-2)	(-2)	(-6)	(0)	(0)

BIBLIOGRAPHY

BOOKS

Anton, Thomas J. The Politics of State Expenditure in Illinois. Urbana, Illinois: University of Illinois Press, 1966.

Appleby, Paul H. Policy and Administration. University, Alabama: University of Alabama Press, 1949.

------ Morality and Administration in Democratic Government. Baton Rouge, Louisana: Louisana State University Press, 1952.

Barber, James David. Power in Committees: An Experiment in the Governmental Process. Chicago, Illinois: Rand McNally & Co., 1966.

Barnard, Chester I. The Functions of the Executive. Cambridge, Mass.: Harvard University Press, 1938.

Bauer, Raymond A.; Pool, Ithiel de Sola; and Dexter, Lewis Anthony. American Business and Public Policy: The Politics of Foreign Trade. New York: Atherton Press, 1967.

Blalock, Hubert M., Jr. Causal Inference in Nonexperimental Research. Chapel Hill: University of North Carolina Press, 1961.

Blau, Peter M. Bureaucracy in Modern Society. New York: Random House, 1956.

Braybrooke, David, and Lindblom, Charles E. A Strategy of Decision: Policy Evaluation as a Social Process. Glencoe, Illinois: The Free Press, 1963.

Burkhead, Jesse. Governmental Budgeting. New York: John Wiley & Sons, 1956.

Chandler, Alfred D., Jr. Strategy and Structure: Chapters in the History of the American Industrial Enterprise. Garden City, N.Y.: Doubleday & Co., Inc. 1966.

Crecine, John P. Governmental Problem-Solving: A Computer Simulation of Municipal Budgeting. Chicago: Rand McNally & Co., 1969.

Crouch, Holmes F. Nuclear Space Propulsion. Granada Hills, Calif.: Astronuclear Press, 1965.

Crozier, Michel, The Bureaucratic Phenomenon. Chicago: University of Chicago Press, 1967.

Cyert, R. M., and March, J. G. A Behavioral Theory of the Firm. Englewood Cliffs, N.J.: Prentice-Hall, 1963.

Dahl, Robert A. and Lindblom, Charles E. Politics, Economics and Welfare: Planning and Politics - Economic Systems Resolved into Basic Social Processes. New York: Harper & Row, Inc., 1953.

Davis, James W., Jr. Politics, Programs, and Budgets: A Reader in Government Budgeting. Englewood Cliffs, N.J.: Prentice-Hall, Inc., 1969.

Devons, Ely. Planning in Practice: Essays in Aircraft Planning in War-Time. Cambridge, England: The University Press, 1950.

Diesing, Paul. Reason in Society: Five Types of Decisions and Their Social Conditions. Urbana, Ill.: University of Illinois Press, 1962.

Doctors, Samuel I. The Role of Federal Agencies in Technology Transfer. Cambridge, Mass.: MIT Press, 1969.

Downs, Anthony. Inside Bureaucracy. Boston: Little, Brown & Co., 1967.

Dror, Yehezkel. Public Policymaking Reexamined. San Francisco: Chandler Pub. Co., 1968.

Dupree, A. Hunter. Science in the Federal Government: A History of Policies and Activities to 1940. New York: Harper Torchbooks, 1964.

Easton, David. The Political System: An Inquiry into the state of Political Science.

Engler, Robert. The Politics of Oil: Private Power and Democratic Directions. Chicago: The Univ. of Chicago Press, 1961.

Etzioni, Amitai. Modern Organizations. Englewood Cliffs, N.J.: Prentice-Hall, Inc., 1964.

Fenno, R. F. The Power of the Purse: Appropriations Politics in Congress. Boston: Little, Brown & Co., 1966.

Friedrich, Carl J. Constitutional Government and Democracy (Fourth edition). Waltham, Mass.: Blaisdell Pub. Co., 1968.

Galbraith, John Kenneth. The New Industrial State. New York: Signet Books, 1968.

Galtung, Johan. Theory and Methods of Social Research. New York: Columbia Univ. Press, 1967.

-335-

Gerwin, Donald. Budgeting Public Funds: The Decision Process in an
     Urban School District. Madison, Wisc.: Univ. of Wisconsin
     Press, 1969.

Green, Harold P. and Rosenthal, Alan. Government of the Atom: The
     Integration of Powers. New York: Atherton Press, 1963.

Hewlett, Richard G., and Anderson, Oscar E., Jr. The New World,
     1939-1946. A History of the USAEC, Vol. I. University Park, Pa.:
     Penna. State Univ. Press, 1962.

Hewlett, Richard G., and Duncan, Francis. Atomic Shield, 1947/1952.
     A History of the USAEC, Vol. 2. University Park, Pa.: Penna.
     State Univ. Press, 1969.

Hitch, Charles J., and McKean, Roland N. The Economics of Defense
     in the Nuclear Age. New York: Atheneum, 1965.

Jacobson, Harold Karen, and Stein, Eric. Diplomats, Scientists, and
     Politicians: The United States and the Nuclear Test Ban
     Negotiations. Ann Arbor, Mich.: Univ. of Michigan Press,
     1966.

Kane, Edward J. Economic Statistics and Econometrics. New York:
     Harper & Row, 1968.

Karl, Barry Dean. Executive Reorganization and Reform in the New
     Deal: The Genesis of Administrative Management, 1900-1939.
     Cambridge, Mass.: Harvard Univ. Press, 1963.

Key, V. O., Jr. Politics, Parties, and Pressure Groups (4th Edition)
     New York: Thomas Y. Crowell Co., 1958.

Lasswell, Harold. Politics: Who Gets What, When, How. New York:
     Meridian Books, 1958.

Lilienthal, David E. Change, Hope, and the Bomb. Princeton, N.J.:
     Princeton Univ. Press, 1963.

------ The Journals of David E. Lilienthal: Vol. II. The Atomic
     Energy Years 1945-1950. New York: Harper & Row, 1964.

Lindblom, Charles E. The Intelligence of Democracy: Decision Making
     Through Mutual Adjustment. New York: The Free Press, 1965.

Loftness, Robert F. Nuclear Power Plants. Princeton, N.J.: Van
     Nostrand Co., 1964.

Lowi, Theodore J. The End of Liberalism: Ideology, Policy, and the
     Crisis of Public Authority. New York: W. W. Norton & Co.,
     Inc. 1969.

Maass, Arthur. Muddy Waters: The Army Engineers and the Nations Rivers. Cambridge, Mass.: Harvard Univ. Press, 1951.

March, James G., and Simon, Herbert A. Organizations. New York: John Wiley & Sons, Inc., 1958.

Martin, Roscoe C. (ed.). Public Administration and Democracy. Syracuse, N.Y.: Syracuse Univ. Press, 1965.

MacAvoy, Paul W. Economic Strategy for Developing Nuclear Breeder Reactors. Cambridge, Mass.: The MIT Press, 1969.

Mackenzie, W.J.M. Politics and Social Science. Baltimore, Md.: Penguin Books, 1967.

Marx, Fritz Morstein (ed.). Elements of Public Administration (2nd edition). Englewood Cliffs, N.J.: Prentice-Hall, Inc., 1959.

McConnell, Grant. The Decline of Agrarian Democracy. Berkeley, Calif.: Univ. of Cal. Press, 1953.

McFarland, Andrew S. Power and Leadership in Pluralist Systems. Stanford, Calif.: Stanford Univ. Press, 1969.

McKinley, Charles. Uncle Sam in the Pacific Northwest: Federal Management of Natural Resources in the Columbia River Valley. (Berkeley, Calif.: Univ. of Calif. Press, 1952.

Mosher, Frederick C. Democracy and the Public Service. New York: Oxford Univ. Press, 1968.

Mosher, Frederick C., and Poland, Orville F. The Costs of American Governments: Facts, Trends, Myths. New York: Dodd, Mead & Co., 1964.

Mullenbach, Philip. Civilian Nuclear Power: Economic Studies and Policy Formation. New York: The Twentieth Century Fund, 1963.

Neustadt, Richard E. Presidential Power. New York: Signet Books, 1964.

Newman, James R., and Miller, Byron S. The Control of Atomic Energy: A Study of Its Social, Economic and Political Implications. New York: McGraw-Hill Book Co., Inc., 1948.

Organization for Economic co-operation and Development. Reviews of National Science Policy: United States. Paris: OECD, 1968.

Orlans, Harold. Contracting for Atoms. Washington, D.C.: The Brookings Institution, 1967.

Ott, David J., and Ott, Attiat F. Federal Budget Policy. Washington, D.C.: The Brookings Institution, 1969.

Parsegian, V. Lawrence. Industrial Management in the Atomic Age: Patterns, Restraints, Opportunities, and Trends in Government - Sponsored Technology. Reading, Mass.: Addison-Wesley, 1965.

Peacock, Alan T., and Wiseman, Jack. The Growth of Public Expenditure in the United Kingdom. Princeton, N.J.: Princeton Univ. Press, 1961.

Price, Don K. The Scientific Estate. Cambridge, Mass.: The Belknap Press of Harvard Univ. Press, 1965.

Price, James L. Organizational Effectiveness: An Inventory of Propositions. Homewood, Ill.: Richard D. Irwin, Inc., 1968.

Quade, E. S., and Boucher, W. I. (eds.). Systems Analysis and Policy Planning: Applications in Defense. New York: American Elsevier Pub. Co., Inc. 1968.

Rourke, Francis E. Bureaucracy, Politics and Public Policy. Boston: Little, Brown & Co., 1969.

------ (ed.) Bureaucratic Power in National Politics. Boston: Little, Brown & Co., 1965.

Sapolsky, Harvey M. Creating the Invulnerable Deterrent. Cambridge, Mass.: MIT Press, 1971.

Sayre, Wallace S., and Kaufman, Herbert. Governing New York City: Politics in the Metropolis.

Schilling, Warner R.; Hammond, Paul Y.; and Snyder, Glenn H. Strategy, Politics, and Defense Budgets. New York: Columbia Univ. Press, 1962.

Schooler, Dean, Jr. Science, Scientists, and Public Policy. New York: The Free Press, 1971.

Schubert, Glendon. The Public Interest: A Critique of the Theory of a Political Concept. Glencoe, Ill.: The Free Press, 1960.

Schultze, Charles L. The Politics and Economics of Public Spending. Washington, D.C.: The Brookings Institution, 1968.

Schultze, Charles L.; Fried, Edward R.; Rivlin, Alice M.; and Teeters, Nancy H. Setting the National Priorities: The 1972 Budget. Washington, D.C.: The Brookings Institution, 1971.

Seidman, Harold. Politics, Position, and Power: The Dynamics of Federal Organization. New York: Oxford University Press, 1970.

Selznick, Philip. TVA and the Grass Roots: A Study in the Sociology of Formal Organization. Berkeley: University of California Press, 1953.

------ Leadership in Administration: A Sociological Interpretation. New York: Harper & Row, 1957.

Sharkansky, Ira. The Politics of Taxing and Spending. Indianapolis: The Bobbs-Merrill Co., Inc.

------ The Routines of Politics. New York: Van Nostrand, 1969.

Shonfield, Andrew. Modern Capitalism: The Changing Balance of Public and Private Power. New York: Oxford University Press, 1965.

Simon, Herbert A.; Smithberg, Donald W.; and Thompson, Victor A. Public Administration. New York: Alfred A. Knopf, 1950.

Simon, Herbert A. Administrative Behavior: A Study of Decision-Making Processes in Administrative Organization. 2nd edition. New York: The Free Press, 1952.

------ Models of Man. New York: John Wiley & Sons, Inc., 1957.

Smith, Bruce L. R. The Rand Corporation: Case Study of a Nonprofit Advisory Corporation. Cambridge, Mass.: Harvard University Press, 1966.

Smithies, Arthur. The Budgetary Process in the United States. New York, McGraw-Hill Book Co., Inc., 1955.

Stern, Philip M. The Oppenheimer Case. New York: Harper & Row, 1969.

Steiner, Gilbert Y. The State of Welfare. Washington, D. C.: The Brookings Institution, 1971.

Stinchcombe, Arthur L. Constructing Social Theories. New York: Harcourt, Brace, & World, Inc., 1968.

Strauss, Lewis L. Men and Decisions. New York: Doubleday & Co., 1962.

Suchman, Edward A. Evaluative Research: Principles and Practice in Public Service and Social Action Programs. New York: Russell Sage Foundation, 1967.

Thayer, Frederick C., Jr. Air Transport Policy and National Security:
A Political, Economic and Military Analysis. Chapel Hill:
University of North Carolina Press, 1965.

Thompson, James D. Organizations in Action. New York: McGraw-
Hill Book Co., Inc., 1967.

Truman, Harry S. Memoirs, Vol. 2. Years of Trial and Hope 1946-1952
Garden City, N.Y.: Doubleday & Co., 1956.

White, Leonard D. The Federalists: A Study in Administrative History,
1789-1801. New York: The Free Press, 1965.

----- The Jeffersonians: A Study in Administrative History, 1801-1829.
New York: The Free Press, 1965.

----- The Jacksonians: A Study in Administrative History, 1829-1861.
New York: The Free Press, 1965.

----- The Republican Era: A Study in Administrative History, 1869-1901
New York: The Free Press, 1965.

Wildavsky, Aaron. The Politics of the Budgetary Process. Boston:
Little, Brown & Co., 1964.

Wilensky, Harold L. Organizational Intelligence. New York: Basic
Books, Inc., 1967.

Wilimovsky, Norman J., and Wolfe, John N., eds. Environment of
Cape Thompson Region, Alaska. Oak Ridge, Tenn.: USAEC
Division of Tech. Information, 1966.

Wilmerding, Lucius, Jr. The Spending Power. New Haven, Conn.:
Yale University Press, 1943.

Wonnacott, Ronald J., and Wonnacott, Thomas H. Econometrics.
New York: John Wiley & Sons, 1970.

Yarmolinsky, Adam. The Military Establishment: Its Impacts on
American Society. New York: Harper & Row, 1971

ARTICLES

Allison, Graham T. "Conceptual Models and the Cuban Missile
Crisis." 63, American Political Science Review, Sept. 1969.

Argyris, Chris. "On the Effectiveness of Research and Development
Organizations." 56, American Scientist, no. 4, 1968.

Bendix, Reinhard. "Bureaucracy and the Problem of Power." 5, Public Administration Review, Summer 1945.

Blau, Peter M. "Structural Effects." 25, American Sociological Review, April, 1960.

Bower, Joseph L. "Descriptive Decision Theory from the 'Administrative' Viewpoint," in, Raymond A. Bauer and Kennath J. Gergen (ed.) The Study of Policy Formation (New York: The Free Press, 1968).

Davis, Otto A.; Dempster, M. A. H.; Wildavsky, Aaron. "A Theory of the Budgetary Process." 60, American Political Science Review, Sept. 1966, pp. 529-547.

Davis, Otto A.; Dempster, M. A. H.; Wildavsky, Aaron. "On the Process of Budgeting: An Empirical Study of Congressional Appropriations," in Gordon Tullock (ed.), Papers on Non-Market Decision Making, (Charlottsville, Va.: Thomas Jefferson Center for Political Economy, 1966).

Finney, John W. "Defense Study Favors Cut in Atomic Weapon Output." New York Times, December 21, 1963.

Friedrich, C. J. "Public Policy and the Nature of Administrative Responsibility," in C. J. Friedrich and E. S. Mason (eds.) Public Policy (Cambridge, Mass.: Harvard Univ. Press, 1940).

Green, Philip. "Science, Government, and the Case of RAND: A Singular Pluralism." World Politics, Vol. 20, no. 2 (Jan. 1968).

Hewlett, Richard G. "Man Harnesses the Atom," in M. Kranzberg and C. W. Pursell, Jr. (eds.), Technology in Western Civilization, (Madison, Wisc.: University of Wisconsin Press, 1967) pp. 256-275.

Hogerton, John F. "The Arrival of Nuclear Power," 218 Scientific American, no. 2, February 1968.

Huntington, Samuel P. "The Marasmus of the ICC: The Commission, The Railroads, and The Public Interest," in Peter Woll (ed.) Public Administration and Policy, (New York: Harper Torchbooks, 1966).

Kaufman, Herbert. "Emerging Conflicts in the Doctrines of Public Administration," in Alan A. Altshuler (ed.), The Politics of the Federal Bureaucracy, (New York: Dodd, Mead & Co., 1968).

Lambright, W. Henry. "Shooting Down the Nuclear Plane," The Inter-University Case Program, #104 (Bobbs-Merrill Co., Inc. 1967).

Lindblom, Charles E. "The Science of 'Muddling Through'." 19 Public Administration Review, Spring, 1959.

Lowi, Theodore J. "American Business, Public Policy, Case-Studies and Political Theory." 16, World Politics, no. 4, July, 1964.

Maass, Arthur. "In Accord with the President's Program," in C. J. Friedrich and J. K. Galbraith (eds.), Public Policy, (Cambridge, Mass.: Harvard University Press, 1954).

Marks, Herbert S. "Public Power and Atomic Power Development," in Law and Contemporary Problems, Winter, 1956, Durham, N. C.: Duke University School of Law.

Merton, Robert K. "Bureaucratic Structure and Personality," in Social Theory and Social Structure, rev. ed. (New York: The Free Press, 1957.

Metzger, Peter. "Project Gasbuggy and Catch-85." New York Times Magazine, February 22, 1970.

Marx, Fritz Morstein. "The Bureau of the Budget: Its Evolution and Present Role," I and II. 30, American Political Science Review, Aug. and Oct., 1945, pp. 653-684 and 869-898.

McKean, Roland N., and Awshen, Melvin. "Limitations, Risks and Problems," in David E. Novick (ed.) Program Budgeting: Program Analysis and the Federal Government, (Cambridge, Mass.: Harvard University Press, 1965).

Miller, Warren E., and Stokes, Donald E. "Constituency Influence in Congress." 57, American Political Science Review, March, 1963.

Natchez, Peter B., and Bupp, Irvin C. "Candidates, Issues, and Voters," in Dryer and Rosenbaum (eds.), Political Opinion and Behavior, 2nd edition, (Wadsworth Publiching Co., Inc., 1970).

Neustadt, Richard E. "The Presidency and Legislation: The Growth of Central Clearance." 48, American Political Science Review, Sept. 1954, pp. 641-671.

Palfrey, John G. "Atomic Energy: A New Experiment in Government-Industry Relations." Columbia Law Review, March, 1956.

Russett, Bruce. "Who Pays for Defense?" 32, American Political Science Review, June, 1969, pp. 412-426.

Sapolsky, Harvey M. "Organizational Competition and Monopoly," in John D. Montgomery and A;bert D. Hirschman (eds.), Public Policy, (Cambridge, Mass.: Harvard University Press, 1968).

Schick, Allen. "Systems Politics and Systems Budgeting." 29, Public Administration Review, no. 2, March/April, 1969.

Selznick, Philip. "Cooptation: A Mechanism for Organizational Stability," in Robert Merton et al. (eds.), Reader in Bureaucracy, (Glencoe, Ill.: The Free Press, 1952.

Simon, Herbert A. "On the Concept of Organizational Goal." 9, Administrative Science Quarterly, 1964.

Spivak, Jonathan. "Nuclear Cutbacks." Wall Street Journal, December 30, 1963.

Staebler, U. M. "Objectives and Summary of USAEC Civilian Power Reactor Programs," in J. Gueran, et al. (eds.), The Economics of Nuclear Power, (New York: McGraw-Hill Book Co., 1957).

Stinchcombe, Arthur L. "Social Structure and Organizations," in J. G. March (ed.), Handbook of Organizations, (New York: Rand McNally & Co., 1965).

Wilson, James Q. "The Bureaucracy Problem." The Public Interest, no. 6 (Winter, 1967) pp. 3-9.

UNPUBLISHED MATERIAL

Crecine, John P. "A Computer Simulation Model of Municipal Resource Allocation." Paper delivered at the Midwest Conference of Political Science, April, 1966.

----- "The Defense Department Budgetary Process." Unpublished paper presented at the 64th Annual Meeting of the American Political Science Association, Washington, D.C., Sept. 1968.

----- "Defense Budgeting: Constraints and Organizational Adaptation." Discussion Paper, Institute of Public Policy Studies, University of Michigan, July, 1969.

Hewlett, Richard G. "The Advent of Nuclear Power in the U.S., 1945-1968." Paper delivered at meeting of the American Association for the Advancement of Science, Dallas, Texas, Dec., 1968.

Jackson, John E. "A Research Strategy on National Priority Determination." Unpublished Paper, Harvard University, 1970.

Mohr, Lawrence B. "The Concept of Organizational Goal." Discussion Paper, Institute of Public Policy Studies, University of Michigan, Sept. 1969.

Natchez, Peter B. "The Reasonable Voter." Unpublished Ph.D. Dissertation, Harvard University, 1969.

Schamndt, Jurgen. "The Dismal State of Energy R & D." Paper delivered at the Southwest Social Science Conference, Dallas, Texas, March, 1971.

Stromberg, John. "Regression Analysis of Department of Defense Budgeting." The RAND Corporation, 1969.

Whitelaw, W. E. "The Determinants of Municipal Finance: A Time-Series Analysis." Program on Regional and Urban Economics, Discussion Paper no. 57, Harvard University, November, 1969.

CONGRESSIONAL DOCUMENTS

(Including "SHORT-TITLE INDEX")

FULL TITLE	SHORT TITLE

U.S. Congress, Hearings before the Joint Committee on Atomic Energy (JCAE), Accelerating the Civilian Reactor Program, 84th Cong., 2d Sess. (1956).

U.S. Congress, Hearings before the JCAE, Civilian Atomic Power Acceleration Program, 84th Cong., 2d Sess. (1956).

U.S. Congress, Hearings before the JCAE, Development, Growth, and State of the Atomic Energy Industry, 85th Cong., 1st Sess. (1957).

U.S. Congress, Senate, Hearings before the Subcommittee on Disarmament of the Committee on Foreign Relations, Control and Reduction of Armaments, 85th Cong., 2d Sess. (1958).

U.S. Congress, Hearings before the JCAE, Development, Growth, and State of the Atomic Energy Industry, 85th Cong., 2d Sess. (1958).

U.S. Congress, Hearings before the JCAE, Development, Growth, and State of the Atomic Energy Industry, 86th Cong., 1st Sess. (1959).

U.S. Congress, Hearings before the JCAE, Development, Growth, and State of the Atomic Energy Industry, 86th Cong., 2d Sess. (1960).

U.S. Congress, Hearings before the
JCAE, Development, Growth, and
State of the Atomic Energy Industry,
87th Cong., 1st Sess. (1961).

U.S. Congress, Hearings before the
JCAE, Development, Growth, and
State of the Atomic Energy Industry,
87th Cong., 2d Sess. (1962).

U.S. Congress, Hearings before the
Subcommittee on Legislation of the
JCAE, AEC Authorizing Legislation
Fiscal Year 1962, 87th Cong., 1st
Sess. (1961).

FY 1962 Authorization
Hearings

U.S. Congress, Senate, Hearings
before the Committee on Foreign
Relations, Nuclear Test Ban Treaty,
88th Cong., 1st Sess. (1963)

U.S. Congress, Hearings before the
Subcommittee on Legislation of the
JCAE, AEC Authorizing Legislation
Fiscal Year 1965, 88th Cong., 2d
Sess. (1964).

FY 1965 Authorization
Hearings

U.S. Congress, Hearings before the
JCAE, Peaceful Applications of
Nuclear Explosives--Plowshare,
89th Cong., 1st Sess. (1965).

Hearings on Peaceful
Applications of Nuclear
Explosives (1965)

U.S. Congress, Hearings before the
Subcommittee on Legislation of the
JCAE, AEC Authorizing Legislation
Fiscal Year 1966, 89th Cong., 2d
Sess. (1966).

FY 1966 Authorization
Hearings

U.S. Congress, Hearings before the
Subcommittee on Legislation of the
JCAE, AEC Authorizing Legislation
Fiscal Year 1967, 89th Cong., 2d
Sess. (1966).

FY 1967 Authorization
Hearings

U.S. Congress, Hearings before the
JCAE, Uranium Enrichment Services
and Related Matters, 89th Cong., 2d
Sess. (1966).

U.S. Congress, Hearings before the
Subcommittee on Legislation of the
JCAE, AEC Authorizing Legislation
Fiscal Year 1968, 90th Cong., 1st
Sess. (1967).

FY 1968 Authorization
Hearings

U.S. Congress, Hearings before the
Subcommittee on Legislation of the
JCAE, AEC Authorizing Legislation
Fiscal Year 1969, 90th Cong., 2d
Sess. (1968).

FY 1969 Authorization
Hearings

U.S. Congress, Hearings before the
Subcommittee on Legislation, JCAE,
Commercial Plowshare Services,
90th Cong., 2d Sess. (1968)

Hearings on Commercial
Plowshare Services

U.S. Congress, Hearings before the
JCAE, Nuclear Explosion Services
for Industrial Applications, 91st
Cong., 1st Sess. (1969).

Hearings on Nuclear
Explosion Services

U.S. Congress, Hearings before the
Subcommittee on Legislation of the
JCAE, AEC Authorizing Legislation
Fiscal Year 1970, 91st Cong., 1st
Sess. (1969).

FY 1970 Authorization
Hearings

U.S. Congress, Hearings before the
Subcommittee on Legislation of the
JCAE, AEC Authorizing Legislation
Fiscal Year 1971, 91st Cong., 2d
Sess. (1970).

FY 1971 Authorization
Hearings

U.S. Congress, Senate, Inquiry of the
Subcommittee on National Security
and International Operations of the
Committee on Government Operations,
Planning - Programming - Budgeting,
91st Cong., 2d Sess. (1970).

U.S. Congress, Senate, Hearings before
the Subcommittee on Air and Water
Pollution of the Committee on Public
Works, Underground Uses of Nuclear
Energy, 91st Cong., 2d Sess. (1970).

U.S. Congress, Hearings before the
Subcommittee on Research, Development, and Radiation of the JCAE,
High Energy Physics Research,
89th Cong., 1st Sess. (1965).

AEC RECORDS

The Office of the Secretary of the USAEC holds what Richard G. Hewlett has termed, "the most important single collection of documents relating to the history of atomic energy in the United States."* All of the official AEC documents, staff papers, correspondence and memoranda cited in the footnotes to the text are in these files. Moreover, all of the data listed in Appendix A was collected from the Secretariat's records. Since the documents actually cited constitute only a fraction of files consulted during the course of my research, there seems little point in listing them item by item. A brief explanation of the Secretariat's general filing system is more appropriate.

All subjects considered by the Commission since 1947 have been separated into distinct files arranged internally in chronological order. Hence, for example, all memoranda and reports, staff papers, correspondence with other agencies and the JCAE, private individuals, and summaries of Commission actions relating to the fiscal year 1967 budget cycle are in a separate chronologically arranged file.

In general, from the context of any particular footnote in the text it would be easy to identify the pertinent Secretariat file, and then, by date, locate the cited document.

The minutes of Commission meetings and the "Summary Notes" of their official discussions with others are not filed as part of the subject series. For the former, however, the unique meeting number

---

* Hewlett and Duncan, op. cit., p. 595. See pp. 595-601 for an important supplement to this note.

is sufficient to locate a particular minute, while in the case of "Summary Notes" (also kept separately) the date is adequate.

Citation in the text of this study should not be taken to imply that the document in question is either unclassified or available for inspection. As noted in the preface, this thesis treads on uneasy ground between open and "privileged" information. In a sense this aspect of it represents as much an experiment as the methodological innovations.

OTHER SOURCES

The following is a list of those interviewed as part of my research. It does not include numerous lower level AEC employees and others with whom I spoke on too casual a basis to be called an "interview":

John P. Abbadessa, USAEC, Hq., Controller
H. H. Aronson, CER Geonuclear Corporation
Roger Batzel, Lawrence Radiation Laboratory
Harvey Brooks, Harvard University
Howard C. Brown, Jr., USAEC, Hq., Assistant
    General Manager
H. D. Bruner, M.D., USAEC, Hq., Director,
    Division of Biology and Medicine
Fred J. Clark, Jr., USAEC, Hq., Division of
    Peaceful Nuclear Explosives
Victor Corso, USAEC, Hq., Office of the
    Controller
Delmar L. Crowson, USAEC, Hq., Director,
    Office of Safeguards and Material Management
Harold B. Curtis, USAEC, Hq., Division of
    Peaceful Nuclear Explosives
J. Keith Davy, USAEC, Hq., Division of Peaceful
    Explosives
Spofford G. English, USAEC, Hq., Assistant General
    Manager for Research and Development
Paul C. Fine, USAEC, Hq., Director, Division of
    Operations Analysis and Forecasting

Edward H. Fleming, Lawrence Radiation Laboratory
Carl R. Gerber, USAEC, Hq., Division of Peaceful
Nuclear Explosives
Gerald W. Johnson, Gulf General Atomic
Antoinette Joseph, USAEC, Hq., Office of the
General Manager
George M. Kavanagh, USAEC, Hq., Assistant
General Manager for Reactors
John S. Kelly, USAEC, Hq., Director, Division
of Peaceful Nuclear Explosives
A. M. Labowitz, USAEC, Hq., Special Assistant
to the General Manager for Disarmament
Willard F. Libby, University of California,
Los Angeles
Paul W. McDaniel, USAEC, Hq., Director,
Division of Research
Robert E. Miller, USAEC, Manager, Nevada
Operations Office
John G. Palfrey, Columbia University
John F. Philip, USAEC, San Francisco Operations
Office
Fred Schuldt, Bureau of the Budget
Milton Shaw, USAEC, Hq., Director of Reactor
Development and Technology
Nicholas S. Stoer, Bureau of the Budget
Edward Teller, Lawrence Radiation Laboratory
Dean Thornbrough, USAEC, Nevada Operations
Office
J. H. Van Santen, USAEC, Hq., Division of
Peaceful Explosives